THE MARYLANDERS

Without Shelter or a Crumb

A SAGA OF THE FASCIST REPRESSION OF A FAMILY
DURING THE AMERICAN CIVIL WAR

Revised Edition

Stephen D. Calhoun

HERITAGE BOOKS
2019

HERITAGE BOOKS
AN IMPRINT OF HERITAGE BOOKS, INC.

Books, CDs, and more—Worldwide

For our listing of thousands of titles see our website
at
www.HeritageBooks.com

Published 2019 by
HERITAGE BOOKS, INC.
Publishing Division
5810 Ruatan Street
Berwyn Heights, Md. 20740

Copyright © 2007 Stephen D. Calhoun

All rights reserved. No part of this book may be reproduced or transmitted in any form or by any means, electronic or mechanical, including photocopying, recording or by any information storage and retrieval system without written permission from the author, except for the inclusion of brief quotations in a review.

International Standard Book Number
Paperbound: 978-0-7884-4392-3

TABLE OF CONTENTS

ACKNOWLEDGEMENTS vii

FROM BIRTH TO THE CIVIL WAR 1

THE COUP D'ETAT AGAINST MARYLAND 19

THE QUIET REVOLUTION 33

THE UNION RAID OF THE PLAINS 51

HOSTAGES AT THE PLAINS 71

FATHER AND SONS IN THE CONFEDERACY 77

THE OCCUPATION OF THE PLAINS 87

THE CLAIM AGAINST THE QUARTERMASTER CORPS 98

AFTER THE CIVIL WAR 109

CONCLUSION 115

APPENDIX 119

BIBLIOGRAPHY 126

INDEX 135

ACKNOWLEDGEMENTS

This book would not have been possible without the dedicated work of archivists and librarians. On my many visits to archives and libraries, I received their excellent help. Much of the additional research of this revised edition was found on the Internet. The dedicated work of the National Archives and Records Administration, The Library of Congress, Cornell University Library and the Abraham Lincoln Papers at the Library of Congress, which are transcribed and annotated by the Lincoln Studies Center, Knox College, A Century of Lawmaking for a New Nation: U.S. Congressional Document and Debates, 1774-1875 at the Library of Congress (Washington, D.C.: American Memory Project, [2000-02]) and are excellent resources that all have copied images of historic works and made them available on the Internet.

Please be aware that original handwritten documents from the National Archives and Records Administration and the Maryland State Archives were transcribed as accurately as possible. Most of the letters from the Archives files were written over a century ago and are characterized by run-on sentences, a lack of punctuation and words that are capitalized contrary to modern usage. A few of the documents either lacked clarity of expression or the handwriting was so poor that they remain open to interpretation. Some of the original records misspelled the surname Sothoron as Sothern and other variations.

I am very grateful to the Fujitsu Computer Systems for their product, the Stylistic Tablet pen based computer. My Fujitsu tablet, with its pen writing ability to convert my script writing input on its screen into typed copy, greatly eased the effort of writing this revised edition. The support staff of Fujitsu guided me through the scare of a software conflict, which was easily overcome because of the superior design of Fujitsu products. The Microsoft Corporation, with their magnificent Word program, made effortless the technical aspects of writing, editing, footnoting and creating a table of contents and index. The Adobe Acrobat system of document creation facilitated the downloading and storage of source materials.

This book is not a defense of slavery, violent action or discrimination based on race or ancestry. It is an illustration of how our system of Constitutional checks and balances was upset during the Civil War by a military-political clique and the resulting impact on the Sothoron family of Maryland. Government by Constitutional law is far more important than the rule of men and women. I have written it in the hope of fostering openness, toleration and understanding. Slavery and all other forms of economic exploitation are an affront to humanity.

The entire story may never be known. Unfortunately, some of the papers of President Lincoln are alleged to have been destroyed by his son, Robert Todd Lincoln.[1]

---

[1] Philip Van Doren Stern, *The Man Who Killed Lincoln*, page 406.

Chapter 1

FROM BIRTH TO THE CIVIL WAR

John Henry Sothoron was born on Christmas Day, 25 December 1807 in Saint Mary's County, Maryland. His parents were James Forbes and Rebecca Ann Maria Sothoron. He was born near or at The Plains, a plantation on the Patuxent River. The Plains was on a peninsula located between two creeks that flow into the Patuxent River. The ancestors of Colonel Sothoron had arrived in Maryland at some point in the 1600s during the British colonial era. .

The Revolutionary War ended British colonial occupation and achieved three significant changes for Marylanders. First, the United Colonies became the United States and the province of Maryland became the state of Maryland. Secondly, the system of land ownership changed from royalty to individuals. Thirdly, civil rights were extended to all individuals except slaves under the Declaration of Independence, the Constitution and the Bill of Rights.

Saint Mary's County was the subject of raiding by British soldiers who were landed by ships. Saint Mary's County was blockaded by the British navy and suffered economically, just as it had during the Revolutionary War.[2] In 1812, a second war broke out between the United States and Great Britain. During August of 1814, The Plains was the scene of fighting. From May to August of 1814, the British navy was engaged in offensive operations on the Patuxent River. The British fleet was opposed by American gunboats and barges commanded by Commodore Joshua Barney. A British ship, the 74-gun *Albion*, drove the gunboats and barges up the Patuxent River and forced them to retreat to Saint Leonard's Creek. The *Albion* was later joined by the 32-gun frigate *Narcissus* on 15 June 1814. On 26 July 1814, Commodore Barney fought his way out of Saint Leonard's Creek with the assistance of land forces and retreated up the river.[3]

British troops landed on 19 August 1814 at Benedict, about one mile up the Patuxent River from The Plains. They then went to Washington, D.C. and burned the nation's capitol. Colonel Sothoron would have been six years old at the time. If he did not personally view the fighting, it is certainly would have seen its effects. In 1836, the events of the fighting at The Plains were described in a report of the Committee of Claims of the United States Senate:[4]

24th Congress (119)
1st Session

IN SENATE OF THE UNITED STATES
February 4, 1836
Read, and ordered to be printed

---

[2] Hammett, Regina Combs, *History of Saint Mary's County, Maryland, 1634-1990*, page 104.
[3] Hammett, page 107.
[4] *National Archives and Records Administration* (cited hereafter as *NARA*), Congressional Series Set, Senate Claims Report Number 119, 24th Congress, 1st Session, Volume 280.

Mr. Naudain made the following
REPORT
with Senate Bill No. 118

The Committee of Claims, to whom was referred the petition of James F. Sothoron, praying compensation for property destroyed by the enemy during the late war, report:

That Alexander Lyon, Joseph B. Burroughs, John B. Burroughs, and Hanson Burroughs, testify that they were private soldiers in a company of Maryland militia commanded by the petitioner, and were encamped, with other troops, under the command of the late General Philip Stuart, near the farms of the said petitioner, during a part of the summer of the year 1814; that, in the early part of July in the said year, they were ordered by Captain Sothoron, the petitioner, together with others, to march down upon his farm on the Patuxent river and occupy his houses, as a corps of observation; that the guard or troops did, according to his orders, occupy the houses, both dwelling and out-houses, for the space of thirty days, when they were driven there from by the enemy landing and attacking them with a superior force; that they effected their retreat with difficulty, leaving behind their baggage, ammunition, and provisions; and that the enemy destroyed the dwelling, and burnt a large barn with upwards of forty hogsheads of tobacco, and pulled down the other houses, such as the granary, quarters, &c.

When the troops were driven from their first position, they retreated to an adjoining farm, also belonging to the said petitioner, and occupied the dwelling-houses and buildings upon it; the next day, the enemy pursued them, drove them from their new position, injured and nearly destroyed the dwelling-house, and burnt a large barn containing one hundred and twenty-three thousand pounds of tobacco. They further testify that the troops under the command of General Stuart had not, at the time they were ordered to occupy Sothoron's houses, any tents at all, and the detachment had no other shelter from the weather than the houses of the petitioner.

John B. Burroughs testifies that, about three or four days after the burning of the petitioner's barns and the damage done to his dwelling-houses, he heard a conversation between his father and three British officers, at his father's house, during which conversation the British officers declared "that it was their orders to burn and destroy all property occupied by the militia in any way, and if that property (meaning the petitioner's) had not so been occupied, they would not have burnt and destroyed it."

The character of the persons who testify to the above facts is vouched for by the certificate of Charles C. Egerton, William Ford, and William Floyd, three justices of the peace.

The petitioner alleges in his memorial that, while under the command of General Stuart and encamped with his company about five or six miles from the river, "he was ordered by General Stuart to detach a portion of his company, under the command of a subaltern officer, to march down upon the said Sothoron's farm, there to occupy his houses and remain as a corps of observation." Against this order the petitioner alleges he remonstrated, stating the consequences that might result from such occupancy, but he was nevertheless obliged to comply with the said order, and did detach a part of his company for that service accordingly, which was the cause of the destruction of the petitioner's property by the enemy.

From a consideration of the whole of the testimony in the case, the committee do not doubt that the buildings upon the farms of the petitioner were occupied as barracks, from necessity, in consequence of the orders given by officers of the militia then in service of the United States; that their destruction by the enemy was the consequence of the orders given by the officers of the militia then in service of the United States; that their destruction by the enemy was the consequence of that occupation, and that the petitioner is entitled to relief for the destruction of the said buildings.

A bill is therefore reported for his relief.

[Gales & Seaton, print.]

From the information given in the report, it appears that the fighting took place at The Plains in the early part of August of 1814. The Plains was used as an observation post and a military barracks by the Maryland militia. The actions of the British naval and land forces at The Plains were part of an effort to neutralize any potential resistance by the Maryland militia to the subsequent landing of British troops on 19 August 1814. It appears that the threat of the British army officers to destroy property effectively resulted in the hesitancy of the local Maryland militia to oppose the invaders. The Plains was unoccupied by the family for a time due to the threat of the invading British forces. The farm that the Maryland militia retreated to was probably Chesley's Hill.

John H. Sothoron attended the Charlotte Hall School (or Military Academy) in Saint Mary's County for his preparatory studies. He later went to the University of Virginia at Charlottesville, Virginia from 1826 to 1828. His name appears in three college catalogues. For the second session commencing on 1 February 1826, he studied modern languages and mathematics. His residence was given as Saint Mary's, Maryland. For the third session of the University of Virginia from 1 February to 20 July 1827, Colonel Sothoron studied modern languages, mathematics and natural philosophy. His residence was given as Charles County, Maryland. For the fourth session from 1827 to 1828, he studied modern languages and natural philosophy. His residence was again listed as Charles County, Maryland.[5] As will later be shown in this book, students of the University of Virginia from this time period were significant as both Unionists and in Confederate government affairs during the Civil War.

Unfortunately, the Federal Census for 1830 of Saint Mary's County does not exist During March of 1831, the courthouse burned down.[6] The census was probably stored there.

It does not appear that his residence physically changed from Saint Mary's to Charles County. The Plains is within Saint Mary's near the Charles County border. The border between the two counties was not definite at that time. In the early 1900s, the Legislature of Maryland defined the border and settled the boundary problem.

In a Chancery Court of Annapolis proceeding in 1832, there was a dispute among heirs of The Plains and other land. It was recorded that Elizabeth and John Henry Sothoron were the children of Rebecca (nee Forbes) Sothoron. From the court record it appears that Rebecca Sothoron died about 1819. The Plains was referred to as the "Plains of Plenty". The complaint was dismissed because the parties had agreed.[7]

*   *   *

On 22 May 1834, Colonel Sothoron married Elizabeth Magruder Somervell at Greenwood, her father's residence in Prince Georges County, Maryland. In the marriage notice printed in the *National Intelligencer* on 11 June 1834, he was referred to as Colonel for the first time.[8] This may have been a hereditary title for a militia appointment dating back to colonial times. The title appears to have originated with Colonel Henry Jowles (or Joles) who was an ancestor of Colonel Sothoron and lived in Saint Mary's County in the 1600s. Colonel Jowles was one of the leaders of the Protestant Revolution of 1689 in Maryland.[9]

The first child of John H. and Elizabeth M. Sothoron was born on 20 April 1835. Rebecca Ann Mariah Sothoron was baptized on 27 April 1835 in Prince Georges County, Maryland.[10] She was named after her paternal grandmother Rebecca Ann Mariah Sothoron.

---

[5] University of Virginia, *A Catalogue of the Officers and Students of the University of Virginia, Second Session, commencing February 1, 1826, Third Session, commencing February 1 to July 20, 1827, Fourth Session, 1827 to 1828.*

[6] Hammett, page 494.

[7] *Maryland State Archives* (cited hereafter as *MSA*), 1832, Chancery Papers 7923.

[8] Fresco, *Marriages and Deaths, Saint Mary's County, 1634-1900*, page 273.

[9] Hammett, page 43.

[10] Brown, *Index of Church Registers, 1686-1885, Vol. II*, page 100.

For the damages sustained to The Plains from the War of 1812, the previously mentioned Committee of Claims report of 4 February 1836 was issued in support of Senate Bill Number 118 to pay James F. Sothoron, the father of Colonel Sothoron, for his losses. On 24 October 1836, the Auditors Office of the Treasury Department disbursed a payment in the amount of $7,500 to James F. Sothoron.[11]

For the Federal Census of 1840 and earlier, only the head of family was listed by name. All other persons were listed not by name, but by category. Colonel and Mrs. Sothoron with their children lived in the Fourth Election District of Charles County, Maryland:[12]

> Head of Family: John H. Sothoron
> 1 white male under age 5
> 1 white male age 20 and under 30
> 1 white female under age 5
> 1 white female age 15 and under 20
> 1 white female age 40 and under 50
> 5 free Blacks
> 7 slaves

It is possible that this farm or plantation was located at Benedict, about one mile up the river from the main plantation house at The Plains. There were five free Blacks and seven slaves. The slaves were not given any racial classification.

Charles and Saint Mary's Counties are next to each other. In the Federal Census of 1840 Colonel Sothoron had an additional household, probably at The Plains. This household was in Saint Mary's County:[13]

> Head of Family: John H. Sothoron
> 1 white male age 20 and under 30
> no white females
> 1 free colored male age 10 and under 24
> 1 free colored male age 24 and under 36
> 1 free colored male age 55 and under 100
> no free colored females
> 5 male slaves age under 10
> 4 male slaves age 10 and under 24
> 2 male slaves age 24 and under 36
> 1 male slave age 36 and under 55
> 3 female slaves age 10 and under
> 7 female slaves age 10 and under 24
> 2 female slaves age 24 and under 36
> 1 female slave age 55 and under 100
> 29 persons total
> 22 persons in each family employed in agriculture

There are three free colored males included in the household of Saint Mary's County. The distinction of the two descriptions by the census taker of the two counties is that they used two names, "Black" and "colored", to

---

[11] *NARA*, RG 217, Misc. Treasury Account 70942.
[12] page 162.
[13] page 167.

describe the same racial category of person. Speculating by ages given, this household may have included in it the father and mother of Colonel Sothoron. Additionally, it appears by counting that no children under age 10 were working.

By 1840, Colonel and Mrs. Sothoron had at least four children: Rebecca Ann Mariah, Mary Elizabeth, Margaret Holliday and James Forbes. It appears that Colonel Sothoron and his wife were living with two surviving children in Charles County. Infant mortality was a significant tragedy at that time. There were no young children included in the household of Saint Mary's County.

The total number of slaves in this census was 32 counting both households. The white male age 20 and under 30 may have been an overseer, farm manager or foreman for the plantation household in Saint Mary's County. The working conditions of the slaves are not known. However, while agricultural work can be strenuous, it is seasonal. There is more labor activity during the planting, growing and harvesting seasons than during the winter. Winter months could have been a vacation for the slaves before the existence of the word.

Some of the free colored persons included in the census of the two households above may be Peter, Susanna or Darky Butler listed below or descendants of them.[14]

Page 4, Certificate Number 16
Negro Susanna commonly called Susanna Butler is five feet three inches high aged thirty three years or thereabouts complexion rather bright, hair short & wooly: make middle size has a small scar about one inch above the left elbow, her right thumb straight with a crooked nail - large full eyes, a gap between her upper and lower fore teeth, dimples in her cheeks, & a pleasing countenance, was raised in Saint Mary's County, has this day produced to me satisfactory proof, in the manner directed in the act of assembly "relating to negroes" and pursuant to the said act I do hereby certify that the said Susanna Butler is a free negro and that she obtained her freedom in Saint Mary's County Court at March Term 1809 of John Sothoron & others.

March 14, 1809
Page 9, Certificate Number 33
Peter commonly called Peter Butler aged twenty two years or thereabouts of the height of five feet six and a quarter inches, complexion dark, hair short, make rather slender, notable marks large aquiline nose, thick lips the under one projected rather more than the upper, remarkable large full eyes and high forehead was raised in Saint Mary's County and obtained his freedom in Saint Mary's County Court at March term 1809 against John Sothoron & others –

March 13, 1810
Page 18, Certificate Number 64
Darky Butler aged twenty one years or there about of the height of five feet two inches, complexion not very black, hair rather long & bushy make rather stout notable marks a scar in the left eye brow, nose of the common size & flat round, visage broad across the temples was raised in Saint Mary's County and obtained her freedom at August Term 1812 from John Sothoron & others—
August 7, 1812

The above slaves had been owned by John Sothoron and possibly other relatives. John Sothoron may have been an uncle of Colonel Sothoron.

In 1843, the sister of Colonel Sothoron, Elizabeth A. Sothoron married Hezekiah Burroughs. According to the National Archives War of 1812 military pension file of Hezekiah Burroughs, he was born on 11 April

---

[14] *MSA*, Saint Mary's County Certificates of Freedom 1806-1864.

1793. The age of Elizabeth A. Sothoron is unknown. The date of their Saint Mary's County marriage license was 23 February 1843.[15] Hezekiah and Elizabeth A. Burroughs had two children who survived to become adults. Hezekiah Duncan Burroughs was born on 17 March 1847 and his sister, Eliza C. Burroughs was born in 1848 or 1849. Their mother, Elizabeth A. (nee Sothoron) Burroughs does not appear in the census of 1850 and it is possible that she died from the birth of her daughter or another child. Hezekiah Burroughs was known as "Deacon Burroughs" because he made his slaves go to church.[16] The church of the Sothoron and Burroughs families was All Faith Church.

According to the *National Intelligencer* of 20 December 1843, James Forbes Sothoron, the eldest son of Colonel Sothoron died at his grandfather's residence in Prince Georges County on 17 December 1843. He was four years old and had been named after his paternal grandfather.

On 6 February 1847, during the Second Session of the 29th Congress, Senator Reverdy Johnson of Maryland introduced legislation on behalf of James F. Sothoron, the father of Colonel Sothoron.[17] The additional legislation was for James F. Sothoron to recover money for additional damages incurred during the War of 1812. Captain Sothoron had been required to use his own dwellings to quarter troops in August of 1814. The dwellings used had been severely damaged by the invading British forces. Ten days later, the father of Colonel Sothoron, Major James F. Sothoron died from falling off his horse. His death occurred on 16 February 1847. He was 63 years old and the death was reported in the *National Intelligencer*.[18] James F. Sothoron died intestate; he did not leave a will.

The legislation that Senator Reverdy Johnson introduced in 1847 was passed by the Senate in 1848. *The Congressional Globe* of Friday, 16 June 1848 reported the bill as having been passed.[19] Because James F. Sothoron was deceased, the payment of the bill for damages passed on to the heirs of his estate. Included in the National Archives file is a document naming John H. Sothoron as the administrator of his father's estate. The document was signed by George Combs, the Registrar of Wills and Henry G. S. Key, the Justice of the Orphan's Court for Saint Mary's County.

The claim was originally introduced in 1836 and then reintroduced in 1847. The Congressional Report of 4 February 1836 indicates that a bill was "reported" for the payment of the claim. However, the second Congressional Committee of Claims report of 6 February 1847 matched exactly the 1836 report except for the last paragraph. In the last paragraph, a distinction was made as to the genre of property that the claim was made for:[20]

> As the facts here set forth apply as well to the loss of the personal as of the real estate of the claimant, it became the subject of inquiry with your committee, why indemnity had been allowed for one and not for the other, and whether the former application had included the personal property. On this point it is in evidence (see deposition of W. B. Scott, the agent for the former claim, herewith filed) that no claim was then made for indemnity for personal property, in consequence of the advice of a Senator from Maryland, and a Senator from Delaware, who deemed it best to limit the application to the buildings, which came clearly within the provisions of the act of 1816. It is impossible, as your committee think, to draw a distinction, in equity, between the loss of houses and of personal property which they contain; and they believe that if the petitioner was entitled, as in their opinion he certainly was, to remuneration in the one case, he is so in the other. Under these circumstances, it is believed that the prayer of the

---

[15] Brumbaugh, page 323.
[16] Duncan Dashiel Burroughs
[17] *CLNN*, The Congressional Globe, February 6, 1847, page 335, spelled as Sotheron, accessed 7 December 2006.
[18] Fresco, page 458.
[19] *The Congressional Globe*, June 16, 1848, page 850.
[20] *NARA*, Congressional Serial Set, Senate Claims Report Number 127, 29th Congress, 2nd Session, Volume 495.

claimant is just, and should be granted; and the passage of the accompanying bill is recommended.

The third and last report of the Congressional Committee of Claims, issued on 4 February 1848, was identical to the others made in 1836 and 1847 except that the last paragraph recommended the passage of the bill which was Senate Bill Number 129.[21] The Comptroller's Office of the Treasury Department paid $12,070 to the heirs of James F. Sothoron on 8 May 1849.[22] From the documents in the National Archives files, it appears that the payment made in 1836 was for "real" property which was buildings. The payment made in 1848 was for "personal" property which was tobacco, crops and timber. The timber was cedar trees cut down and taken by the British army. An issue mentioned in the papers was determining the value of tobacco during 1814. There were letters in the file from Benjamin M. Hodges, John R. Magruder, Robert Bowie and others stating the price of tobacco during the War of 1812.

When the legislation was introduced and passed in 1847 and 1848, Abraham Lincoln and Andrew Johnson both were congressmen in the House of Representatives. Both later became Presidents. During the Civil War, President Abraham Lincoln was involved with making decisions regarding the Sothoron family. After the Civil War, President Andrew Johnson made a decision about the Sothoron family. During the era, Jefferson Davis was a Senator and the future president of the Confederate States.[23]

Surviving photographs of The Plains show that it had a gambrel (or Mansard) style of roof, which is not a common roof style for houses in Saint Mary's County. Possibly, the roof was replaced as a result of compensation paid by the Federal government. Mansard roofs appear in American architecture around the decade preceding the Civil War and the roof of The Plains may have been replaced during that time. Because it appears that in 1840 Colonel Sothoron and his family did not reside at The Plains, it may be that the house may have remained in an uninhabitable condition due to the fighting in August of 1814 during the War of 1812.

* * *

The Census of 1850 differed greatly from prior enumerations. All persons were counted individually and their age and sex was recorded. Free persons had their name listed while slaves did not. Free persons had other information included such as income, occupation and birthplace. Financial value was also recorded on the census.

In the Federal Census of 1850 Colonel Sothoron and his family are found in the Fifth Election District of Saint Mary's County. The enumeration was taken on 29 October 1850 and the value of Colonel Sothoron's real estate was given as $40,000. The household composition was follows:[24]

Name	Age	Sex	Occupation	Birthplace
John H. Sothoron	43	M	Planter	Saint Mary's County
Mary E. Sothoron	34	F		Prince Georges County
Webster Sothoron	8	M		Saint Mary's County
Marshall Sothoron	6	M		Prince Georges County
Robert Sothoron	4	M		"
Fanny Sothoron	2	F		Saint Mary's County
John Cocoran	62	M	Teacher	Ireland
John Gardner	47	M	None	Saint Mary's County

---

[21] *NARA*, Congressional Serial Set, Senate Claims Report Number 57, 30th Congress, 1st Session, Volume 512.
[22] *NARA*, RG 217, Misc. Treasury Account Number 100974.
[23] *BDUSC*, accessed 22 December 2006.
[24] page 348, reverse unnumbered:

       John Fowler   24   M   Manager   Calvert County

The census has an error. The census taker omitted the name of Colonel Sothoron's wife which was Elizabeth and instead listed the name of his daughter which was Mary E. and gave the correct age for Elizabeth. . Another child of the Sothoron family resided in the First Election District of Saint Mary's County. Margaret H. Sothoron, age twelve, lived at the Saint Mary's Female Seminary and her birthplace is given as Saint Mary's County. John Cocoran, born in Ireland, probably taught the other Sothoron children at home. John Gardner may have been related to the Sothoron family. There was a marriage on 16 September 1800 between Henry Gardener and Eleanor Sothoron.[25]

In the 1850 Federal Slave Schedules there is enumeration by age, sex and color for each individual slave:

Owner: John H. Sothoron

Line Number	Age	Sex	Color
35	70	Male	Black
36	48	Male	Black
37	40	Female	Black
38	18	Male	Black
39	16	Male	Black
40	16	Female	Black
41	12	Male	Black
42	10	Male	Black
1	8	Female	Black
2	6	Male	Black
3	3	Female	Black
4	38	Male	Black
5	45	Female	Black
6	13	Female	Black
7	11	Female	Black
8	4	Female	Black
9	30	Male	Black
10	25	Female	Black
11	2	Female	Black
12	20	Female	Black
13	3	Male	Mulatto
14	60	Female	Black
15	16	Female	Black
16	21	Male	Black
17	24	Male	Black
18	34	Female	Black
19	16	Male	Black
20	14	Female	Black
21	12	Female	Black
22	10	Male	Black
23	4	Male	Black

---

[25] Brumbaugh, Vol. I, page 344.

24	2	Male	Black
25	22	Female	Black
26	4	Female	Black
27	2	Male	Black
28	60	Female	Black
29	21	Male	Black
30	21	Male	Black
31	24	Male	Black
32	18	Male	Black
33	18	Female	Black
34	30	Male	Black
35	25	Female	Mulatto
36	10	Male	Black
37	50	Male	Black
38	40	Female	Black
39	12	Male	Black
40	8	Female	Black
41	5	Female	Black
42	35	Male	Black
1	38	Female	Black
2	8	Male	Black
3	6	Male	Black
4	2	Male	Black
5	25	Female	Black
6	5	Male	Black
7	2	Female	Black
8	25	Female	Black
9	6	Male	Black
10	33	Male	Black
11	28	Female	Black
12	18	Male	Mulatto
13	13	Male	Black
14	10	Male	Black
15	8	Female	Black
16	4	Female	Black
17	2	Female	Black
18	35	Male	Black
19	28	Male	Black
20	22	Male	Black
21	20	Male	Black
22	30	Male	Black

Unfortunately, the census does not list any names for the slaves. Colonel Sothoron owned 72 slaves.

The slaves listed on line 13, 35 and 12 were Mulatto. They were of mixed racial ancestry. On line 12, there is a twenty year old female Black slave. Just beneath her, on line 13 is a three year old Mulatto male. She may have been a "femme covert", which is translated as "secret woman". Plantation owners, with complete control over the lives of their slaves, had mistresses. The worst fear of a slave owner was that a child born from his sexual relationship with a slave was a potential heir if slavery was abolished. This may have been the motive (and for financial gain) to break up families and sell children. Other persons, such as overseers or neighbors could also have had liaisons with slaves.

The census recorder of the above slaves appears to have enumerated them by family or household group. Beginning at the top line number 35 there appears to be the logical age sequence for a family or household group that extends to line number three. Other family or household groups extend from line number 4 to 8, 9 to 11, 12 and 13, 14 to 24, 25 to 27, 28 to 33, 34 to 36, 37 to 41, 42 to 4, 5 to 7, 8 and 9, 10 to 17; and a group of males from line number 18 to 22. I have entered lines in the census list to delineate the family or household groups. The number of family or household groups is fourteen and equals the number of structures given in the Census of 1860 that housed slaves.

In the Federal Census of 1850, the Agricultural Schedules give two line entries for John H. Sothoron in Saint Mary's County. Unfortunately, some of the figures were somewhat blotted out and are represented in the following figures by enclosing them with parenthesis:

	Line 7 - John H. Sothoron	Line 8 - John H. Sothoron
Improved Acres	(230)	250
Unimproved Acres	(230)	450
Cash Value of Farm	(20,000)	10,000
Value of Implements	800	200
Hogs	9	6
Asses and Mules	2	2
Mulch Cows	13	6
Working Oxen	12	8
Other Cattle	10	
Swine	75	40
Value of Live Stock	1326	620
Wheat, bushels of	2100	384
Indian Corn, bushels of	6,000	2,000
Tobacco, lbs. of	25,000	50,000
Peas & Beans bush. of	10	5
Irish Potatoes bush. of	800	75
Sweet Potatoes bush. of		100
Butter, lbs. of	260	
Beeswax and Honey lbs. of	100	
Value of Animals slaughtered	540	465

The method used to determine the figures for Line 7 in parenthesis was to use the totals at the bottom of the census sheet, not shown here, to mathematically compute the blotted entries.

The fact that there are two line entries for Colonel Sothoron's plantation is because there were two separate tracts of land. One of the plantations was The Plains, while the other was Chesley's Hill. According to this census, Colonel Sothoron owned 1160 acres of land. The number of slaves owned by Colonel Sothoron in 1840 was 32 and the increase to 72 in 1850 could be the result of inheritance, population increase or purchase.

On 2 October 1854 a murder occurred near The Plains. William Webster was shot on a road in the lands owned by Colonel Sothoron. Apparently, the perpetrator of the crime was never found. A coroner's inquest, led by George Alvey, had among its members Michael Woodburn and Hezekiah Burroughs.[26]

On 15 April 1856, a son John Henry Sothoron, Jr. was born to John Henry and Elizabeth M. Sothoron. He was baptized 13 July 1856 in Prince Georges County.[27]

The aristocratic gentry of Saint Mary's County retained traditions that found their source in English chivalry. On 25 November 1857 the *Philadelphia Press* reported a gala jousting tournament. Colonel Sothoron was the "marshal" of the event, attended by 4,000 people. They were described as the "*elite*" of Maryland. Twenty-five knights on horses tilted with lances on horseback in a competition for the privilege to crown the Queen of Love and Beauty, who was Miss Slanna Mattingly of Washington, D.C. Miss Cecilia Mudd of Charles County, was the first maid of honor. When the competition ended, a speech was given by James Compton and the queen and maids of honor were crowned. After a supper and ball, the celebration ended at 3 AM.[28] Colonel Sothoron was the leader of the Maryland landed gentry.

The origins of the November event were probably from the early English settlement times of Maryland. During colonial times in Maryland, November was the month when farmers paid "quit rent" to the Lord of the Manor, who was the leader of the English colony. The Lord of the Manor had been given a large tract of land by the king of England. Persons were subsequently granted land held by the lord, provided that they pay for the transportation of additional new immigrants from Great Britain (and sometimes other countries) and pay annual "quit rent". The new immigrants worked to pay for their transportation for a time period, usually about 7 years. The November rent payment was comparable to a yearly property tax.

The land grant program had promoted the growth of the colonies in the British colonial province of Maryland during the 1600s. The Revolutionary War changed the system. There was no longer a Lord of the Manor to collect quit rents from Resurrection Manor, which was the large tract of land that included The Plains. Colonel Sothoron was celebrating and honoring the love and beauty of women with the tradition of an event from earlier times.

North of Maryland, in the New England state of Massachusetts, there was also a day in the fall that was observed as a holiday. Persons came together for a feast of thanksgiving. However, Massachusetts had a sinister history of persecution. During the 1630s, women were executed in Salem, Massachusetts because they had been accused of practicing witchcraft. In 1861, descendents of the puritanical witch hunters of Massachusetts invaded Maryland. The men of Maryland would fight to protect their women and freedom.

Barnes Compton and Margaret Holliday Sothoron married on 27 October 1858. Margaret Holliday Sothoron was the daughter of Colonel John H. Sothoron.[29] The ceremony was held at The Plains and the marriage was performed by Rev. James W. Hoskins.[30]

Barnes Compton later became a member of the Maryland state house of delegates and a United States congressman. He was also a Maryland state tobacco inspector and State treasurer. A graduate of Charlotte Hall Academy and Princeton College, New Jersey, in 1851, he later became the naval officer at Baltimore appointed by President Cleveland.[31]

Barnes Compton may have attended Princeton College (now University) with Henry Sothoron. Henry Sothoron, age 18, is listed in the 1850 Census for New Jersey as living in Princeton Township, Mercer County. His occupation is that of a student and his birthplace was given as Medford.[32] His relationship to the Sothoron

---

[26] Knott, *Saint Mary's Coroners Inquest, 1821-1921*, page 33.
[27] Brown, page 101.
[28] *Philadelphia Press*, November 25 1857, "A Tournament in American Style", page 2, accessed 29 December 2006
[29] Hollowak, *Index to Marriages in The (Baltimore) Sun 1851-1860*, page 42.
[30] Wearmouth, *Abstracts from the Port Tobacco Times and Charles County Advertiser, 1855-1869*, pages 98-99.
[31] *Biographical Directory of the United States Congress, 1774-1989*, United States Congress, page 813., available online as the *Biographical Directory of the United States Congress, 1774 to present*, United States Congress, accessed 5 December 2006, cited hereafter as *BDUSC*, available on the Internet.
[32] page 34B, line 35.

family of Maryland is unknown.

The Census of 1860 records the occupation of Colonel Sothoron as a farmer and planter and gave his personal value as $70,000 and his real estate value as $33,000. The household composition was as follows:[33]

Name	Age	Sex	Occupation	Birthplace
John H. Sothoron	52	M	Farmer & Planter	Maryland
Elizabeth M. Sothoron	44	F	w.	Maryland
Mary E. Sothoron	22	F	Lady	Maryland
Webster Sothoron	18	M	Student	Maryland
Marshall Sothoron	16	M	do	Maryland
Robert Sothoron	14	M		Maryland
Fanny Sothoron	12	F		Maryland
Amelia Sothoron	10	F		Maryland
Ellen Sothoron	7	F		Maryland
John H. Sothoron, Jr.	4	M		Maryland
Virginia Anderson	25	F	Teacher	Virginia

Webster and Marshall Sothoron most likely were attending Charlotte Military Academy, located a few miles from The Plains. The other Sothoron children were probably educated at home by Virginia Anderson.

The Census of 1860 also reveals an out of the ordinary living arrangement for Colonel Sothoron's youngest son, Forbes Sothoron, age seven months. Forbes lived with a free Black family by the surname of Curtis who was neighbors of the Sothoron family:[34]

Name	Age	Sex	Color	Occupation	Birthplace
Sarah Curtis	35	Female	Black	Farm hand	Maryland
Ann Curtis	10	Female	Black	same	Maryland
Loney Curtis	8	Male	Black		Maryland
Elijah Curtis	5	Male	Black		Maryland
Forbes Sothoron	7/12	Male			Maryland
Alice Curtis	3	Female	Black		Maryland
Jim Curtis	1	Male	Black		Maryland

This living arraignment proves that a mutually trusting relationship existed connecting the Sothoron and Curtis families of diverse color races. Mrs. Sothoron at age 44 may have had an inability to care for her infant child Forbes. There were also other free Black families living in the area and throughout Saint Mary's County at this time.

Sarah Ann Curtis had obtained her freedom on 3 September 1845. Her age was given as seventeen and the witness at the Saint Mary's court was Henry M. Lyon.[35] She does not appear in the 1850 census for Saint Mary's or Charles counties.

The 1860 Federal Slave Schedules give less information than the 1850 census. The line entries are grouped by descending age rather than individual slave:

Line Number	Number of Slaves	Age	Sex	Color

---

[33] page 180.
[34] page 180-181.
[35] *MSA*, Saint Mary's County Certificates of Freedom, certificate 549.

31	1	95	Male	Black
32	1	75	Female	Black
33	2	60	Male	Black
34	1	80	Female	Black
35	1	52	Female	Black
36	1	50	Male	Black
37	1	46	Male	Black
38	1	44	Male	Black
39	1	44	Female	Black
40	2	40	Female	Black
1	2	40	Male	Black
2	1	36	Male	Black
3	2	36	Female	Black
4	1	35	Male	Black
5	1	32	Male	Black
6	1	32	Female	Black
7	1	30	Female	Black
8	1	28	Female	Black
9	1	27	Male	Black
10	2	26	Male	Black
11	1	26	Female	Black
12	5	24	Female	Black
13	1	22	Female	Black
14	1	22	Male	Black
15	1	21	Male	Black
16	3	20	Male	Black
17	1	19	Male	Black
18	4	18	Female	Black
19	1	16	Female	Black
20	2	16	Male	Black
21	3	15	Male	Black
22	2	14	Male	Black
23	3	14	Female	Black
24	2	13	Female	Black
25	3	12	Female	Black
26	1	12	Male	Black
27	1	11	Male	Black
28	1	11	Female	Black
29	2	10	Female	Black
30	3	10	Male	Black
31	1	9	Male	Black
32	2	8	Male	Black
33	1	8	Female	Black
34	3	6	Female	Black
35	3	6	Male	Black
36	1	5	Male	Black

37	1	5	Female	Black
38	5	4	Female	Black
39	1	4	Male	Black
40	1	3	Female	Black
1	1	1	Male	Black
2	1	1	Female	Black
3	1	2/12	Female	Black
4	1	8/12	Female	Black
5	1	7/12	Female	Black
6	1	7/12	Male	Black
7	2	3/12	Female	Black

The ages of the elderly slaves are surprising evidence of the longevity of slaves. Colonel Sothoron owned 95 slaves according to the seat of government classification system of socioeconomic status.

No Mulatto slaves were enumerated in the above census. It is possible that the fear at the seat of government, that a child born of a female slave might in the future be granted the legal right to become heir to his estate, changed the results of the census. Consequently, it appears possible that for enumeration purposes, Mulattos could become Black. The lack of Mulattos may also be an indication that racist polarization occurred during the decade between 1850 and 1860.

The overseer of slaves at the plantation was John Goodrich. He and his family are listed just above Colonel Sothoron on the same census page, but living in a separate house. John Goodrich was the witness listed in Saint Mary's court records for the freedom given to Charles Barns, age 23, on 13 September 1853.[36]

In Maryland as a whole there were many free Blacks. The 1860 population figures for Maryland, Delaware, Virginia and the District of Columbia were:[37]

	Whites	Free Negroes	Negro Slaves
Maryland	515,918	83,942	87,189
Delaware	90,589	19,829	1,789
Virginia	1,047,411	58,042	490,865
District of Columbia	60,764	11,131	3,185

For the total combined population of Maryland, approximately one tenth of the population was in slavery but an almost equal number of Blacks were free persons. The figures for Delaware, Virginia and the District of Columbia are given as a comparison.

By comparison, New Jersey had 18 slaves in 1860. In New Jersey, there may have been an economic class defined by state law. In 1861, the legislature of New Jersey passed a law titled "An act for the more easy partition of lands held by co-parceners, joint tenants and tenants in common." From a definition in Black's Law Dictionary, published in 1951, a coparcener was an heir. However, the fact that two other groups existed and were known as joint tenants and tenants in common, but are not heirs, supports this idea. These two groups were apparently occupying land that was legislated for the act title words "easy partition". The legislation passed from one judge or justice who had "expired" to another judge or justice the power to appoint commissioners to sell the real estate (land) from underneath the serf persons who had worked on it as farmers, thereby causing

---

[36] *MSA*, Saint Mary's County Certificates of Freedom, no number on certificate.
[37] *Preliminary Report of the Eighth Census, 1860*, page 131, United States Bureau of the Census, accessed 20 December 2006, available on the Internet.

homelessness.[38]

It may be that New Jersey had a serf economic class tied to the land and called them by a name other than slave or serf. Serfs differ from slaves because in a transaction both they and land are sold, while a slave is sold without land. It would be interesting to discover if the joint tenants and tenants in common were evicted and where they went or where they were deported to. There is a third category which describes workers. A servant, during the time of the Civil War, was an unpaid "at will" person who could leave a master. A chief servant is a butler. "Easy partition" may have been an escheat pogrom.

In the Agricultural Census of 1860, it is apparent that there was a significant increase in the productivity of the plantation, particularly for the amount of tobacco produced and in many other categories:

<u>Line 7, John H. Sothoron</u>
Improved acres of land	600
Unimproved acres of land	300
Cash value of land	33,000
Value of farm implements and machinery	500
Horses	18
Asses and mules	6
Much cows	18
Working oxen	24
Other cattle	26
Sheep	45
Swine	150
Value of live stock	4,300
Wheat, bushels of	1,800
Indian corn, bushels of	5,000
Tobacco, lbs. of	120,000
Wool, lbs of	200
Peas and beans, bushels of	50
Irish potatoes, bushels of	200
Sweet potatoes, bushels of	75
Wine, gallons of	3
Butter, lbs. of	1,000
Hay, tons of	30
Hops, lbs. of	10
Value of homemade manufactures	100
Value of animals slaughtered	1,000

It appears that this Agricultural Census combined the land acres for both The Plains and Chesley's Hill. A number of the slaves at The Plains must have been involved with fishing. In 1868, when Colonel Sothoron filed a claim for damages against the government, he included boats and fishing nets in an inventory of items that were stolen by the Union army during the Civil War.

A Black woman may have been informally freed by Colonel Sothoron. There is no record of her receiving a certificate of freedom in Saint Mary's County. A marriage was recorded on 29 February 1840 at Sacred Heart Church for a Black couple. The groom was Ignatius Hutchins and the bride was Clara, a "servant"

---

[38] *Acts of the Eighty-fifth Legislature of the State of New Jersey and Seventeenth Under the New Constitution*, approved February 1, 1861, Session of 1861, Chapter IX, page 19.

that belonged to Colonel Sothoron. There is no record of a marriage license for Ignatius and Clara Hutchins in the civil records of Saint Mary's County. It appears that their marriage was recognized by the church and not by the government.[39]

As a result of Saint Mary's County court action Ignatius Hutchins was given his freedom on 7 February 1843:[40]

> Page 128, Certificate Number 522
> Ignatius Hutchins aged about twenty five years, five feet eight inches high of a dark Copper almost olive has a mole near the right corner of his mouth about the size of a pea has a long scar on the shin bone of the right leg and has a mole on the inside of his left arm a little below the Joint was born free and raised in Saint Mary's County,
> Jerome Russell Feb 7, 1843

The married couple, with the husband having legally gained his freedom, may have moved out of the area. Clara Hutchins, while not having received her certificate of freedom, was probably considered free due to the freedom of her husband. Ignatius and Clara Hutchins do not appear in the 1850 Federal Census for Saint Mary's or neighboring Charles County.

The wording of this certificate of freedom is remarkable compared to other St Mary's County certificates. Other certificates use the word "obtained" to describe how the slave became free. The certificate of Ignatius Hutchins has the words "born free and raised in Saint Mary's County" to describe the legal grounds of his freedom.

In 1840, Ignatius Hutchins, a slave, had married Clara, a servant. It was the marriage of a slave, who worked at the will of another person; to a servant, who worked for another person but was allowed leave the person she served. It was the marriage of persons of two different economic classes.

Col. Sothoron was a member of the Maryland House of Delegates in 1831, 1833 and 1834. From 1852 to 1856 he was a member of the Maryland Senate.[41]

* * *

Prior to the Civil War, Colonel Sothoron was a Whig. The Whigs were the political party who represented the aristocratic landed gentry. Slavery was one of the main issues that dominated American political attitudes in that era. The landed gentry needed slavery to maintain their economic status while northern interests increased their pressure for the abolition of slavery. In 1856 John Brown and others hacked to death with swords five proslavery settlers in Kansas. Slave owners responded self protectively to the grisly and fanatical terrorist attack. Colonel Sothoron attended a convention in Baltimore, Maryland on 8 June 1859. He opposed "free-negroism".[42]

In the later part of 1858, a "manifesto" was published by Boston lawyer Lysander Spooner. The propaganda sheet was sent to about 200 slave owners. It included threats of murder, kidnapping and organized attacks. John Brown and others may, or may not, have been the author(s) of the written threats.[43] It is not known if Colonel Sothoron was the recipient of the vile threats.

---

[39] Callum, *Black Marriages of Saint Mary's County, Maryland*, page 59.
[40] *MSA*, Certificates of Freedom, Saint Mary's County, certificate 522, page 128.
[41] Hammett, page 523-526.
[42] Annual report of the American Anti-Slavery Society: by the executive committee, for the year ending May 1, 1860., American Anti-Slavery Society., New York, 1861, page 208, accessed 7 December 2006, available on the Internet at the Cornell University Library, Samuel J. May Anti-Slavery Collection(cited hereafter as *SJMASC*).
[43] Renehan, Jr., *The Secret Six, The True Tale of the Men Who Conspired with John Brown*, pages 173 to 175.

In New England during the 1850s, a conspiratorial group of abolitionists known as "The Secret Six" were plotting to invade slave states. The six were Franklin Sanborn, Thomas Wentworth Higginson, Dr. Samuel Gridley Howe, Gerrit Smith, George Luther Stearns and Theodore Parker. Their activities were material support of terrorism. Their terrorism included attacking police stations to free slaves who were prisoners, attacking and exterminating families who owned slaves, recruiting the slaves into their death squads and taking all the property they could steal. Over time, their ambitions grew and they were sending groups of settlers into Kansas. They also planned and financially supported a slave revolt in Virginia for their stated purpose of creating disunion. They met with and supported John Brown, a murderer.[44] As early as 1857, Thomas Wentworth Higginson organized a convention in Massachusetts advocating disunion.[45]

In 1854 the New England Emigrant Aid Company sent groups of mostly Irish settlers to Kansas. The company was formed by Eli Thayer and financially backed by Amos Lawrence and others. On the surface, the goals of the company appeared benevolent. However, Renehan, Jr., characterizes their goals as to "ban black citizenship and property ownership", which are words that partially describe apartheid. Dr. Samuel Gridley Howe was on the board of directors of the New England Emigrant Aid Company.[46]

Financially supported by New England abolitionists known as the "Secret Six", John Brown raided Harper's Ferry, Virginia in 1859.[47] His raid was an attempt by fanatical terrorists to invade Virginia and begin a slave revolt. During the raid, Brown took hostages. The attempt failed and Brown was tried, found guilty of murder and treason against the state of Virginia. He was executed. After his capture, Brown was interrogated by a group of government officials. One of the members of the group was congressman Clement L. Vallandigham. Vallandigham asked Brown about his financial supporters.[48]

The political crisis exacerbated with the election of Abraham Lincoln to the presidency in 1860. The states of the South seceded and began to form the Confederate States of America. Because it was a Border State, Maryland was in the middle of the conflict. Saint Mary's County sided with the interests of the south. In the presidential election of 1860, Abraham Lincoln received only one vote from Saint Mary's County.[49]

Nationwide, the ratio of whites to colored persons was changing. In 1790, the ratio of white persons to colored persons was 4 to 1. By 1860, the ratio increased to 6 to 1. After the Civil War, in 1870, the ratio again increased to 6.89 to 1 (see chart in Appendix). Within Saint Mary's County the combined number of Blacks, slave and free, exceeded the number of whites from 1810 to 1870. In 1860, there were 6,798 white, 6,549 slaves and 1,866 free Blacks in Saint Mary's County (see chart in Appendix).[50] Demographically, emancipation would result in a free Black majority.

In 1805, the Maryland legislature had passed a law that provided for the granting of certificates of freedom to slaves. From 1806 to 1864 about one thousand slaves gained their freedom in Saint Mary's County. Some of the slaves released had two middle names, which may be an indication of a rise in social status. The use of two middle names could also have been necessary because of the existence of two persons in the same locality with identical first and last names. In addition, a few of the slaves, in physical descriptions given of them in their freedom certificates, had vaccination marks on them. Other slaves were described as having injuries on them that could have been from accidents; or evidence of physical abuse by owners and overseers.

---

[44] Edward J. Renehan, Jr., *The Secret Six, The True Tale of the Men Who Conspired with John Brown*, Brown's disloyalty is throughout the book and is specifically mentioned on page 93.
[45] Ibid, page 115.
[46] Renehan, Jr., *The Secret Six, The True Tale of the Men Who Conspired with John Brown*, page 81 and 82.
[47] Wikipedia, "Secret Six" or "Committee of Six", accessed 1 January 2007, available on the Internet; also see Edward J. Renehan, Jr., *The Secret Six, The True Tale of the Men Who Conspired with John Brown*.
[48] Renehan, Jr., *The Secret Six, The True Tale of the Men Who Conspired with John Brown*, page 206.
[49] Evitts, *A Matter of Allegiances*, page 150.
[50] United States Census Bureau, Census of Population and Housing, Census of 1870, page, 5-to 7 (download file 1870a-03), pages 36 to 37 (1870a-03), accessed 20 December 2007. .

During the presidential election year of 1860 alone, about one hundred slaves were given their freedom in Saint Mary's County, particularly in the months of October and November. This is about one-tenth of the total number freed from 1805 to 1864. A search of the certificates of freedom for Saint Mary's County did not reveal any slaves given their freedom by Colonel Sothoron. During the 1850s, the name of Benjamin Gwinn Harris appears frequently in Saint Mary's County Court records in regards to the freeing of slaves. Harris later became a congressman and was a friend of Colonel Sothoron.

Slavery was an extremely profitable enterprise for Colonel Sothoron. In 1868, when he filed a claim against the government, he valued his yearly tobacco crop of 120,000 pounds to be worth $14,700. Tobacco was a cash crop and earned income. It is possible he could have freed his slaves and began to pay them.

To determine the wages paid for farm labor, *The New York Times* of 28 November 1863 published orders concerning the treatment and pay of former slaves who had come under the suzerain jurisdiction of the Union army. The military orders were issued by Lorenzo Thomas, the Adjutant-General of the Union army. Men over age fifteen received seven dollars per month. Women over age fifteen received five dollars per month. Children between the ages of twelve and fifteen received half the pay of adults.[51]

The orders also provided that clothing would be furnished at cost. By applying the above wage formula to the slaves of Colonel Sothoron listed in the 1860 census and excluding all under age 12, it would have cost him $313.50 per month or $3,762 yearly in wages. However, with freedom, his slaves could have left the farm if urban areas provided competitive pay. Additionally, food, clothing, rent for housing or a boarding fee would have increased living costs for employees.

It has to be kept in mind that the costs of the era may have created a completely different aspect for the freeing of slaves. If the cost of basic necessities exceeded the income of a freed slave, then freedom may have been accompanied by the abject poverty of wage slavery.

---

[51] *The New York Times*, November 28, 1863, page 2.

Chapter 2

THE COUP D'ETAT AGAINST MARYLAND

The war that existed in the United States from 1861 to 1865 had the name of it changed to reflect evolving viewpoints. During the war the conflict was described as a national emergency, civil war, rebellion and insurrection. The records both of the Union and Confederate armies were published by the United States Government Printing Office with the title of *The War of the Rebellion: a Compilation of the Official Records of the Union and Confederate Armies*. In the early 1900s the name changed from the War of the Rebellion to the Civil War. The conflict has also been referred to as the War Between the States.

In records made during the war, Confederates were given a variety of names to describe them by politicians, the Union army and others. Those names, other than Confederate, were disunionist, secessionist, rebel, insurgent, guerilla, bushwhacker and Tory. Tory was a name from the Revolutionary War and it described an American who fought against the revolution on the side of the British.

In the years before the Civil War, one group was targeted and demonized by abolition fanatics of the north. The fanatics propagandized extensively against southern and Border State slave owners while completely ignoring any and all employment exploitation in their own geographical area. Fanaticism resulted in absolutist actions to dominate opponents, real or imagined.

In 1887 the book, *Memories of the Men Who Saved the Union*, by Donn Piatt was published. Piatt had worked for the election of Lincoln for president in Illinois and remained politically connected to Lincoln during the Civil War.[52] Lincoln, after he was elected, did not believe that the south would secede.[53] Lincoln was characterized by Piatt as "blind to the coming storm."[54]

The events of 1861 in the South and Maryland roused public sentiment in Saint Mary's County against the northern states. The southern states began to secede and form the provisional government of the Confederate States of America. In February, President-elect Lincoln traveled secretly through Baltimore during the night on his way to Washington because of threats of assassination.

On 12 April 1861, United States Fort Sumter, located in Charleston Harbor, South Carolina was bombarded by the secessionists. Fort Sumter surrendered the next day and the garrison was munificently released to return to the United States. In response to this, on 15 April 1861, a chagrined President Lincoln issued a proclamation calling for 75,000 militia troops of the states to suppress the combination which opposed and obstructed the laws of the United States. The "deep south" seven states of South Carolina, Georgia, Alabama, Florida, Mississippi, Louisiana and Texas he identified as being where the combination existed. He commanded "those" who were involved to return to their "abodes" within twenty days. Lincoln ordered both chambers of Congress to convene on 4 July 1861. Lincoln promised the "utmost care will be observed" to avoid

---

[52] Donn Piatt, *Memories of the Men Who Saved the Union*, page 28, accessed 28 December 2006, available on the Internet.
[53] Donn Piatt, ibid., page 33, accessed 28 December 2006.
[54] Donn Piatt, ibid., page 34, accessed 28 December 2006.

the devastation, destruction or interference with property.[55] His promise was soon to prove specious.

On 17 April 1861, after the surrender of Fort Sumter, the state of Virginia adopted an ordinance of succession and detached from the United States.[56] Virginia was geographically separated from Maryland by the Potomac River but economically linked by their mutual trade in the tidewater region of the Chesapeake Bay and the Potomac River with the tributary rivers that lead into them.

At the beginning of the Civil War, the United States had a standing army of about 13,000 soldiers. It was the regularly constituted military establishment which was professionally trained and stationed within our national boundaries. Individual states had their own military units consisting of militia organizations which were haphazardly organized and trained. Northern state militia units began traveling from northern states to Washington, D.C., while southern militia units went to Richmond, Virginia. Most United States military officers from seceded states or northerners married to a woman of the south resigned their commissions and returned home.

Massachusetts Union general and politician Benjamin Franklin Butler was known as "Spoons" to his adversaries because of his reported theft of silverware.[57] The nickname of Butler does not accurately describe him. When in New Orleans during 1862, Butler ordered the execution of William B. Munford for removing the United States flag.[58] Later during the Civil War, Butler approved of the illegal taking of civilian hostages within his military command to secure the safety of telegraph lines. His direct order was "to execute them if necessary on the spot."[59] Butler also earned the nickname "Beast Butler" because his actions towards women were chauvinistic and vile. True to the tradition of his Massachusetts forbearers who falsely accused women of witchcraft and then murdered them, puritanical Butler threatened to classify the entire female population of New Orleans as prostitutes and then take repressive action against them.

On 19 April 1861 there was a riot in Baltimore, Maryland between Massachusetts militia soldiers traveling from the north to Washington, D.C. and civilians of the city.[60] One day later, on 20 April 1861 Butler arrived in Annapolis, Maryland with his army.[61] On 23 April 1861 Brigadier General Butler of the "United States Army" made a propaganda offer to use United States troops in cooperation with the Governor of Maryland to oppose a slave rebellion.[62] On 27 April 1861 Brigadier General B. F. Butler of the "Massachusetts Militia" was assigned to suzerain command the Department of Annapolis.[63] Annapolis was the capital of Maryland and where the Maryland Legislature normally met. The reason for the sudden transformation of Butler's military status from the United States Army to the Massachusetts Militia is not known.

---

[55] A Century of Lawmaking for a New Nation: U.S. Congressional Documents and Debates, 1774-1875 (cited hereafter as *CLNN*). Statutes at Large, April 15, 1861, page 1258, A Century of Lawmaking for a New Nation: U.S. Congressional Document and Debates, 1774-1875 at the Library of Congress (Washington, D.C.: American Memory Project, [2000-02]), available on the Internet, accessed 5 December 2006; see also Abraham Lincoln Papers at the Library of Congress (cited hereafter as *ALPLC*). Transcribed and Annotated by the Lincoln Studies Center, Knox College. Galesburg, Illinois (cited hereafter as *ALSC*). Abraham Lincoln, Monday, April 15, 1861 (Proclamation on State Militia) [Draft], available on the Internet at Abraham Lincoln Papers at the Library of Congress, Manuscript Division (Washington, D.C.: American Memory Project, [2000-02]), accessed 5 December 2006, available on the Internet.
[55] Basler, *Vol. VII*, page 255.
[56] *The War of the Rebellion: a Compilation of the Official Records of the Union and Confederate Armies*, United States War Department, United States, Record and Pension Office, United States, War Records Office, *et al.*, Government Printing Office, (cited hereafter as *OR*), Series 1, Volume 2, 1880, Summary of the Principal Events, page 1, available at Cornell University Library, Making of America, accessed 2 December 2006, available on the Internet.
[57] Boatner, *Civil War Dictionary*, page 109.
[58] *OR*, Series 1, Volume 15, 1886, June 5, 1862, Wm. H. Wiegel, Special Orders No. 70, by command of Major General Butler, page 469, accessed 2 December 2006.
[59] *OR*, Series 1, Volume 40, Part III, 1892, July 26, 1864, G. S. Innis (of Fort Powhatan) to Benj. F. Butler, page 500, accessed 2 December 2006.
[60] *OR*, Series 1, Volume 2, 1880, Summary of the Principal Events, page 1, accessed 2 December 2006.
[61] *OR*, Series 1, Volume 2, 1880, Summary of the Principal Events, page 1, accessed 2 December 2006.
[62] *OR*, Series 1, Volume 2, 1880, April 23, 1861, B. F. Butler to Thos. H. Hicks, page 593, accessed 2 December 2006.
[63] *OR*, Series 1, Volume 2, 1880, Summary of the Principal Events, page 1, accessed 2 December 2006.

President Abraham Lincoln convened a secret emergency meeting with his constitutional advisors and department heads on 20 or 21 April 1861 at the office of the Navy Department. The secret meeting was revealed by Lincoln to Congress one year after it occurred. Washington was in a state of "siege" because all mail and telegraph communications were "cut off by the insurgents". Land travel was blocked by "treasonable resistance" in Maryland. At the meeting, Lincoln ordered that an armed revenue cutter be sent to sea to protect commerce, especially "the California treasure ships" on their way to the east coast of the United States.

Lincoln ordered that a total of fifteen armed steamships be chartered by the commandants of the navy yards at Boston, Philadelphia and New York. Commander Gillis and Commodore DuPont were to purchase additional ships, with the goal of lifting the siege of Washington by opening the water route of the Potomac River. Lincoln directed his government to listen to and receive the services of the Governor of New York, Edwin P. Morgan or his second, George D. Morgan, William M. Evarts, R. M. Blatchford, and Moses H. Grinnell. The group had been "especially empowered" to respond to the crisis. Governor Morgan and Alexander Cummings were authorized by Secretary of War Simon Cameron to arrange for the transportation of troops and military supplies. Lincoln dictated that the Secretary of the Treasury was to give two million dollars to John A. Dix, George Opdyke, and Richard M. Blatchford of New York to achieve his plan for the defense of Washington. Businessmen and politicians were among the group members. The orders to achieve Lincoln's goal were sent by private messengers.[64]

The private messengers may have been the Pony Express, also known as Russell, Majors and Waddell, and by the alias name given to them by Congress as the "Floyd acceptances".[65] From February of 1861 to at least 1874, the United States Congress received many petitions and "memorials" for the payment of bills of exchange from banks, financial groups and one individual that remained unpaid because of over drafts by Russell, Majors and Waddell.[66] In 1874, then Representative Benjamin F. Butler introduced a memorial in the House of Representatives for Pierce & Bacon of Boston, Massachusetts to be indemnified for drafts made by Russell, Majors and Waddell which had been accepted by John B. Floyd, the former Secretary of War is the Buchanan administration. The memorial was sent to the Committee on Claims.[67]

On 20 April 1861, President Lincoln received a message from James H. Lane offering that he could organize a coup d'état "from the North through Maryland" to secure the capital city of Washington.[68] James Henry Lane of Kansas was a Senator and was appointed by Lincoln as a brigadier general of volunteers. Charged with financial irregularities, Lane committed suicide in 1866.[69] To protect himself and Washington, Lincoln allied with extremist and northern economic interests.

On 25 April 1861, Lincoln wrote to Winfield Scott, the commanding general of the United States army. President Lincoln referred to Scott as "Commander in Chief" in the communication even though the

---

[64] *CLNN*, Journal of the Senate, May 28, 1862, pages 534 to 536. The meeting was revealed to the United States Senate on May 28, 1862, as a message from President Lincoln brought by his secretary John Nicolay. The Journal of the Senate copy of Lincoln's message states the meeting occurred on a Sunday while April 20, 1861 was actually a Saturday. The message from Lincoln was to the Senate is reply to their proposed censure of Simon Cameron., accessed 5 December 2006. Secretary of War Simon Cameron and Secretary of the Navy Gideon Welles were both defendants in lawsuits filed in Philadelphia, Pennsylvania. See *OR*, Series 2, Volume 2, 1897, pages 505 to 509, wells was sued by Pierce Butler, a Philadelphia native who owned land in Georgia, for trespass, *vi et armis*, assault and battery and false imprisonment.

[65] *CLNN*, Journal of the Senate, March 25, 1862, page 335, accessed 5 December 2006.

[66] *CLNN*, Journal of the Senate, February 18, 1861, "petition of Pierce & Bacon" (Senator Wilson), page 247, accessed 2 December 2006.

[67] *CLNN*, Journal of the House of Representatives, March 9, 1874, memorial of Pierce & Bacon (Representative Benjamin F. Butler), page 576, accessed 2 December 2006.; William H. Russell, Alexander Majors and William B. Waddell were the company principals; a case related to Russell, Majors and Waddell was heard by the United States Supreme Court is 1872, see U.S. Supreme Court ALLEN v. U S, 84 U.S. 207 (1872).

[68] *ALPLC, ALSC*, James H. Lane to Abraham Lincoln, Saturday, April 20, 1861 (coup d'état) From James H. Lane to Abraham Lincoln, accessed 5 December 2006.

[69] *BDUSC*, accessed 2 December 2006.

Constitution designates the President as having the title. Technically, Scott was the highest ranking general in the army while Lincoln was the "Commander in Chief", according to the United States Constitution.[70] In his message to Scott, Lincoln was indecisive regarding any decision to arrest or disperse the Legislature of Maryland. Lincoln suggested to Scott that he preferred non-intervention in the future meeting of the Maryland legislature However, if the legislature was to "arm their people against the United States", Lincoln advocated an aggressive military response: the "bombardment of their cities" and the "suspicion suspension of the writ of habeas corpus".[71]

The response of Lincoln was aggressive and not measured. The Confederates had bombarded a Federal military fort located on an island in a harbor. The bombardment of a city is an attack on a civilian target. To suspend habeas corpus was a questionable action itself. The constitutionally guaranteed right of habeas corpus prevented incarceration of citizens without judicial intervention. Lincoln wanted the military to secretly arrest citizens and not try them in a court of law. The basis for arrest was to be legally groundless and vague "suspicion"!

On 27 April 1861, Lincoln communicated again to Winfield Scott. He repeated his authorization for the general or his designee to suspend the writ of habeas corpus and to counter "resistance" along the "military line" between the cities of Washington and Philadelphia because of an "insurrection against the laws of the United States".[72] The orders for the suspension of habeas corpus may have been confidential or secret. This author uses the words "confidential or secret" because of the wording of legislation passed by the United States Congress on 6 August 1861, months after Lincoln's authorization order to Scott. The legislation was titled "An Act to confiscate Property used for Insurrectionary Purposes." The word "if" is used in the first sentence of the legislation. The act required the President to make a proclamation declaring that an insurrection existed in order for the act to become operative.[73] Neither the legislation nor the proclamation mentioned the constitutionally guaranteed right of habeas corpus.

At 2 AM on 25 May 1861, John Merryman was arrested by military authorities in Cockeysville, Maryland. On 27 May 1861, a writ of habeas corpus was filed with the United States Supreme Court. Chief Justice Roger Brooke Taney, in the decision titled Ex Parte Merryman, found that the military was resisting and obstructing the process of law. Furthermore, Taney determined that the power to suspend habeas corpus rested with Congress and not with the President. Merryman remained imprisoned at Fort McHenry in Baltimore. Chief Justice Taney ordered that his decision be delivered to President Lincoln.[74]

On 28 June 1861 Captain George N. Hollins and Colonel Richard Thomas (alias Zarvona) of Saint Mary's County captured the steamship *St. Nicholas* in the Chesapeake Bay and transported it to the seceded state of Virginia. Prior to the capture, on 18 June 1861, Hollins had visited the plantation of "Colonel S." on the Patuxent River. "Colonel S." advised Hollins that his plan to capture the U.S. Navy steamship *Pawnee* was not advisable because there were many Union men in the area. Hollins subsequently conceived another of his plans to capture the *St. Nicholas*.[75] The action of capturing ships during that time was called privateering.

Privateering was used during the War of 1812 by American patriots against the British. Richard Thomas was later captured and imprisoned at Fort McHenry, Baltimore on 8 July 1861.[76] He was captured while

---

[70] Article II, Section 2.

[71] *ALPLC, ALSC,* Abraham Lincoln to Winfield Scott, Thursday, April 25, 1861 (Arrest of Maryland Legislature) From Abraham Lincoln to Winfield Scott [Copy in Lincoln's hand], accessed 5 December 2006.

[72] *OR*, Series 2, Volume 2, 1897, April 27, 1861, Abraham Lincoln and William H. Seward to The Commanding General Army of the United States, page 19, accessed 2 December 2006.

[73] *CLNN*, Statutes at Large, 37th Congress, 1st Session, page 319, accessed 2 December 2006.

[74] *OR*, Series 2, Volume 1, 1894, Ex Parte John Merryman, page 577 to 585, accessed 2 December 2006.

[75] *Official records of the Union and Confederate Navies in the War of the Rebellion.*, Series I, Volume 4, United States Naval War Records Office, Government Printing Office, 1896 (cited hereafter as *ORN*), Extracts from notes by Commander George N. Hollins, C. S. Navy, pages 553 to 555, accessed 5 December 2006, available on the Internet.

[76] *OR*, Series 2, Volume 2, 1897, Summary of Principal Events, page 1, accessed 2 December 2006.

traveling into Baltimore on the steamship *Mary Washington*. The ship was diverted to Fort McHenry. Other passengers were also arrested who apparently were innocent, among them Edward Johnson, an employee of the United States Custom House.[77]

On 21 July 1861, a battle was fought in northern Virginia, which was inside of seceded states territory. One side of it called it the Battle of Bull Run and the other called it the Battle of Manassas. Bull Run was the stream that the Union army crossed over after its invasion of Virginia to get to the battle and very quickly retreated over after their defeat. Manassas was the name of the railroad junction where the secessionist Confederate provisional army arrived at and then defended.

Unionists thought their invasion of the Confederate states would result in a rapid victory and they would parade into Richmond, the capitol of the provisional government. Many civilians accompanied the Union army to watch the battle. Among them were northern politicians who came to the battle to observe what was predicted to be the final solution of the secession insurrection of the Confederacy. One of them, Alfred Ely, a congressman from New York, was captured by the Confederates and sent to Richmond.[78] The battle was a surprise victory won by the newly created Confederate States.

On 5 August 1861 Representative Henry May of Maryland submitted a resolution to the United States House of Representatives concerning the civil war. The resolution blamed "republicans" for "our present national misfortunes." May's resolution said that it was impossible to "subjugate" the seceded slates and called for commissioners to establish an "armistice" to lead to the reconstruction of the United States. His motion was disagreed to by the House and a resolution by Representative Alexander Samuel Diven was introduced. Diven's resolution called for resolutions such as Representative May's to be demonized as "cowardly or treasonable." His motion failed also.[79] Ironically, the abolition terrorist John Brown had been found guilty of treason in 1859. The Union definition of treason became extended to words attempting to bridge the chasm between north and south. In the south, the definition of treason was abolitionists invading and creating slave revolts. In the north, the definition of treason was disunion, secession, slave owning and dissent against the Republican political party line.

The next day, on 6 August 1861, the United States Congress passed a confiscation act. The legislation was titled "An Act to confiscate Property used for Insurrectionary Purposes." The law allowed property used for the insurrection to be confiscated. However, the person whose property was to be confiscated would have to use his property "in aiding, abetting, or promoting such insurrection or resistance to the laws." Any property taken by confiscation would have to be "condemned in a circuit or district court of the United States." An "informer" was entitled to half the proceedings from the condemnation. Owners of slaves used for service or labor against the United States would lose any future claim to ownership. The legislation had the word "if" in it. The legislation would become operative only if President Lincoln made a proclamation declaring the existence of insurrection.[80] The wording of this legislation made "material support" of the insurrection punishable by confiscation through a required court proceeding. This legislation was the first of two confiscation acts.

The propaganda that the Maryland legislature was meeting for the purpose of secession has persisted to this day. However, the *Philadelphia Press* of 6 August 1861 reported that Mr. Wallis of the Maryland legislature had prepared a report about the usurpation of the Baltimore police and the imprisonment of the city Police Marshal and Commissioners by the Union army. The "Union members" of the Maryland legislature voted for the Wallis report to be printed and distributed to Congress and state governors.[81]

---

[77] Anonymous, *The Bastille in America; or, Democratic Absolutism, London, 1861, by an eye-witness,* available on the Internet at the Cornell University Library, Samuel J. May Anti-Slavery Collection (cited hereafter as SJMASC), accessed 12 December 2006, for an excellent summary of Civil War privateering, see William A. Tidwell, *April '65, Confederate Covert Action is the American Civil War*, pages 84 to 93.
[78] *OR*, Series 2, Volume 2, 1897, Fulton to Thomas A. Scott, December 18, 1861, page 479, accessed 2 December 2006.
[79] *CLNN*, Journal of the House of Representatives, August 5, 1861, pages 241 and 242, accessed 7 December 2006.
[80] *CLNN*, Statutes at Large, 37th Congress, 1st Session, page 319, accessed 7 December 2006.
[81] *Philadelphia Press*, August 6, 1861, "Maryland Legislature", page 2, accessed 30 December 2006.

On 15 August 1861, Secretary of the Navy Gideon Welles gave instructions to Thomas T. Craven, the commander of the Union Potomac Flotilla. Welles ordered Craven "to destroy every vessel or boat within your reach . . . without regard to passes given". Welles stated that forty-eight "permits" had been given for trade on the Potomac River. Welles also gave Craven the power to cancel the permits.[82] Wells had ordered the senseless mass destruction of all nautical shipping on the Potomac River.

The next day, 16 August 1861, President Lincoln issued a proclamation declaring that insurrection existed in the eleven seceded Confederate states of Georgia, South Carolina, North Carolina, Alabama, Florida, Mississippi, Louisiana, Texas, Virginia, Tennessee and Arkansas. He classified parts of western Virginia as where there was loyalty to the Union. The number of seceded states had increased from seven to eleven since the surrender of Fort Sumter.

Lincoln's proclamation banned "commercial intercourse" with the Confederate states with a notable exception. Trade between the states was prohibited unless a "special license and permission of the President" was obtained. Lincoln used the phrase "will be forfeited" two times in his proclamation. Lincoln was referring to any "vessel or vehicle" to be forfeited. Lincoln did not mention what would happen to the cargo or freight of the carrier.[83] The proclamation made the confiscation act operative. The proclamation was a blockade of the Confederacy and Lincoln's exclusive economic monopoly of excerptions to the blockade. It may, or may not, be that the exceptions to the blockade made by Lincoln were to benefit northern business interests trading in cotton and tobacco, the two main agricultural products of the south. By December of 1863, the Union navy had captured more than 1,000 ships.[84] The fact that Secretary of Navy Welles had issued orders canceling permits and passes the day prior to Lincoln's proclamation announcing a blockade with presidential licenses may, or may not, be proof that a secret blockade with exemptions existed prior to 16 August 1861.

A survey of Pennsylvania newspapers of the period revealed articles about a blockade but no mention of presidential exemptions. The public was not being told the truth about Lincoln's proclamation. In 1874, part of the truth was made known. John D. Sanborn and G. W. Lane were recipients of the monopoly of exceptions. Sanborn was a general agent and detective of the Adams Express Company. They were trading to obtain cotton.[85] Cotton, an agricultural product of the south used to make cloth, was needed by northern industrial garment manufacturers.

In early of August 1861, the former American diplomat to France, Charles J. Faulkner, returned to the United Status at the port of New York. On 12 August 1861, he was arrested in Washington, D.C. and later sent to Fort Lafayette in New York harbor.[86] Charles J. Faulkner was a citizen of Virginia, a state that had seceded from the Union. His purpose in visiting Washington was to finalize the tasks as a government diplomatic employee. He was told he was being held hostage for the return of two persons held in Richmond, Virginia. Faulkner wrote a letter to William H. Seward and asked that his arrest be brought to the attention of President Abraham Lincoln.[87] Charles James Faulkner was a congressman before and after the Civil War.[88]

Lincoln's pledge that the "utmost care will be observed" to avoid the devastation, destruction or interference with property was soon broken by the Union army in Maryland. On or about 12 and 13 September of 1861, Massachusetts Union cavalry troops under the command of Colonel William Dwight were at Benedict,

---

[82] *ORN*, Series 1, Volume 4, 1896, August, 15, 1861, Instructions from the Secretary of the Navy to Commander Craven, U.S. Navy, commanding Potomac Flotilla, in view of information received from the Assistant Secretary of War regarding intentions of the enemy., Gideon Welles to Captain T. T. Craven, page 612, accessed 6 December 2006.
[83] *OR*, Series 3, Volume 1, 1899, page 417 to 418; *CLNN*, Statutes at Large, 36th Congress, Appendix, page 1262, accessed 2 December 2006.
[84] *OR*, Series 3, Volume 3, 1889, December 8, 1863, Message to Congress, Abraham Lincoln pages 1144 to 1155, page 1147, accessed 16 December 2006.
[85] *CLNN*, Congressional Record, May 27. 1874, speech of Hiester Clymer, page 377, accessed 15 January 2007.
[86] *OR*, Series 2, Volume 2, 1897, Summary of Principal Events, page 1, accessed 2 December 2006.
[87] *ALPLC, ALSC*, Charles J. Faulkner to William H. Seward, Monday, August 19, 1861 (Imprisonment), accessed 5 December 2006.
[88] *BDUSC*, accessed 22 December 2006.

in Charles County, Maryland. Benedict was a small town on the same side of the Patuxent River as The Plains. The area of The Plains and the town of Benedict are separated by Indian Creek. The distance between The Plains and Benedict is about one mile by a direct water route. The Union soldiers of Colonel Dwight robbed slaves and horses along with destroying property.[89] Colonel Robert Cowden, of the First Regiment Massachusetts Volunteers, reported that Union cavalry on "detached duty" had committed the plundering attacks while "intoxicated".[90]

Maryland Representative Henry May of Congress was arrested in a midnight raid on Friday, 13 September 1861 because of his position advocating "a discontinuance of the inhuman war".[91] His name appears on a list of prisoners at Fort Lafayette in New York harbor on 14 October 1861 with the status of "on parole" and a reception date of 26 September 1861.[92] Fort Lafayette was on an island in New York harbor and the 34 political prisoners transported there from Fort Monroe in Virginia were guarded by inexperienced and "raw German recruits". By the order of Secretary of State William H. Seward, letters written by prisoners were censored. Letters that were approved by censors for mailing were required to have a disclaimer in the handwriting of the prisoner against any newspaper publishing the contents of it. No "invidious" language about Union politicians was allowed.[93] Political criticism of the Union government had become heresy.

Henry May, a Unionist, had openly and publicly opposed the riot that took place in Baltimore on 19 April 1861 between city residents and Massachusetts militia soldiers. A delegate to the 1860 Democratic National Convention and Stephen A. Douglas supporter, he was strongly against secession and disunion. He sympathized with "Southern Constitutional right" but believed those rights should be maintained within the Union. May had been "menaced" by riot supporters and told them he was armed and "ready to defend his rights in the Union". Henry May was the Peace candidate in the special election to Congress of June 1861 with a platform against secession and coercion. He advocated a National Convention to settle the differences between north and south. Sometime after the battle at Bull Run on 21 July, May calmed a crowd that was on the brink of becoming a riot.[94]

Unable to meet in Annapolis because Benjamin F. Butler had taken military control of the capitol city, the Maryland legislature tried to convene at a different location. Thirty thousand copies of the Wallis report were printed by the legislature for distribution to Congress and state governors. The report was demonized as a "treasonable document" and all the copies of it were seized by the Union army on 17 September 1861 at Frederick, Maryland. Maryland legislators who voted for its publication were arrested in September of 1861.[95] The Union army military coup d'état had prevented exposure of its illegal actions and depredations by a mass arrest of Maryland citizens and legislators.

On 17 September 1861, Clarke J. Durant, the Maryland state legislator from Saint Mary's County was arrested with other members of the body.[96] On 27 September 1861, he arrived at Fort Lafayette in New York harbor.[97] Durant refused to take a loyalty oath and he was transferred to the custody of the War Department on

---

[89] *OR*, Series 1, Volume 1, 1881, November 11, 1861, Geo. Sykes through Silas Casey to Headquarters, Second Brigade, Casey's Division, pages 387 and 388, accessed 2 December 2006.

[90] *OR*, Series 1, Volume 5, 1881, September 20, 1861, Robert Cowdin to Joseph Hooker, page 605, assessed 3 December 2006.

[91] *ALPLC, ALSC*, John A Dix to Simon Cameron, Friday, September 13, 1861 (Arrests made in Baltimore), accessed 8 December 2006.

[92] *OR*, Series 2, Vol. 2, 1897, page 102, accessed 2 December 2006.

[93] *SJMASC*, The Bastille in America; or, Democratic Absolutism, London, 1861, page 16, accessed 12 December 2006.

[94] *ALPLC, ALSC*, Series 1. General Correspondence. 1833-1916. Robert J. Brent, Monday, September 16, 1861 (Affidavit concerning Henry May), accessed 10 December 2006.

[95] *The Huntington Globe*, September 19, 1861, "Arrest of the Officers of the Legislature", page 1, accessed 30 December 2006.

[96] *OR*, Series 2, Volume 2, 1897, List of prisoners of state at Fort Warren, Boston Harbor, November 27, 1861, page 154 and 155, accessed 2 December 2006.

[97] *OR*, Series 2, Volume 2, 1897, List of prisoners confined at Fort Lafayette, New York Harbor, October 14, 1861, page 102. Durant was confined by the Secretary of State, accessed 2 December 2006.

15 February 1862.[98] It has long been maintained by propaganda that Maryland legislators were meeting for the sole purpose of seceding and not to protest the depredations of the Union army.[99] The population of Maryland was learning a lesson about fascist tyranny because the Union army could not be trusted. The Union army was making secret midnight arrests, moving prisoners to secret locations, using censorship, changing the location and custody status of prisoners and pillaging the countryside. On 20 September 1861, John A. Dix, who was given money in April by President Lincoln for the defense of Washington, advised a subordinate that he preferred house searches to be done by the "police" and not by the Union army.[100]

The "police" were the secret police and detectives of Lafayette C. Baker. In early October of 1861 the post office at Great Mills, Saint Mary's County was raided by Union secret police chief Lafayette C. Baker. Mail was found that was to be sent to both north and the south. John S. Travis was arrested.[101] There were many other political arrests in Saint Mary's County. Some Marylanders chose to resist the fascist tyranny by crossing the Potomac River into Virginia and joining the Confederate army because it was their only hope for restoring freedom to their state. Two sons of Colonel Sothoron went to Virginia and joined the Confederate army.

During October of 1861, Colonel Sothoron was in Richmond, Virginia and wrote a letter of recommendation for his son, S. Webster Sothoron. Richmond was the capitol of the Confederate States of America. The letter was sent to Confederate Secretary of War Judah Philip Benjamin for his son to receive a commission as a Lieutenant in the Confederate army.[102] This letter is from the military service file of Webster Sothoron in the National Archives:

Richmond, Va.
21st Oct 1861
Hon J.P. Benjamin
Secretary of War
Sir

I have the honor to present the name of my son Mr. S.W. Sothoron of Maryland for a First or Second Lieutenancy in the regular army of the Confederate States.

With the commencement of the war my son has been in active service as a private in Captain Murray's company of the First Maryland Regiment and has participated in every engagement upon the Potomac, where he has won the commendation of his officers for gallantry and general good conduct as a soldier.

Mr. S. has been a student at the Charlotte Military Academy and was the Captain of a company there when hostilities began between this Government and the United States.

I am authorized to say that the officers of the company regiment or brigade to which he is attached regard him fully competent to the position he desires. This will appear more to your satisfaction from letters hereafter to be filed with this application.

I have the honor to be your obedient servant
John H. Sothoron
Through General S Cooper, Adjutant General, C. S. Army

---

[98] *OR*, Series 2, Volume 1, 1894, page 668 and 669; Durant was a prisoner of state before the transfer of custody, accessed 2 December 2006.
[99] Union records in *OR* states that the purpose of the meeting was to pass the "Wallis resolutions". This topic deserves further research. S. Teackle Wallis was a member of the Maryland legislature. See *OR*, Series 2, Volume 1, 1894, September 28, 1861, H. Morris Copeland to Major General Banks, page 693, accessed 6 December 2006.
[100] *OR*, Series 2, Volume 1, 1894, September 20, 1863, John A. Dix to Capitan Bragg, page 597, accessed 24 December 2006.
[101] *OR*, Series 2, Volume 1, 1894, October 10, 1861, To the Honorable Secretary of State from L.C. Baker, page 600, accessed 2 December 2006.
[102] *NARA*, Civil War Confederate military service record of Webster Sothoron.

There are other letters of recommendation in the military service file but no record of a promotion to lieutenant until December of 1863. Webster Sothoron eventually attained the rank of major. Colonel Sothoron was a servant of Benjamin.

The prior service for Webster Sothoron was in a Confederate unit from Maryland known as the First Maryland Infantry (later reorganized into the Second Maryland Infantry and also known as the Maryland Line). He was a member of Company "H" and his rank is given as private.[103] Company "H" was also known as "Winder Rangers".[104] The commanding officer of Company "H" was William H. Murray, who died later in the war at the Battle of Gettysburg.[105] Coincidentally, the above letter was written the day of the Battle of Ball's Bluff, which was a second surprise Confederate victory over an attempted Union army invasion of Virginia.[106] The battle gave a false sense of the military superiority of the Confederate army. The north had the superiority of a larger population and an industrial establishment to support an army with recruits and equipment.

The person whom the above letter was sent through, General Samuel Cooper, was born in Hackensack, New York in 1798. He was the highest ranking General in the Confederate army and a close associate of the President of the Confederate States, Jefferson Davis. He was among a few persons from the North who served the Confederacy in a leadership position.[107] Samuel Cooper graduated in 1815 from the United States Military Academy at West Point. He was promoted over the years and served as the adjutant general of the United States army from 1852 to 1861 with the rank of colonel. In 1836, he wrote *A Concise System of Instruction Regulations for Militia and Volunteers of the United States*. Samuel Cooper died at Cameron, Fairfax County, Virginia in 1876.[108] During the war, his home in Virginia was torn down and a Union fort was built on the former location of his house.[109]

On 22 October 1861, B. L. Hayden was arrested in Saint Mary's County. Arrested at his home by order of the Secretary of State, he was taken to Fort Lafayette in New York. Hayden was charged with "disloyalty". It was alleged he belonged to a group known as the Lower Maryland Vigilance Committee. He was released on 2 January 1862.[110] A Blackman by the name of Lewis Hayden was connected with Thomas Wentworth Higginson, a member of the Secret Six. Hayden was the subject of inquiry by the Senate in connection with the investigation of Franklin Sanborn, another member of the Secret Six, during 1860.[111] It appears that Lewis Hayden acted as a bodyguard for Higginson.

Webster Sothoron also received a recommendation letter from Maryland Confederate Lieutenant Colonel Bradley T. Johnson:[112]

> To The Honorable Secretary of War
> Richmond
> Sir
>
> S. Webster Sothoron of Co - H. 1st Md Regt is an applicant for commission of Lieutenant in the Provisional Army of the Confederate States He is a young gentleman of highly respectable family, has served in this Regiment with his Company since its formation at the Battle of Manassas under my own eyes behaved with gallant & courage.
>
> I respectfully recommend him for the appointment

---

[103] Goldsborough, *The Maryland Line in the Confederate Army, 1861-1865*, page 80.
[104] Amann, *Personnel of the Civil War, Vol. I*, page 165.
[105] Goldsborough, page 80, 110.
[106] Farwell, *Ball's Bluff, A Small Battle and Its Long Shadow*
[107] Boatner, page 175.
[108] *Who Was Who In America, Historical Volume, 1607-1896*, page 190.
[109] Frobel, *The Civil War Diary of Anne S. Frobel*, page 195.
[110] *OR*, Series 2, Volume 2, 1897, page 312 and 313, accessed 2 December 2006.
[111] Renehan, Jr., *The Secret Six, The True Tale of the Men Who Conspired with John Brown*, page 68 and 257.
[112] *NARA*, Civil War Confederate military service record of Webster Sothoron.

Your obedient servant
Bradley T. Johnson
Lt Col 1st Md Regt.
Oct 27. 1861
I concur with Lt Col Johnston in every particular
Geo. H. Steuart
CC 1st Md Regt

Bradley Tyler Johnson, in the above letter, established the date of the formation of the First Maryland Infantry Regiment as the day of the Battle of Manassas which was 21 July 1861. Due to the efforts of the wife of Bradley T. Johnson, the unit was supplied with weapons provided by the state of North Carolina. Mrs. Johnson was originally from North Carolina.[113] Bradley T. Johnson was a servant of the Confederate Secretary of War.

Marylanders who fought for the Confederacy were in a tenuous position. Because Maryland never seceded, their actions could have been construed as disloyal or treasonable by Union authorities. Confederate authorities may have never completely accepted them because of their legalistic viewpoint that Maryland, a state which never seceded, was not a part of the Confederate States.

On 6 November of 1861, state elections were held in Maryland. Union soldiers were at Charlotte Hall, near The Plains.[114]

In December of 1861, former diplomat Charles J. Faulkner was imprisoned at Fort Warren in Massachusetts. He was released to the Confederates for the exchange of Alfred Ely. Ely was the congressman from New York who had been captured by the Confederates on 21 July 1861.[115] Later during the war, on 17 July 1864, the house of Charles J. Faulkner, in Martinsburg, West Virginia, was ordered burned by Major General D. Hunter through Chas. G. Halpine, Assistant Adjutant General. The order was to be carried out by Captain F. G. Martindale and the First New York (Lincoln) Cavalry. The order included burning the dwelling house and outbuildings with everything inside them "except the family" of Faulkner.[116]

After the Civil War, General Bradley T. Johnson wrote about the Battle of Winchester. He mentioned the marksmanship ability of Webster Sothoron during fighting in the Shenandoah Valley of Virginia near Harrisonburg on 6 June 1862.[117] The Confederates fought the "Bucktails", a Union infantry unit from Pennsylvania officially designated as the 13th Pennsylvania Reserves.[118] The commanding officer of the Bucktails, General Thomas Leiper Kane was wounded and captured during the battle. Kane had made himself a prominent target during the battle while attempting to rally his soldiers by waving his sword.[119]

On 2 August 1862, two prisoners were registered at Fort McHenry in Baltimore, Maryland. James Waring (Warring) of Saint Mary's County was described as a "political prisoner". He was released or 5 August 1862.[120] B. G. Harris of Baltimore was also registered on that day. Harris was released on 12 August 1863 and gave and oath of allegiance.[121] In the Maryland state elections of 4 November 1863, Benjamin Gwinn Harris ran as a Conditional Unionist.[122] Fort McHenry had a reputation as the "Americans Bastille".

In November of 1862 the home of James Raley, about three miles inland from the Patuxent River, was

---

[113] Manakee, *Maryland in the Civil War*, page 133.
[114] *OR*, Series 1, Volume 1, 1881, November 11, 1861, Geo. Sykes through Silas Casey to Headquarters, Second Brigade, Casey's Division, pages 387 and 388, accessed 2 December 2006.
[115] *OR*, Series 2, Volume 2, 1897, December 18, 1861, Fulton to Thomas A. Scott, page 479, accessed 2 December 2006.
[116] *OR*, Series 1, Volume 37, Part II, 1891, July 17, 1864, Special Orders No. 128, Chas. G. Halpine by order of Major General Hunter, page 367 and 368, accessed 2 December 2006.
[117] *Southern Historical Society Papers, Vol. X, 1882*, Bradley T. Johnson, "Memoir of the First Maryland Regiment", page 104-105.
[118] Boatner, page 636.
[119] Boatner, page 447.
[120] Fort McHenry prisoners, accessed 3 November 2006, available on the Internet.
[121] Fort McHenry prisoners, accessed 9 November 2006.
[122] Scharf, *History of Baltimore City and County*, page 145.

raided by Union marauders. A Union officer, with two white and two Black men, came to his house during the night. They speciously claimed Raley had a "rebel flag" and searched the house. During the "search" the vile home invaders tore the clothing of his wife and children. The officer demanded all the paper in the house and told Raley he would return the next day to arrest him. The "paper" had a value of $17,000. On 21 November 1862, G. E. McConnell, the Acting Ensign of the *U.S.S. Jacob Bell*, went to the house, apologized and returned the property stolen by the five vile thieves. In addition to Raley's, six other homes were raided by the Union brigands.[123]

The Civil War created problems that caused difficulty for the ability of ordinary and peaceful citizens in Union controlled territory to distinguish between authentic government agents and imposter brigands. On 2 December 1862, the United States Congress passed Joint Resolution S. R. 103. The Joint Resolution identified the problem of persons "pretending" to have the authority of the United States. Imposters of government authority had falsely arrested citizens and placed them in "military prisons and camps" without "any public charge being preferred against them". The resolution denounced the false arrests as "a usurpation of power never given by the people to the President". Congress "demanded" that the secret arrests cease and that the prisoners be immediately freed or tried.[124] The "imposters" may, or may not, have been fascist Republican political operatives.

The National Archives military service file for Webster Sothoron shows that he appears on a "Receipt Roll for commutation of rations while on furlough; received from Lieutenant J. Johns, A.A.C.S., C.S.A., at Richmond, Va." from 9 February to 16 March 1862.

In December of 1862, Webster Sothoron was appointed to the rank of sergeant in the Confederate Signal Corps. The Signal Corps, headed by Major William Norris, also had secret assignments. The letter for his appointment is from the records of Letters Received by the Confederate Adjutant and Inspector General in the National Archives:[125]

> Signal office Richmond
> Dec. 16. 1862
> Hon Jas A Seddon
> Secretary of War
> Sir
> Sergeants (Daniel G.) Morrow and (Davis) Blashear having declined their appointments in the Signal Corps, I respectfully request that the vacancies be filled by the appointment of
> 1st Webster Sothoron of La
> 2 K. Owen Norris of Texas –
> Very Respectfully
> William Norris
> Major & Chief: Signal Corps

The identifying of Webster Sothoron as being from Louisiana is either an indication that he had dual state residency to satisfy Confederate legalistic requirements or that it was part of a cover story. The Signal Corps had the responsibility for the operation of the "Secret Line", through which mail, agents and supplies were transported into and from Union controlled territory. Part of the route of the Secret Line was through Saint Mary's and Charles Counties in Maryland. Later during the war in 1864, the house of the Major John Seddon,

---

[123] *ORN*, Series I, Volume 5, 1897, November 24, 1862, Report of Acting Ensign McConnell U.S. Navy, U.S.S. Jacob Bell, of a visit to the house of James Raley, near Patuxent River, page 167, accessed 6 December 2006.
[124] Joint Resolutions, December 2, 1862, 37th Congress, 3rd Session.
[125] *NARA*, Letters Received by the Confederate Adjutant and Inspector General, M474, Microfilm 49, letter 3025-8-1862.

the deceased brother of letter addressee James A. Seddon, was burned by the Union army.[126] James Alexander Seddon was a former United States congressman.[127]

The diary of William Wilkins Glenn mentions a Sothoron in the city of Baltimore during the Civil War. Wilkins met a Sothoron in Baltimore and warned him or her about being arrested as a spy.[128] The author of the diary, William Wilkins Glenn, was the editor and owner of *The Baltimore Exchange*, a newspaper. Glenn had been arrested on 14 September 1861 by Union authorities.[129] Glenn was taken in the mass arrests of that time because the Union army imposed censorship by arresting newspaper owners and editors to conceal from the public their illegal mass arrest of members of the Maryland Legislature.

Another son of Colonel Sothoron, Marshall Lyles Sothoron, served in Company "I" of the First Maryland Infantry.[130] His National Archives Confederate army military record shows he was enlisted by Captain Robertson on 4 August 1861 for the duration of one year. Marshall Sothoron was seventeen years old at the time. One of the three cards in his file shows that his name appears on a list of sick sent to Manassas, Virginia on 5 October 1861 and that he had "remittent fever". The second card is a company muster roll for September and October of 1861 and shows that he was "absent sick in General Hospital". The muster roll shows that he was paid by J. D. Skinner up to 31 August 1861. The third and last card again shows him on the company muster roll for November and December 1861 as "absent sick at Richmond since 1 October 1861" and that he was paid by Captain McElrath to 31 October 1861. His rank is given as private. There is no other information in the army record. However, there is a separate National Archives Confederate naval military record for Marshall Sothoron. Colonel Sothoron's presence in Richmond in October of 1861 was due to the illness and hospitalization of his son.

The First Maryland Infantry was disbanded on 11 August 1862. There are two reasons for the disbandment. First, the enlistment time length of one year had expired. Secondly, a proclamation had been made by President Lincoln on 25 July 1862 with a threat of punishment against Confederates if they did not return their allegiance to the United States. If Confederates did not return their allegiance, Lincoln proclaimed that they faced "pain of the forfeitures and seizures" of the confiscation legislation passed by Congress.[131]

The second confiscation act was passed on 17 July 1862. It was titled "An Act to suppress Treason and Rebellion, to seize and Confiscate the Property of Rebels, and for other Purposes." The legislation said it was "the duty" of the President to "cause the seizure of all the estate and property . . . for the support of the army". The legislation was a justification of the previous depredations of the Union army to support itself and the harbinger of a dismal future for persons in areas occupied by the Union army.

Section 6 of the second confiscation act set a time limit of 60 days after a "public warning and proclamation" made by President Lincoln persons to return their allegiance to the United States and to cease aid, countenance and abetting of the rebellion. Excluded from the group to return allegiance were Confederate government officials, seceded state government officials, army and navy officers and property owners is loyal states who "assist and give aid and comfort " to the rebellion.[132] The sixty day time limit made by Congress was omitted and not mentioned by President Lincoln in his proclamation of 25 July 1862.

By proclamation, President Lincoln on 24 September 1862 suspended the writ of habeas corpus for persons already imprisoned and to be imprisoned in the future. He made a category of persons "guilty of disloyal practices . . . subject to martial law and liable to trial and punishment by courts-martial or military

---

[126] *OR*, Series 1, Volume 43, Part I, 1893, August 13, 1864, James A. Seddon to J. A. Early, pages 998 and 999, accessed 14 December 2006.
[127] *BDUSC*, accessed 22 December 2006.
[128] Marks and Schatz, *Between North and South, A Maryland Journalist Views the Civil War*, page 82.
[129] *OR*, Series 2, Volume 2, 1897, September 14, 1861, J. A. Dix to Hon. W. H. Seward, page 779, accessed 2 December 2006.
[130] Goldsborough, page 81.
[131] *OR*, Series 3, Volume 2, 1899, July 25, 1862, A Proclamation, Abraham Lincoln, page 274, accessed 6 December 2006.
[132] *CLNN*, Statutes at Large, 37th Congress, 2nd Session, page 589 to 592, accessed 7 December 2006.

commission."[133] It was a draconian proclamation.

Colonel Sothoron returned to his home at The Plains prior to October of 1862. From The Plains, he allegedly wrote a letter to President Jefferson Davis of the Confederate States in Richmond, Virginia. The following letter was found in the Unfiled Papers and Slips Belonging in Confederate Compiled Service Records found at the National Archives:[134]

> St Mary's County Maryland
> October 13th 1862
> His Excellency
> Jeff. Davis, President C.S.A.
>
> My Dr Sir Allow me to introduce to you my friend, Lieutenant Colonel Wm. T. Magruder of Maryland late of the US Army, who has very recently throws up his commission for the purpose of joining the army of the Southern Confederacy –
>
> I have known Col Magruder from his boyhood and it gives me great pleasure to commend him to your <u>especial</u> consideration — It would require more space than can be allotted to the purpose in an ordinary letter, to state in full all the reasons which have operated upon my friend Col Magruder to restrain him from taking that step, which from the beginning of our unfortunate difficulties, his heart and his sense of right have instilled him to take - Suffice it to say, that in my judgment - if my judgment is worth any thing - these causes afford an ample and thorough excuse for his conduct - They are such as appear to me, as would have actuated any man of that high sense of honor and delicacy of feeling which I know Col Magruder to possess - He has now however taken the steps, and determined to cast his fortunes with the South, and makes an offering of his <u>services and his life</u> if need be; in the defense of <u>his rights</u> - Officers of your Army know him well and from them you will be able to obtain a more correct idea of his Military Capacity then I can give you — Permit me however to bespeak for him, as a gentleman and a friend, your kind attention, and as a Soldier an appointment to show the sincerity and earnestness of the motives which impel him to his present purpose <u>What remains to be done</u> then, <u>must be left for himself to do</u> –
> <u>With Great Respect</u> -
> I am Yours
> <u>John H. Sothoron</u>

On the surface, it appears that "Lieutenant Colonel Wm. T. Magruder of Maryland late of the US Army", allegedly a commissioned officer, was a defector who had switched sides during the Civil War from the Union to the Confederate army. Magruder was the middle name of the wife of Colonel Sothoron.

However, William T. Magruder remains a mysterious person. There was a William Magruder, residence "unknown", who was a "political prisoner" and a "blockade runner". He was registered at Fort McHenry on 26 June 1863 and he "escaped" on 1 November 1863.[135] A search for a Union or Confederate Civil War military record failed to reveal a soldier matching his name. These facts cast doubt on the authenticity of the letter.

On 25 February 1863, the United States Congress passed a law prohibiting correspondence "with the pretended rebel Government". It was titled "An act to prevent Correspondence with Rebels."[136] If Colonel Sothoron wrote the letter, he was not in violation of the law because the Constitution prohibits the use of an ex post facto law, which is a law that makes an action a crime after the action is made.

---

[133] *CLNN*, Statutes at Large, 38th Congress, Appendix, page 730, page not numbered, accessed 7 December 2006.
[134] *NARA*, Unfiled Papers and Slips Belonging in Confederate Compiled Service Records, M347, Microfilm 73, letter 1012-S-1862.
[135] Fort McHenry prisoners, accessed 3 November 2006.
[136] *CLNN*, Statutes at Large, An act to prevent Correspondence with Rebels, 37th Congress, 3rd Session, page 696, accessed 7 December 2006.

In the Union state of Maryland, military occupation, midnight arrests and secret detention, depredations, despoliation of farm areas and draconian laws and proclamations followed the Union military coup d'état which lifted the siege of Washington in April of 1861. However, Maryland, while occupied and oppressed by the Union army, was not subjugated. To secure and consolidate their gains, the Union army needed a quiet revolution with a reign of terror.

Chapter 3

THE QUIET REVOLUTION

When the Constitution was written in 1787, none of the Founding Fathers saw the terrible future conflict that would result from the inclusion of slavery in it. Unfortunately, slavery was sanctioned in Article I, Section 2, concerning representation and taxes, Article II, Section 9, concerning slave trade and Article IV, Section 2, concerning fugitive slaves. There were repeated attempts to reach a compromise about the issue of slavery. All of them failed. The Thirteenth Constitutional Amendment prohibiting slavery was not finally ratified until after the Civil War ended.

The causes of the Civil War remain the subject of debate. Slavery, sectionalism and secessionism are often cited as causes. However, the conflict may also be viewed as the clash of northern morality and southern legalism. The north felt that slavery was morally wrong, while the south claimed slavery to be a legal and constitutional right. At the time of the Civil War, slave owning was equated with disloyalty and treason by Radical Republicans. During the Civil War, the Union army demanded all property from owners of it to prove "loyalty".

A strictly economic interpretation of the causes of the Civil War is the view that it was a battle not to free the slaves, but to determine how and which ruling class would exploit them. In the north, indenturing and bonding persons, the use of an immigrant or other person as an unpaid servant, were common practices. Indenturing and bonding persons could be as exploitive as slavery. In the south, slaves were owned by a number of Blacks, mostly on coastal islands. Abolition extremists demonized slave owners. The Civil War may have been the clash of northern industrialists and merchants, suffering economic hardship from a shortage of inexpensive labor, against southern agriculture.

In 1849, twelve years before the Civil War, then congressional Representative Abraham Lincoln drafted legislation for the compensated emancipation of the slaves of Washington, D.C., our national capitol. Compensated emancipation was the purchase of slaves from owners to give them freedom. Lincoln abandoned his proposal after discovering that former supporters of it had changed their position.[137]

In his first inaugural speech, Lincoln stated his position on slavery. He said that he would not "interfere" with existing slavery.[138] In November of 1861, a draft copy of proposed legislation for the compensated emancipation of the slaves of the Union state of Delaware was written by John Nicolay, a secretary to President

---

[137] ALPLC, ALSC, Abraham Lincoln, [January 1849] (A Bill to Abolish Slavery in the District of Columbia) Abraham Lincoln, A Bill for Abolishing Slavery in the District of Columbia [Draft], [January 1849] accessed 5 December 2006.
[138] ALPLC, ALSC, Abraham Lincoln, [March 1861] (First Inaugural Address, Final Version) Abraham Lincoln, First Inaugural Address, Final Version, [March 1861], 5 December 2006.

Lincoln.[139] President Abraham Lincoln took the position that slavery was a state issue to be decided by states and not the federal government. This is contrary to the hagiography that portrays Lincoln as "The Great Emancipator" of slaves. Lincoln had a position more concerned with the political and military objective of preservation of his political power and the Union, rather than one of advocating freedom and emancipation.

The Union army pre-empted Lincoln. On 30 August 1861 Major General John C. Fremont of the United States Army proclaimed martial law in Missouri and declared his purpose to confiscate the property and liberate the slaves of owners. President Lincoln responded and on 11 September 1861 issued an order to modify the proclamation of Fremont to conform to an act of Congress.[140]

On March 6, 1862, Lincoln presented to Congress his plan for the gradual abolition of slavery by the legislative mechanism of compensated emancipation. In his message to Congress, he used the phrase "gradual abolishment of slavery". He encouraged Congress to cooperate with states beginning programs for his objective.[141]

On 16 April 1862, shortly after the Union victory at the Battle of Shiloh, a plan of compensation was passed by Congress to free the slaves in the District of Columbia. The bill was titled "An Act for the Release of certain Persons held to Service or Labor in the District of Columbia". The legislation freed all persons of "African descent". Within ninety days of the passage of the act, slave owners could apply for compensation from three commissioners appointed by President Lincoln and approved by Congress. The slave owners had to be loyal persons and declare their allegiance to the Union government. The three appointed commissioners were authorized to pay up to three hundred dollars for each freed person. Disputes of ownership were to be settled in the circuit court of the District of Columbia. One million dollars was appropriated to implement the provisions of the bill. A provision for voluntary emigration to Haiti or Liberia was made and one hundred dollars could be spent for the transportation of each individual. The amount of $100,000 was appropriated for colonization. Any slave owner in the district attempting to evade manumitting his slaves could be imprisoned for five to twenty years.[142]

President Lincoln signed the legislation on the day it was passed by Congress. The legislation raised the false optimism of Maryland slave owners to be compensated in exchange for freeing their slaves. *The New York Times* of 17 April 1862 printed President Lincoln's message to Congress informing them of his acceptance and signing of the bill. President Lincoln affirmed his belief of the legality of freeing slaves in the District of Columbia with the "two principles of compensation and colonization".[143] The colonization "principle" would eventually become a labor deportation program to benefit northern business interests.

An article on the same page of *The New York Times* reported that the Commissioners appointed by President Lincoln were the former Mayor of Washington, James G. Berret (Berrett), the Honorable Samuel F. Vinton of Ohio and Daniel R. Goodlow (Goodloe), formerly of North Carolina. The article expressed doubts that Congress would approve the appointment of James G. Berret, because he had been imprisoned by Union authorities at Fort Lafayette in New York. In his message, President Lincoln expressed his concern for femmes coverts, the mistresses of slave owners and Foggy Bottom politicians. Lincoln also expressed his concern for other categories of former slaves, such as insane persons. On 24 April 1862, Lincoln withdrew the nomination

---

[139] *ALPLC, ALSC*, Abraham Lincoln, November 1861 (Draft of Bill for Compensated Emancipation in Delaware) Abraham Lincoln, Draft of Bill for Compensated Emancipation in Delaware [Copy in John Nicolay's Hand], November 1861, accessed 5 December 2006.

[140] *OR*, Series 1, Volume 3, 1881, September 11, 1861, A. Lincoln to John C. Fremont, pages 485 and 486, accessed 2 December 2006.

[141] *CLNN*, House Journal, March 6, 1862, pages 413 and 414, accessed 7 December 2006.

[142] *CLNN*, Statutes at Large, 37th Congress, 2nd Session, pages 376 to 378, accessed 7 December 2006.

[143] *The New York Times*, April 17, 1862, page 8, column 2.

of Berrett and replaced him with Horatio King.[144] Berret had been the mayor of Washington from 1858 to 1861.[145]

In May of 1862, Union army Major General David Hunter exceeded his authority. He issued a printed proclamation freeing the slaves of Florida, Georgia and South Carolina. President Lincoln responded with a proclamation repudiating and nullifying Hunter's emancipation proclamation. In his writing on the subject, Lincoln called for the "gradual" elimination of slavery. In the same statement, Lincoln affirmed his position that the states had the "discretion" to compensate for the abolition of slavery. Lincoln did not begrudge Hunter for his proclamation.[146]

On 12 July 1862, Lincoln gave an address to congressmen of the Border States. Lincoln reaffirmed his support of "gradual emancipation" and colonization. He mentioned his repudiation of the emancipation proclamation of General Hunter.[147] In his communications, public and private, Lincoln maintained his position. He was not diverted away from compensated emancipation.

Later, on July 16, 1862, Congress appropriated additional money for the emancipation and colonization of former slaves from Washington, the District of Columbia. The amount of $500,000 was to be repaid to the Federal Treasury from confiscated property. Colonization was declared to be a "right" of the former slaves.[148] Their "right" transformed into disaster and tragedy.

The colonization schemes were clearly exploitative. In October of 1863, Lincoln agreed to a contract with Bernard Kock, who wanted to transport and colonize freedmen in Haiti. Kock transported himself and 500 former slaves to the island of Ile a Vache on the coast of Haiti, known for Mangrove trees. The United States diplomatic Consul James De Long reported that Kock was trying to declare himself "Governor" of the island, much to the chagrin of the Haitian authorities, and that the former slaves were exploited.[149] Apparently, Lincoln issued a proclamation repudiating his contract with Kock on 16 April 1863. The proclamation was "omitted by oversight" from congressional records and not published until 1867 or 1868.[150] It may be that the real promoter of the Ile a Vache scheme was Jacob R. S. Van Vleet, who was the "Agent" for the scheme.[151] In regards to the freed slaves, Van Vleet wanted to "surround them by all the institutions of New England civilization." Of the 500 former slaves who went to Haiti, only 350 returned alive.[152] The ethic of the institutions of New England civilization failed to protect the lives of many of the former slaves transformed into colonists.

Lincoln also agreed to a contract with the Chiriqui Improvement Company, which wanted to transport and colonize freedmen to Panama to mine coal.[153] The Ile a Vache and Chiriqui schemes may be cited as an example that the Civil War was fought to decide which economic ruling class, industrial or agricultural, would exploit the freedmen. Freedmen had been abandoned by the Union government to the oppressive yoke of

---

[144] *CLNN,* Senate Executive Journal, April 24, 1862, page 255, 5 December 2006. Foggy Bottom is used to describe Washington, D.C.
[145] Wikipedia, Mayors of Washington, accessed 1 January 2007, available on the Internet.
[146] *ALPLC, ALSC,* Abraham Lincoln, Monday, May 19, 1862 (Proclamation revoking General David Hunter's General Order No. 11 on military emancipation of slaves) [Draft], accessed December 5, 2006.
[147] *ALPLC, ALSC,* Abraham Lincoln, Saturday, July 12, 1862 (Address to Border State Representatives), 5 December 2006.
[148] *CLNN,* Statutes at Large, 37th Congress, 2nd Session, page 582, accessed 7 December 2006.
[149] *ALPLC, ALSC,* James De Long to Henry Conard, June 25, 1863 (Bernard Kock and colony on Ile a Vache), accessed 5 December 2006.
[150] Statutes at Large, 40th Congress, Appendix, Proclamations, Volume XV, page 697 (not numbered), accessed 14 December 2006.
[151] *ALPLC, ALSC,* Jacob R. S. Van Vleet to Abraham Lincoln, Thursday, December 11, 1862 (Seeks interview to discuss colonization), accessed 5 December 2006.
[152] *ALPLC, ALSC,* Jacob R. S. Van Vleet to Abraham Lincoln, Saturday, October 04, 1862 (Colonization) Office of the National Republican, accessed 5 December 2006
[153] *ALPLC, ALSC,* Ambrose W. Thompson to Abraham Lincoln, Tuesday, June 02, 1863 (Enlistment of black soldiers; endorsed by Lincoln, June 3, 1863 and Henry W. Halleck) [With Endorsement by Lincoln], accessed 5 December 2006.

expansionist fascist exploiters. Donn Piatt, a political associate of Lincoln, portrayed Lincoln as a racist and a teller of "vulgar" stories.[154]

An article titled "Emancipation in the District" in *The New York Times* on 15 January 1863 gave details of the efforts to promote compensated emancipation in the District of Columbia. The article referred to slaves as "servants". About three thousand slaves were freed.[155] Compensated emancipation was implemented with very few problems in the capitol city and federal district itself. However, slaves from nearby plantations in Maryland escaped to the federal district to the freedom the city was reputed to offer.[156]

On 30 January 1863, an article appeared in the *Richmond Enquirer* titled "Compensated Emancipation". Newspaper articles published in the Confederate States about the possibility of payment for giving slaves their freedom may have falsely encouraged slave owners that the Civil War could be ended peacefully and without more bloodshed.

The New York Times of 5 March 1863 printed an article titled "Compensated Emancipation - The Condition of Missouri". The article reported the failure of legislation to be passed for compensated emancipation by Congress for the Border States of Maryland and Missouri. Democrats were blamed for the failure and the word "filibustered" was used. The article also stated that the government of Missouri had been strengthened by the "liberal overtures" of President Lincoln.[157] In another article on the subject, *The New York Times* of 22 March 1863 published an article titled "Political History" and blamed Republican dominated Congress for the disappointment to pass legislation for compensated emancipation. A letter was printed within the article from former congressman Albert S. White, whose term had recently expired and was involved in the attempt to pass the legislation. The last paragraph of his letter was prophetic and said that "Republican altars" would never be blamed for the failure. Hagiographic propaganda has blamed anyone or anything but Republicans for the Civil War.[158]

On 18 February 1863 Maryland paroled political prisoner and congressional Representative Henry May gave an oration to the House of Representatives. He denounced a proposed bill giving President Lincoln the power to suspend the writ of habeas corpus. May eloquently said Maryland was "the bright morning star of civil and religious freedom" but now a "subjugated province" ruled by oppressors who were the "skulking minions of power". The rump Union government in Maryland had restricted trade by imposition of fees paid to politicians and by requiring oaths. The Union army had seized property and then returned it for ransom. Slaves in Maryland were being enticed into camps and hospitals by the Union army and then transported out of the state.[159] The slaves of Maryland who were transported out of state may have alleviated the labor shortage in the northern Union states.

Later, in his message to Congress of 8 December 1863, President Lincoln confirmed the existence of the labor shortage by stating that a "great deficiency of laborers in every field of industry, especially in agriculture" was prevalent in the north. He said that government encouragement of immigration would solve the problem. Lincoln said that "confusion and destitution" had occurred because of differences between state and federal policy for emancipation and said that "a total revolution of labor throughout whole States" must occur. He also glorified the war by praising the "sharp discipline" it had created.[160]

---

[154] Donn Piatt, *Memories of the Men Who Saved the Union*, page 31 and 35, accessed 28 December 2006.
[155] *The New York Times*, January 15, 1863, page 1, column 5.
[156] ALPLC, ALSC, Charles B. Calvert to Abraham Lincoln, Tuesday, May 06, 1862 (Fugitive slaves), accessed 5 December 2006.
[157] *The New York Times*, March 5, 1863, page 4, column 4.
[158] *The New York Times*, March 22, 1863, page 2, column 1.
[159] CLNN, Congressional Globe, February 18, 1863, pages 1069 to 1072, accessed 10 December 2006
[160] OR, Series 3, Volume 3, 1889, December 8, 1863, Message to Congress, Abraham Lincoln pages 1144 to 1155, page 1147, accessed 16 December 2006.

Henry May persisted with his opposition to the maneuvers of the Union military political administrator in Maryland, Major General Robert C. Schenck. On 3 March 1863, Representative May introduced to Congress a resolution for the Judiciary Committee to investigate the fascist intrusion into the churches of Maryland by Schenck to establish state control of religion.[161] Schenck had issued an order requiring the United States flag to be displayed inside churches. A Methodist Episcopalian minister, the Reverend John H. Dashiell (or Dashiel) had removed a flag that was surreptitiously placed in his church.[162] Dashiell was arrested and then released from the American Bastille, Fort McHenry on 17 February 1863.[163]

In April, Schenck was pressured by Catholic Archbishop Frances Patrick Kenrick to release a priest. The Most Reverend Thomas A. Becker of Martinsburg was allegedly accused of praying for Confederate President Jefferson Davis and refusing to pray for President Lincoln and the Union authorities. Schenck had personally interrogated Becker and wanted Stanton to approve his deportation to the Confederacy.[164] There was no end to the machinations of Schenck and his efforts to invade and control every aspect of society.

* * *

One of the other influences that prevented the implementation of compensated emancipation was the severe need for new recruits by the Union army. On 3 March 1863, Congress passed a conscription act. The act was titled "An Act for enrolling and calling out the national Forces, and for other Purposes." All male citizens and persons of foreign birth between the ages of 20 and 45 formed the group of draft eligible. A notice was required to be given to the draftee to report at an induction station. Many government officials were exempt from military service. The Vice President was specifically exempted but the President was not.

Others gained exemption because they were needed to financially support family members. Recruitment officers were to have the military rank of colonel in the cavalry. The President was given the power to set quotas of the number of draftees from draft districts. A bounty was authorized to encourage current soldiers to re-enlist.

Section 21 of the legislation removed from President Lincoln the power to "carry into execution" the decision of a court martial and gave that power to a "commanding-general in the field". The legislation was unconstitutional because the Constitution assigns to the President the authority as Commander in Chief of the military. This appears to have been the beginning of the quiet Radical Republican legislative revolution against President Lincoln and lawful Constitutional authority. The Radical Republicans were civilians without a formal military background who advocated fascist militaristic solutions to problems caused by their war. Piatt wrote that Lincoln was completely aware of Congress removing presidential authority from him.[165]

Punishments were enacted for abetting desertion or resisting the draft. A provision was made for deserters to return to their units without punishment. Persons found "lurking or acting as spies" could be tried by a military commission or court martial and sentenced to death. The provision was draconian and inclusive. Anyone pausing for a moment in public could be falsely accused of "lurking".

The conscription act also had a provision for substitutes to be hired or money paid so that a person could avoid military service. For the legally set price of not more than $300, paid to the Union government, a conscripted person could avoid military service.[166] The substitute exemption of the conscription legislation

---

[161] *CLNN*, Journal of the House of Representatives, March 3, 1863, pages 618 and 619, accessed 14 December 2006.
[162] *CLNN*, Congressional Globe, February 18, 1863, page 1072, accessed 10 December 2006.
[163] Fort McHenry prisoners, accessed 10 December 2006
[164] *OR*, Series 2, Volume 5, 1899, April 10, 1863, Robert C. Schenck to E. M. Stanton, page 458, accessed 12 December 2006.
[165] Donn Piatt, *Memories of the Men Who Saved the Union*, page 38, accessed 28 December 2006.
[166] *CLNN*, Statutes at Large, 37th Congress, 3rd session, pages 731 to 737, accessed 7 December 2006.

caused opposition to it.[167] In April of 1863, it was reported to Lincoln that New York City was 18,000 men short of its quota for the draft and that there was extensive draft resistance which could necessitate future military intervention in the city.[168] Because he was not exempted from the draft by the legislation, a substitute was hired for Lincoln in the fall of 1864.[169]

* * *

The conscription act failed to alleviate the troop shortage of the Union army. The Union army continued to experience declining numbers. The army classified its personnel into three statistical categories. The category of "fit for duty" included officers and men. The second category was "aggregate present". A third category was "aggregate present and absent". The number of men fit for duty and also in the other two other categories continued to diminish. From 31 December 1862 to 30 June 1863 the number of "fit for duty" declined from 529,110 to 500,843.[170] The subtraction continued into the fall of 1863. By 31 December 1863, the army had 473,190 men in its "fit for duty" category.[171] Casualties from battles, disease, soldiers returning home because of expired enlistments and desertion created a manpower crisis for the Union political military leadership (see chart in Appendix).

Events of the previous year of 1862 may have contributed to the decline in numbers of the Union army. The morale of the Union army in the northern Virginia theatre of combat fell. Repeated defeats by the Confederates of the Union army combined with the interplay between President Lincoln, politicians and military officers created a doubtful future and demoralizing atmosphere. Scapegoats were needed to divert blame away from Radical Republican policy.

On 28 January 1862 Secretary of War Edwin McMasters Stanton made a written order for the arrest of Union army Brigadier General Charles P. Stone. On 8 February 1862, the Union commanding general, Major General George B. McClellan ordered the arrest of Stone and his internment at Fort Lafayette in New York harbor with restrictions on his communication. Stone was arrested by General Sykes at night and transported to prison. In prison, he repeatedly requested the grounds of his arrest and asked to be returned to duty. Stone never received a copy of the charges against him and vague mention was made that a refugee from Leesburg, Virginia had reported something negative about him. Stone was finally released after 189 days of confinement on 16 August 1862.[172] In a communication of 30 September 1862, General in Chief H. W. Halleck stated that it was his understanding that the order for the arrest of Stone was made by President Lincoln.[173]

A second Union army general was made a scapegoat of politics. On 9 April 1862 Lincoln wrote to Union Major General George B. McClellan, who was leading the Peninsula Campaign, which later failed to capture Richmond, the capital of the Confederacy. In response to a request for more soldiers, Lincoln expressed his fear that the Confederate army would "sack Washington" because only "20,000 unorganized men" would be

---

[167] *ALPLC, ALSC,* Max F. S. Gunther to Abraham Lincoln, Saturday, February 28, 1863 (Telegram protesting the exemption clause of the Conscription Bill), accessed 5 December 2006.

[168] *ALPLC, ALSC,* James W. White to Abraham Lincoln, Thursday, April 02, 1863 (Draft resistance in New York), accessed 5 December 2006.

[169] *ALPLC, ALSC,* Noble D. Larner to James B. Fry, Saturday, October 08, 1864 (Hiring of Lincoln's substitute; with note from Fry to John G. Nicolay), accessed 5 December 2006.

[170] *OR*, Series 3, Volume 2, 1899, Consolidated abstract from returns of the U.S. Army on or about December 31, 1862, page 957; *OR*, Series 3, Volume 3, 1899, Consolidated abstract from returns of the U.S. Army for June 30, 1863, page 460, accessed 2 December 2006.

[171] *OR*, Series 3, Volume 3, 1899, Consolidated abstract from returns of the U.S. Army for December 31, 1863, page 1198, accessed 2 December 2006.

[172] *OR*, Series 1, Volume 5, 1881, pages 341 to 344, accessed 14 December 2006.

[173] *OR*, Series 1, Volume 5, 1881, September 30, 1862, H W. Halleck to Charles P. Stone, page 344, accessed 14 December 2006.

left for the defense of the city. Lincoln said these circumstances "drove me to detain" Union army Major General Irvin McDowell.[174] The "20,000 unorganized men" may have been marauding Union army deserters who were in the statistical category of "aggregate present and absent". Lincoln's phrase about his detaining McDowell powerfully suggests that he was the decider of the order for his arrest.

On 6 September 1862, Union army Major General Irvin McDowell wrote to President Lincoln. An unnamed Senator had told McDowell that an unnamed dying cavalry colonel had written a note in pencil saying that he had died because of "McDowell's treachery". The Senator also claimed that the soldier's last request was that the note be delivered to Lincoln. McDowell requested a court to investigate the matter. In his letter, McDowell specifically requested that his conduct and policy be investigated in regards to the inhabitants of areas occupied by the Union army in Virginia.[175]

A military court of inquiry convened or 21 November 1862. The court of inquiry, composed of military officers, considered the following:

1. Correspondence by McDowell with Confederates.
2. The conduct of McDowell towards the property of inhabitants in areas occupied by the Union army.
3. If McDowell was derelict in his duty as an officer.
4. If McDowell failed to aid or send reinforcements to "a brother commander".[176]

Additionally, because of a letter to the editor of a newspaper written by Colonel R. D. Goodwin concerning events of early July 1861, the court of inquiry was to investigate charges of drunkenness.[177]

The court of inquiry revealed the shocking disrespect for person and property by the Union army in northern Virginia. On 13 May 1862, McDowell issued orders that bricklayers repair a graveyard. Union soldiers had broken into the tomb of a deceased female and despoiled it.[178]

More depredations of Union army deserters were exposed by the court inquiry. Robert E. Scott, a Union man of Fauquier County, Virginia was murdered while trying to apprehend a group of Union army deserters who had raped two women. On 16 May 1862, McDowell issued General Orders Number 12. His order established a military commission with the power to sentence a soldier or camp follower to death for rape.[179] The Union army rapist deserters may have been part of the "20,000 unorganized men" Lincoln wrote about to McClellan. Testimony given in the case described Union army depredations at and near Belle Plain, Virginia. McDowell had issued orders to stop Union soldiers who were looting and to punish the offenders.

After 67 agonizing days of hearing testimony, the McDowell Court of Inquiry gave its facts and opinions. On 14 February 1863, the court completely vindicated Major General Irvin McDowell.[180] The court of inquiry found the charge of drunkenness against McDowell to be "ridiculous".[181] As to his conduct towards the property of inhabitants, the court found that his actions "merit commendation".[182] McDowell was found to have

---

[174] *OR*, Series 1, Volume 12, Part I, 1885, Record of the McDowell Court of Inquiry, April 9, 1862, A. Lincoln to Major General McClellan, pages 230 and 231, accessed 2 December 2006.

[175] *OR*, Series 1, Volume 12, Part I, 1885, Record of the McDowell Court of Inquiry, pages 39 and 40, accessed 2 December 2006.

[176] *OR*, Series 1, Volume 12, Part I, ibid, pages 43 and 44, accessed 2 December 2006.

[177] *OR*, Series 1, Volume 12, Part I, ibid, pages 44 and 45, accessed 2 December 2006.

[178] *OR*, Series 1, Volume 12, Part I, ibid., May 13, 1862, Special Orders No. 65, Saml. Breck by command of Major General McDowell, page 53, accessed 2 December 2006.

[179] *OR*, Series 1, Volume 12, Part I, ibid, pages 51 and 52, accessed 2 December 2006.

[180] *OR*, Series 1, Volume 12, Part I, ibid, pages 323 to 332, accessed 2 December 2006.

[181] *OR*, Series 1, Volume 12, Part I, ibid, page 331, accessed 2 December 2006.

[182] *OR*, Series 1, Volume 12, Part I, ibid, page 327, accessed 2 December 2006.

been "energetic, intelligent, faithful, and without reproach in the performance of the duties of his station."[183] As for the charge of failing to help "a brother commander", the court changed that into a charge of disloyalty and found that McDowell was loyal and a victim of rumor.[184] The reputation of an excellent Union army major general had been dishonored. The effect of a political show trial and kangaroo court of a ranking Union army officer on enlistments, morale and retention of Union soldiers could only be detrimental.

In November of 1862 a controversy erupted because an order issued by Major General U. S. Grant. Grant's order expelled Jewish merchants from Union military controlled areas. In a communication of 21 January 1863, Union army General in Chief H. W. Halleck explained President Lincoln's position. Halleck wrote that Lincoln had "no objection to your expelling traitors and Jew peddlers" and that Lincoln had revoked it only because it "proscribed an entire religious class", some of who were fighting in the Union army.[185] It may be that Lincoln, a Presbyterian, had latent anti-Semitic feelings.

* * *

The slaves of Maryland, a border state, were viewed by the Union political military leadership as an unexploited resource of manpower. The need to increase the "fit for duty" category of the Union army was dominant.

April and May of 1863 were months of more Union army edicts and events predicting a troubled future for anyone within Union controlled territory who did anything that could be misinterpreted as benefiting the Confederacy or who owned property coveted by Radical Republican military political generals. On 13 April of 1863, Union army Major General Ambrose Burnside issued his General Orders Number 38 from Cincinnati, Ohio, through Louis Richmond, Assistant Adjutant General. Any persons found to have committed any act "for the benefit" of the "enemies" of the Union were to be treated as "spies or traitors" and after conviction to be executed. Persons who had the "habit of declaring sympathy for the enemy" would be sent into Confederate territory. The category of "implied" treason was included.[186]

Burnside convened a "military commission" on 23 April 1863. Clement L. Vallandigham was arrested on 5 May 1863 and the military commission tried him. On 1 May 1863, at Mount Vernon, in Knox County, Ohio, Vallandigham had made a speech and he charged among many other things that the Lincoln administration rejected a peace proposal by France to mediate between the Union and the Confederacy. A Writ of Certiorari was brought before the United States Supreme Court but was denied.[187] Vallandigham was deported to the Confederacy and later went to Canada.[188]

Fredericksburg was the battle fought in December 1862 where Burnside was the Union commanding general and had lost the battle. The battle tactic Burnside used was massed "human wave" frontal assaults against entrenched Confederates. There were thirteen futile assaults ordered by Burnside that day. Burnside needed to bolster his diminished reputation.

In the Border State of Missouri, the Union army issued Order Number 30 on 22 April 1863. Order Number 30 was written by H. Z. Curtis, Assistant Adjutant General, for Major General Samuel R. Curtis. The

---

[183] *OR*, Series 1, Volume 12, Part I, ibid, page 324, accessed 2 December 2006.

[184] *OR*, Series 1, Volume 12, Part I, ibid, page 331, accessed 2 December 2006.

[185] *OR*, Series 1, Volume 24, Part I, 1889, January 21, 1863, H. W. Halleck to Major General Grant, page 9.

[186] *OR*, Series 1, Volume 23, Part II, 1889, April 13, 1863, General Orders No. 38, Louis Richmond by command of Major General Burnside, page 237, accessed 2 December 2006.

[187] *ALPLC*, Series 1, General Correspondence. 1833-1916., U. S. Supreme Court, December 1863 (Printed Opinion: Ex Parte Vallandigham) accessed 5 December 2006; see also Journal of the Senate, February 10, 1863 (French mediation), page 226, 5 December 2006.

[188] *BDUSC*, accessed 22 December 2006.

order described a variety of categories describing the status of rebel combatants. However, at the end of the order were detestable forms to be used to blackmail allegiance to the United States.

The first part of the form was a loyalty oath "to be administered by the military authority". No variation of the wording of the form was to be allowed. The form required loyalty to "national sovereignty" and "the Federal Union". The form ended with the statement that the person compelled to agree with the loyalty oath was required to "pledge my honor, my property, and my life to the sacred performance of this my oath of allegiance to the Government of the United States of America." The "loyalty oath", because of the pledge concerning property, was the transfer of property from a private owner of it to the United States government. The Union army demanded all property from owners of it to prove absolute loyalty by financial support of the army.

The second form was a performance bail bond for a person who was arrested and imprisoned. Money and property were required to be pledged as collateral for the bail bond. It allowed a "military commission or tribunal" to judge a person guilty of "words . . . against the authority of the United States". After verdict, "any officer in the military service" could "seize and sell" the property of the signer of the loyalty oath. The wording of the bond made any turn of phrase critical of the Union army and government and many other actions grounds for seizure.[189] It was the final economic blackmail to silence freedom of speech and legitimate peaceful opposition to the military government orgy of expropriation and theft. Samuel Ryan Curtis, who was behind the order, was a former congressman and a member of the peace convention held in 1861 in Washington.[190]

The Confederate government was aware of the recruiting actions of the Union government both in the United States and abroad. In a communication of 29 April 1863, the Secretary of State of the Confederacy, Judah P. Benjamin, advised his diplomatic official James M. Mason in Great Britain that the Union was making "extensive enlistments" in Ireland. The Union conscription act had allowed for the drafting of persons of foreign birth but Benjamin advised Mason to raise the question of international treaty obligations to Lord Russell of the British government.[191] There was also Union recruiting in the German states. To increase their numbers, foreign mercenary soldiers were hired is Europe to fill the ranks of the Union army.

* * *

Along the Patuxent River in Maryland in May of 1863, an event foreboding the future occurred. Secretary of War Edwin McMasters Stanton communicated to Union army Major General Robert Cumming Schenck about an extremely important action that he ordered Schenck to take. A riverfront plantation owner was confined in the Old Capitol Prison (the site of the Old Capitol Prison is now the Supreme Court Building). Three rebel officers were apprehended with him. He was accused of having rebel mail and uniforms in his house. During the raid of the plantation, a man who was under the authority of Schenck was killed.

The important action that Schenck was ordered to take was described as "the object" of the communication from Stanton. Schenck was to seize the plantation and convert it to "military uses". He was to send the family of the plantation owner beyond United States military lines. Stanton's order to Schenck was to be "executed with diligence and efficiency".

The name of the plantation owner, according to Union military records, was J. H. Warring (Waring). The date of the communication from Stanton to Schenck was 25 May 1863.[192] This is most likely the same

---

[189] *OR*, Series 1, Volume 22, Part II, 1888, April 22, 1863, General Orders No. 30, H. Z. Curtis, page 237 to 244, page 243 has copy of loyalty oath, accessed 3 December 2006.

[190] *BDUSC*, accessed 22 December 2006.

[191] *ORN*, Series II, Volume 3, 1922, April 29, 1863, No. 21, Department of State, Richmond, J. P. Benjamin to James M. Mason, London, pages 753 and 754, accessed 6 December 2006.

[192] *OR*, Series 2, Volume 5, 1899, May 25, 1863, Edwin M. Stanton to R. C. Schenck, page 696, accessed 2 December 2006.

person as the John Waring of Saint Mary's County who was incarcerated at Fort McHenry as a "political prisoner" from the 2nd to the 5th of August 1862.[193] Military training centers would be needed for the anticipated number of recruits brought into the Union army by the draft act, importation of foreign mercenaries and illegal military methods.

The desired result of the imprisonment of the owner and the deportation of his family were obvious. There would be no one to legally oppose the Union military in a judicial court condemnation proceeding from taking the property. The main plantation house would probably become officer's quarters.

Union army Colonel William Birney played a central role in the formulation of plans in the decision to recruit slaves for the Union army from the farms and plantations of their Maryland owners. On 5 June 1863, President Lincoln sent a written message to Secretary of War Stanton and asked him to "please see and hear" Colonel William Birney about his plans for Black soldiers in the Union army. It appears that President Abraham Lincoln personally met with Colonel William Birney.[194]

Colonel Birney's origins were from an anti-slavery family of Alabama and Kentucky. He had participated in the 1848 revolution in France. The father of Colonel Birney, James Gillespie Birney, had been a presidential candidate in the elections of 1840 and 1844.[195] Colonel Birney was a revolutionary and a Union army political officer. He had no formal military training.

President Lincoln had taken political advantage of the military victory of the Union army at Antietam in September of 1862 to issue the preliminary Emancipation Proclamation. The final Proclamation took effect on 1 January 1863. The Emancipation Proclamation was limited and to be put into effect only in certain geographical areas. The border states of Maryland, Delaware, Kentucky and Missouri were not included. It freed slaves in specified areas of rebellion only.

Apparently, Secretary of War Stanton saw Birney, approved of his plan and assigned him to organize Black units for the Union army. In the National Archives Union military service record for Colonel William Birney of the Second Regiment, United States Colored Troops are found copies of orders authorizing him to recruit within specific geographical locations. The first order was issued the day after President Lincoln wrote to Stanton:

> War Department Adjutant General's Office
> Washington, June 6, 1863
> Special Orders}
> No. 258} Extract.

5. Colonel <u>William Birney</u> 2nd Regt U.S. Colored Troops will proceed without delay to organize and complete the 1st Regiment of Colored Troops in the District of Columbia. He will be guided by the rule governing the organization and muster of Volunteers into the service of the United States.

> By order of the Secretary of War:
> Capt Foster}   E D Townsend
> Assistant Adjutant General.
> copy sent Colonel Birney at Ebbit House.

Other documents in the file directed Colonel Birney to recruit at Fortress Monroe and Norfolk in Virginia for the 1st United States Colored Troops.

The second order was dated 22 June 1863 stated that Colonel Birney "will make requisition upon Major

---

[193] Fort McHenry prisoners, accessed 3 November 2006.
[194] Basler, *Supplement*, page 190.
[195] Boatner, page 65.

General J. A. Dix for the necessary transportation and subsistence" and was signed by C. W. Foster, Assistant Adjutant General. The third order was dated 26 June 1863 and directed Colonel Birney to "make to the Adjutant General of the Army the reports and returns called for by the Regulations for the Recruiting Service." and was signed by E. D. Townsend, Assistant Adjutant General. The third order was also signed by Townsend and dated 26 June 1863 and states that the "Quartermaster Department will furnish the necessary transportation". A letter from Colonel Birney to Major Stearns dated 29 June 1863 stated that Colonel Birney wanted to open an office in Baltimore so that he could send recruits from Norfolk, Virginia to there. The relationship of Major Stearns to George Luther Stearns, the member of the Secret Six, is unknown at this time.

On 23 June 1863, Henry Halleck, the General in Chief of the Union army made a directive that he claimed was consistent with "general orders in force". He ordered that "military supplies" in areas where they might fall into the hands of the Confederates should be taken by the Union army. He specifically mentioned beef cattle and horses as the desired objects of Union army seizure. He gave the order to Major General Schenck in Baltimore and three other Union generals.[196] On 25 June 1863, he followed up his first order with a message to General Hooker to confiscate horses in Loudoun County, Virginia and adjacent areas in Maryland.[197]

June of 1863 was a month that began with growing national resistance to Union draft recruiters. In Pennsylvania, Union army civilian recruiters were assaulted. In the village of Newkirk in Schuylkill Township recruiters were shot at.[198] In another incident, a person was mistakenly shot and arrests were made.[199]

The draft resistance spread to Midwestern Union states. On 10 June 1863 in Rush County, Indiana, John F. Stephens, a deputy provost marshal and Richard M. Craycraft, special agent of provost marshal, were shot while escorting a draft enrolling officer into a district. Stephens was killed and Craycraft was mortally wounded.[200] The previous day a warning shot had been fired at an enrolling officer.[201] In his communication to James B. Fry in Washington about the incident, Acting Assistant Provost Marshal General Conrad Baker told of the apprehension of Democrats because "certain" Republicans had threatened them with military draft.[202] James V. Hilligoss, Isaac Hilligoss and Sylvester Hilligoss were arrested for draft resistance in connection with the shooting of Stephens and Craycraft.[203] Conrad Baker later became the governor of Indiana from 1867 to 1873.[204]

In Indiana, on or about 15 June in Fulton County, a Union enrolling officer, described as "obnoxious", was "captured" by local citizens and had his enrolling lists taken from him. A company of the Union army was sent to protect him.[205] On 15 June 1863, at Whitestown in Boone County, an enrolling officer was surrounded by a mob of men while women pelted him with eggs. The Union army returned during the night of 16 June and arrested the four or five citizens they had writs for and eleven others. The Acting Assistant Provost Marshal, Conrad Baker, alleged that an armed mob of 100 to 125 citizens of Whitestown were present during the day but had dispersed before nightfall and the arrival of the army.[206] In Sullivan County, enrolling officer Fletcher

---

[196] OR, Series 1, Volume 27, Part III, 1889, June 23, 1863, H. W. Halleck to Schenck, pages 275 and 276, accessed 2 December 2006.
[197] OR, Series 1, Volume 27, Part I, 1889, June 25, 1863, H. W. Halleck to Hooker, page 57, accessed 2 December 2006.
[198] OR, Series 3, Volume 3, 1899, June 4, 1863, W. K. Jones to C. Tower, esq., page 332, accessed 2 December 2006.
[199] OR, Series 3, Volume 3, 1899, June 10, 1863, C. Tower to James B. Fry, page 330 to 332, accessed 2 December 2006.
[200] OR, Series 3, Volume 3, 1899, June 11, 1863, Conrad Baker to James B. Fry, page 338 to 340, accessed 2 December 2006.
[201] OR, Series 3, Volume 3, 1899, June 11, 1863, Conrad Baker to James B. fry, page 339, accessed 2 December 2006.
[202] OR, Series 3, Volume 3, 1899, June 11, 1863, Conrad Baker to James B. fry, page 340, accessed 2 December 2006.
[203] OR, Series 3, Volume 3, 1899, June 13 1863, John C. McQuiston to Brigadier General Wilcox, page 355 to 356, accessed 6 December 2006.
[204] Indiana Historical Bureau website, accessed 1 January 2007, available on the Internet.
[205] OR. Series 3, Volume 3, 1899, June 22, 1863, Conrad Baker to James B. Fry, page 396 and 397, accessed 2 December 2006.
[206] OR, Series 3, Volume 3, 1899, June 17, 1863, Conrad Baker to James B. Fry, page 375, accessed 2 December 2006.

Freeman was killed on 18 June 1863.[207] On 19 June 1863, in Brown County, an enrolling officer was reported murdered but a later report claimed the original report of his murder to have been false.[208]

In Ohio, draft resistance against the Union was armed and organized. On 16 June 1863 the chief draft enrollment officer for Ohio, Acting Assistant Provost Marshall General Ed. A. Parrott, requested a force of 300 soldiers from Captain John Green, Assistant Adjutant General, because a group of 700 to 900 "insurgents" had concentrated in Holmes County.[209] Draft resistors were labeled as insurgents, who were then demonized as traitors to the Union "cause".

Other areas of Ohio demonstrated their resistance to the draft in June of 1863. In Morrow County, four resistors were arrested. In Crawford County, draft enrolling officers were "mobbed". In Holmes County a group of seventy draft resistors rescued four persons arrested by the marshal. The draft enrolling officer of Knox County resigned because of a negative reception. Union authorities identified Mansfield, in Richland County, as a center of resistance.[210] Governor David Tod of Ohio, fearing for his safety, requested from Secretary of War Stanton an increase for his Governor's Guard.[211]

Union army soldiers were sent to suppress the political emergency of the northern insurrections because of draft resistance. From 16 to 20 June 1863, Colonel William Wallace of the 15th Ohio Infantry went to Holmes County with a composite force totaling 380 soldiers, 100 of them from the Governor's Guard and artillery unit. Near the town of Napoleon, in Henry County, there was a skirmish with about 50 insurgents. The Unionists took prisoners and sent them to Cleveland. Wallace, in his report of 20 June 1863, admitted that soldiers under his command committed "irregularities" against "private property". Wallace excused the "irregularities" of his Union soldiers because they were veterans of fighting in the Confederacy.[212]

Colonel Wallace left about 75 to 100 men behind in the area. D. P. Leadbetter of Millersburg, in Holmes County, sent Governor Tod a letter on 22 June 1863. During the raid of Wallace, Leadbetter had negotiated the surrender of 13 insurgents who he described as "French". The Union soldiers in the area remained despite the agreement of Wallace to withdraw them and they were "stealing" from local citizens. Leadbetter said that some of the soldiers were justifying their actions because of "religion".[213] In a state proclamation of 22 June 1863, Governor Tod said that a regiment of "colored men" was being enlisted in Ohio and was to be sent to a camp at "Delaware", which are both a town and county in Ohio.[214] Any pretext was being used to absolve the Union army soldiers of criminal acts.

General Robert E. Lee and the Confederate army had invaded western Maryland during June of 1863. Because the Union army had difficulty knowing where Lee was moving his army to, concern grew for defense of Baltimore. The invasion panicked the Union military political leadership to resort to ill-disguised threats to force workers to fortify the eastern Maryland city of Baltimore.

In a reply of 20 June 1863 to John L. Chapman, the mayor of Baltimore, Major General Robert C. Schenck expressed his willingness to convert the offer of Chapman to provide paid or voluntary labor to build fortifications to protect the city. Schenck gave Chapman a diktat ultimatum with no choice: provide 1,000 men by 4 PM or he would provide the "military force" to begin "impressments".[215]

---

[207] OR, Series 3, Volume 3, 1899, June 18, 1863, R. W. Thompson to Conrad Baker, page 393 and 394, accessed 2 December 2006.
[208] OR, Series 3, Volume 3, 1899, June 20, 1863, Conrad Baker to James B. Fry, page 392 and 393, accessed 2 December 2006.
[209] OR, Series 1, Volume 23, Part I, 1889, June 16, 1863, Ed. A. Parrott to John Green., page 396, accessed 2 December 2006.
[210] OR, Series 3, Volume 3, 1899, June 12, 1863, Parrott to Fry, page 349 and 350, accessed 2 December 2006.
[211] OR, Series 3, Volume 3, 1899, June 12, 1863, Tod to Stanton, page 349, accessed 2 December 2006.
[212] OR, Series 1, Volume 23, Part I, 1889, June 20, 1863, "June 16-20. 1863.- Affairs in Holmes County, Ohio.", Report of Colonel William Wallace, Fifteenth Ohio Infantry, commanding United Steles Forces in Ohio., page 395 and 396, accessed 2 December 2006.
[213] OR, Series 3, Volume 3, 1899, June 22, 1863, Leadbetter to Tod, page 403, accessed 2 December 2006.
[214] OR, Series 3, Volume 3, 1899, June 22, 1863, Tod to the People of Ohio (proclamation), page 402, accessed 2 December 2006.
[215] OR, Series 1, Volume 27, Part III, June 20, 1863, Robt. C. Schenck to John L. Chapman, page 235, accessed 3 December 2006.

Schenck was not satisfied. On 6 July 1863, he requested permission from the chief of the Union army, Henry Halleck, to use Confederate prisoners of war to build fortifications rather than "negroes". Schenck wrote that there was no problem with the Confederates learning about the Union defenses while they were building them. Henry W. Halleck, General in Chief of the Union army, replied that he knew of no instance in which the Confederates used Union prisoners of war to construct fortifications. Halleck was implying to a dense Schenck his action would provoke Confederate retaliation.[216]

Major General Robert Cumming Schenck (1809-1890) held two positions from 4 March 1863 to at least the beginning of December 1863. He was both a member of Congress in the House of Representatives and a Union army officer. Robert C. Schenck was a Union army political general. Schenck's chief of staff was Colonel Donn C. Piatt. Both Schenck and Piatt had worked in 1860 for the election of Lincoln to be president in Illinois and remained politically connected to Lincoln during the Civil War.[217]

After the Union army victory at Gettysburg, Pennsylvania on 3 July 1863, resistance to the Union draft and impressments of slaves into the Union army became increasingly violent. On 11 July 1863, in Union army occupied Norfolk, Virginia, Union army Lieutenant Anson L. Sanborn of the 1st United States Colored Volunteers was shot and killed by Dr. David M. Wright.[218] The Union version was that Wright shot Sanborn because he was marching "colored" Union soldiers down the main street in Norfolk.[219] The Confederate version was that an elderly Wright said "My God, did ever I expect my country to come to this? Did ever I expect to see such a regiment on the streets of the city of Norfolk?" and that Sanborn tried to slap Wright's cheek with his sword.[220] Norfolk was the Virginia city from where Birney had asked to send Black recruits to Baltimore, Maryland beginning 29 June 1863. The area was under the command of Benjamin F. Butler. The relationship of Anson L. Sanborn to Franklin Sanborn, the member of the Secret Six, or John D. Sanborn is unknown at this time. On 16 February 1860 the United States Senate had voted to arrest Sanborn. He fled.[221] John D. Sanborn was a "provost messenger" between Baltimore and Fortress Monroe.[222]

A search of Union army records failed to reveal a military service record for Anson L. Sanborn, which may, or may not, be because Sanborn was a civilian recruiter and a political operative. This raises the possibility that Colonel William Birney, the revolutionary, was involved in provoking an incident or confrontation in Norfolk. One of the orders given to Birney during June authorized him to form the 1st Regiment of Colored Troops in the District of Columbia, while Sanborn was leading the 1st United States Colored Volunteers.

Draft riots occurred in New York City from 13 to 16 July 1863 and many Blacks were murdered.[223] Union soldiers who recently fought the battle at Gettysburg were sent to New York City to quell the disturbance. Rioting also broke out in Boston, Massachusetts. Resistance to the draft was reported at other locations. Slaves were desperately needed to fill the ranks of the Union army.

On 16 July 1863, Isaac Hilligoss of Rush County, Indiana died according to family records. In early June he had been arrested for draft resistance. The circumstance and the cause of his death remain unknown.

On 27 July 1863, Colonel Birney began illegal recruiting activities in the city of Baltimore, Maryland. Maryland was excluded from the zone in which slaves could be freed by the geographical limitation of the

---

[216] *OR*, Series 2, Volume 6, 1899, July 6, 1863, R. C. Schenck to H.W. Halleck, page 85, accessed 3 December 2006.
[217] Donn Piatt, *Memories of the Men Who Saved the Union*, page 28, accessed 28 December 2006.
[218] *ALPLC, ALSC*, Lemuel J. Bowden to Abraham Lincoln, Friday, July 31, 1863 (Case of David Wright), 5 December 2006.
[219] *OR*, Series 2, Volume 6, 1899, August 19, 1863, J. Holt to His Excellency the President (Abraham Lincoln), page 216, accessed 5 December 2006.
[220] *OR*, Series 2, Volume 6, 1899, August 7, 1863, Mrs. Stark A. W. Peighton to President Davis, page 188, accessed 3 December 2006.
[221] Renehan, Jr., *The Secret Six, The True Tale of the Men Who Conspired with John Brown*, page 257.
[222] *CLNN*, Congressional Record, May 27, 1874, speech of Hiester Clymer, page 377, accessed 15 January 2007.
[223] Boatner, page 245.

Emancipation Proclamation. Birney raided five slave jails of Baltimore and forced the newly freed slaves immediately into the Union army. Birney's orders for his action came from Major General Schenck.[224] Birney was forming the vanguard of his revolution with criminals. Running away from an owner was not the only reason slaves were put into jail.

The military recruiters met with conflict from the civil authorities in Maryland. A letter from imprisoned recruiter J. P. Creager was sent to Colonel Birney. J. P. Creager had been arrested by Maryland civil authorities, apparently for an action or crime associated with recruiting slaves from their owners for the Union army. The amount of his bail was $1,000.[225] The Union War Department refused to bail Colonel Creager out of jail.[226] It is not known how long Colonel Creager remained in jail. Creager may have been a civilian recruiter and political operative who was given the cavalry title of colonel.

On 20 August 1863, Judge Advocate General J. Holt wrote to Stanton regarding a letter that was sent by Judge Hugh L. Bond of Maryland to Stanton and was published in several newspapers. The letter of Bond advocated the enlistment of both free and slave Blacks. Holt's communication to Stanton provided justification for what Bond was promoting. Holt cited the "twelfth section" of legislation of 17 July 1862 which allowed the President to "receive into service" persons of "African descent". However, the legislation described non-combatant work but with the all inclusive phrase of "or any other labor or military or naval service".

On the issue of financial compensation made to loyal slave owners, Holt advocated it. Holt's position was that the compensation should be "entirely to exhaust" any future claims of slave owners to prevent re-enslavement at the conclusion of the war. Holt argued that because slaves were represented numerically in Congress by a provision of the Constitution that they were persons. Holt concluded his writing with his statement that Blacks would have their freedom at the end of the war "once they lay down their arms".[227] The "twelfth section" Holt referred to was part of legislation titled "An Act to amend the Act calling forth the militia to Execute the Laws of the Union, suppress Insurrections, and repel Invasions, approved February twenty-eight seventeen hundred and ninety-five, and acts amendatory thereof, and for other Purposes".[228]

A banquet was given in Baltimore on 31 August 1863 to celebrate the launching of two ships. The banquet was attended by both civilian and military notables. Judge Bond, the Union advocate of unrestricted military mobilization, was there.[229] Col. Birney had already commenced recruitment and enlistment activities prior to the celebration.

Hugh Lennox Bond graduated from the University of the City of New York in 1848. From 1860 to 1868, he served as a judge for the Maryland Criminal Court. Later, he was a judge for the 4th United States Circuit Court. From 1876 to 1893, he was a chief justice and was instrumental in the destruction of the South Carolina Ku Klux Klan by severe judicial sentences.[230] In 1866, Hon. Hugh L. Bond attended a meeting of the Southern Republican Association in New York.[231]

The financial consideration for the recruitment of slaves specifically from the lower (southern) counties of Maryland was known before and during the time illegal recruitment occurred. An argument used by abolitionists was that the recruitment of only slaves would create economic hardship in the city of Baltimore, the northern and the western parts of Maryland. Colonel Birney's actions were discussed by government officials of the city of Baltimore, Governor Bradford and ex-governor Francis Thomas, an anti-slavery

---

[224] Scharf, *History of Baltimore City and County*, page 144.
[225] Berlin, Reidy and Rowland, *Freedom, The Black Military Experience*, pages 203-205.
[226] Glatthaar, *Forged In Battle*, page 68.
[227] *OR*, Series 3, Volume 3, 1899, August 20, 1863, J. Holt to Hon. E. M. Stanton, page 695 and 696, accessed 5 December 2006.
[228] *CLNN*, Statutes at Large, 37th Congress, 2nd Session, pages 597 to 600, accessed 7 December 2006.
[229] Scharf, *History of Baltimore City and County*, page 145.
[230] *Who Was Who In America, Historical Volume, 1607-1896*, page 131.
[231] *The New York Times*, November 27, 1866, page 5.

Democrat.[232] Newspapers also reported the controversy. It was viewed that the "disloyal" slave owners of lower Maryland would economically benefit if their slaves were not recruited. Judge Bond advocated the recruitment of all Blacks, both free and slave.[233] The view of Judge Bond was more obsessed with economic issues than with the issue of freedom for slaves.

On 2 September 1863, President Lincoln communicated in writing to his Secretary of the Treasury, Salmon P. Chase. Secretary Chase was having concerns about extending the Emancipation Proclamation to certain areas of Virginia and Louisiana. In areas of those states, the Emancipation Proclamation was exempted from enforcement and the proclamation did not take effect. President Lincoln's political sensitivity to the issue that slavery remained legal in Delaware, Maryland, Kentucky, Tennessee and Missouri is clearly stated in the letter. Lincoln wrote that the proclamation had no foundation in law or the constitution. He confessed to the military necessity of it. His speculation was that the proclamation might lead to law by proclamation, other than legislative enactment. He stated the risk of losing political support and elections because of the use of proclamation rather than enacted law.[234] The trend that President Lincoln was concerned about was the creation of a fascist military state without him leading it. Chase had been a member of the peace convention of 1861, which was held in Washington.[235]

President Lincoln was an astute observer of the political effects of his decisions and of the military need of recruiting Black slaves and freemen for the Union army. He asked many questions of himself in his letter to Salmon P. Chase. His admission that the Emancipation Proclamation was a "military measure" reflects his resignation to the fact that the Union army was needed for the political uprisings the Union faced in the north and to invade the Confederate south.

On the same day, 2 September 1863, C. W. Foster, Assistant Adjutant General, wrote to Schenck in Baltimore. Foster directed Schenck to order Birney to stop using civilian recruiters of slaves on the Eastern Shore of Maryland and to replace them with commissioned military officers. The reason Foster gave was that Birney's civilian recruiters were "creating trouble".[236] This confirms Birney's use of civilian recruiters and supports the allegation that Anson L. Sanborn, killed by Dr. Wright, was a civilian recruiter and not a soldier in the Union army.

In *The New York Times* of 17 September 1863, a letter titled "Employment of Slaves in the Army" was printed and responded to some of the issues raised in Hugh L. Bond's letter to Secretary of War Stanton. The letter was addressed to Judge Bond. It gave practical and legal reasons for recruiting slaves. In practical terms, if the Union did not employ slaves then the Confederacy would. The legal scholar Blackstone was quoted as saying that all persons born within a country owed allegiance to it. However, the last paragraph of the letter advocated compensation for "loyal" slave owners.[237] The author of the letter was James A. Hamilton, the son of Alexander Hamilton.[238] The idea that the Confederacy might enlist slaves was a possibility. On 11 January 1865, General Robert E. Lee sent a letter to a member of the Virginia Senate advocating the enlistment of Black slaves in exchange for their emancipation.[239]

On 28 September 1863, Augustus W. Bradford, the governor of Maryland communicated to Lincoln. Bradford described a recruiting method he became aware of. Steamboats, hired by the government, were transporting recruiting officers and squads of Black soldiers to areas near farms and plantations that had slaves.

---

[232] Wikipedia, "Frances Thomas", accessed 1 January 2007, available on the Internet.
[233] Scharf, *History of Maryland, Vol. III*, page 570-571.
[234] Basler, *Vol. VI*, page 428-429.
[235] *BDUSC*, accessed 22 December 2006.
[236] *OR*, Series 3, Volume 3, 1899, September 2, 1863, C. W. Foster to R. C. Schenck, pages 760 and 761, accessed 3 December 2006.
[237] *The New York Times*, September 17, 1863, page 5, column 3.
[238] *Who Was Who In America, Historical Edition, 1607-1896*, page 300.
[239] Tidwell, *April '65*, page 232, footnote 3.

At night, the soldiers would secretly go to slaves who were potential recruits and entice them into leaving their farm or plantation. Bradford complained about the practice.[240]

On 1 October 1863 Stanton communicated to Lincoln regarding the recruitment of "free persons of color" and slaves into the Union army from the Border States of Maryland and Tennessee. Stanton referred to the communication of Governor Bradford of Maryland of the 28th and a meeting in Washington with him. Stanton cited the agreement of Bradford to recruit Maryland Blacks, both free and slave, with certain conditions. President Lincoln wrote a memorandum outlining his position:

> To recruiting free negroes, no objection.
> To recruiting slaves of disloyal owners, no objection.
> To recruiting slaves of loyal owners, with their consent, no objection.
> To recruiting slaves of loyal owners without consent, objection, unless the necessity is urgent.
> To conducting offensively, while recruiting, and to carrying away slaves not suitable for recruits, objection.

Stanton wrote of a problem of the Union army: "White soldiers are suffering from the malarious influences of the locality at Fortress Monroe, and require all the power of the Government to supply their places by black troops."[241]

By 1 October 1863, President Lincoln was increasingly aware of the activity of the Union army recruiting slaves in Maryland. On that day he communicated to both Erastus B. Tyler and Colonel Birney. President Lincoln's written instructions to them were to provide for the Black soldiers they had already recruited, but to "do nothing further about that branch of affairs". His instructions were to cease recruiting. He specifically requested that nothing be done about General Vickers of Kent County, Maryland. A copy of his communication to Tyler was addressed to Colonel Birney.[242]

General Erastus Bernard Tyler was temporarily in command of the Union Middle Department from 28 September to 10 October 1863. Tyler commanded during the leave of absence of Schenck. Major General Schenck returned and commanded the Middle Department from 10 October to 5 December 1863.[243] There is no known written message from President Lincoln ordering the resumption of the recruitment of Maryland slaves.[244] Lincoln was countermanding the orders of the Union army.

A few days later, President Lincoln made a written communication to Colonel Birney. On 3 October 1863, he asked Colonel Birney in Baltimore to provide him with the number of slaves he had recruited and not to include the number of free Blacks. Colonel Birney replied on the same day that "between 1250 and 1300" had been recruited. It should be noted that the recruitment numbers of Black freemen in Maryland was not requested by President Lincoln.[245]

On 3 October 1863, General Orders No. 329 was issued from the Adjutant General's Office of the War Department. The orders made the Bureau for Organizing Colored Troops responsible for establishing recruiting stations in Maryland, Missouri and Tennessee. Item four of General Orders 329 allowed the Union army to

---

[240] *ALPLC, ALSC,* Augustus W. Bradford to Abraham Lincoln, Monday, September 28, 1863 (Enlistment of freedmen in Maryland; endorsed by Lincoln, Oct. 1, 1863), accessed 5 December 2006.
[241] *OR*, Series 3, Volume 3, 1899, October 1, 1863, Stanton to Mr. President, page 855 and 856, accessed 15 December 2006.
[242] Basler, *Vol. VI*, page 494.
[243] Boatner, page 549.
[244] Boatner cites Tyler. However, *OR* Series 1, Volume 29, Part II, 1890, cites Brevet Brigadier General W.W. Morris as the officer assigned to the Middle Department by E. D. Townsend, page 224, accessed 5 December 2006.
[245] *OR*, Series 3, Volume 3, 1899, October 3, 1863, A. Lincoln to Colonel Birney, October 3, 1863, Wm. Birney to His Excellency A. Lincoln, page 862, accessed 15 December 2006.

recruit both free and slave persons, provided the owner of slaves gave "written consent". A maximum of $300 was allowed to compensate an owner for each slave. The reason for the order was "the exigencies of the war" and it was considered "confidential" at the time it was issued. The order was given under the signature of E. D. Townsend, Assistant Adjutant General and made "By order of the President".[246] On 15 October 1863, Townsend, by order of Stanton, extended the geographical limit of General Orders No. 329 to Accomack and Northampton, Virginia.[247]

On 12 October 1863, Hugh L. Bond communicated to Stanton. He advised Stanton to delay the draft until after the election of 4 November 1863. The reason Bond cited was that the congressional election would be lost excepting one candidate. Bond expressed his disappointment that Stanton was not at a meeting the previous Saturday. He blamed Donn Piatt for Stanton's absence from the meeting.[248] On the same day, Stanton wrote that Brigadier General Andrew Johnson, the Military Governor of Tennessee, who had authorized the establishment of recruiting stations for "colored troops", could modify General Orders No. 329 to promote enlistments. Stanton was writing "By order of the President".[249]

On 13 October 1863 Birney wrote to an unnamed Adjutant General of the Union army. Birney confirmed receiving Lincoln's communication of early October and included a copy of it. He claimed that he had fully complied with the order and was not recruiting. Birney denied knowledge of General Vickers prior to the communication from Lincoln. Birney then described his knowledge of Vickers that he learned subsequent to Lincoln's communication. He speciously described Vickers as a former "noisy constitutional man" and a "virulent enemy of the Government". Birney then accused Judge Carmichael of the Maryland Eastern Shore as a "vindictive and dangerous enemy of the Government". Birney, sounding like a promoter of class warfare, claimed the "mass of the population" wanted the enlistment of Blacks, both free and slave.[250] The language of Birney, the revolutionary, sounded extreme and on the precipice of insubordination. Birney was willing to make any false accusation to further his revolutionary goal of military domination.

The next day, 14 October, the ominous clouds thundering from Maryland over the White House were pierced by a brief ray of light from the Midwest. Election returns from Indiana were improving the Union political position, as had returns from Ohio shortly before. Lincoln received the news through Secretary of War Stanton.[251]

From the months of July to October the case of Dr. David M. Wright was the subject of the attention of the Union army and President Lincoln. Wright had been sentenced to death by a military commission and his civilian lawyers withdrew from the case. Lincoln had Wright examined by a doctor to determine his sanity. Petitions from the citizens of Norfolk, Virginia had been filed with the Union army and Lincoln to commute his sentence to life imprisonment. On 7 October 1863, Lincoln authorized his execution. Dr. Wright remained alive because Lincoln had granted a stay of execution to 23 October.[252]

The Radical Republican quiet revolution had achieved its preliminary goals and was to solidify its gains

---

[246] *OR*, Series 3, Volume 3, 1889, October 3, 1863, General Orders No. 329, E. D. Townsend, pages 860 and 861, accessed 3 December 2006.
[247] *OR*, Series 3, Volume 3, 1889, October 15, 1863, E. D. Townsend by order of the Secretary of War, page 887, 3 December 2006.
[248] *OR*, Series 3, Volume 3, 1889, October 12, 1863, Hugh L. Bond to Hon. E. M. Stanton, page 877, accessed 3 December 2006.
[249] *OR* Series 3, Volume 3, 1889, October 12, 1863, Edwin M. Stanton, page 876, accessed 5 December 2006.
[250] *OR*, Series 3, Volume 3, 1889, October 13, 1862, William Birney to adjutant General U.S. Army, page 881, 882, accessed 6 December 2006.
[251] *ALPLC, ALSC*, Oliver P. Morton to Edwin M. Stanton, Wednesday, October 14, 1863 (Telegram reporting Indiana election results),
[252] *OR*, Series 2, Volume 6, 1899, October 8, 1863, E. D. Townsend to J. G. Foster with "remarks" of Abraham Lincoln of October ?, 1863, pages 360 and 361, accessed 5 December 2006; also see *OR*, Series 2, Volume 6, 1899, October 15, 1863, A. Lincoln to Major General Foster, page 380, accessed 5 December 2006.

in a reign of terror by invading The Plains in Saint Mary's County.

Chapter 4

THE UNION RAID OF THE PLAINS

Located about a mile upstream on the Patuxent River from The Plains at Benedict was Camp Stanton, a Union base for the training of Black troops. Camp Stanton was established on 19 October 1863. The day after, on 20 October 1863, one white officer, an unidentified "young white man" and two Black soldiers from Camp Stanton arrived at The Plains in a rowboat. Union Lieutenant Eben White of Company "B", 7th United States Colored Troops and two Black soldiers went to the house. The unidentified "young white man" remained at the rowboat. Words were exchanged between Colonel Sothoron and Lieutenant White. Lieutenant White and the two soldiers proceeded to the fields in an attempt to recruit the slaves working there. Colonel Sothoron and his son Webster followed them shortly afterwards. More words were exchanged. Colonel Sothoron was armed with his "fowling piece"; a double-barreled shotgun.

A confrontation took place that has been described by various sources ranging in description from "murder" to "justifiable homicide". The following is a most likely what transpired based on the various sources.

Moving towards the Sothorons, one of the Black soldiers urged White to kill them. Armed only with a sword, Lieutenant White took a musket from one of the Black soldiers and attempted to shoot Colonel Sothoron. The gun either misfired or shot a bullet that put a hole in Colonel Sothoron's hat. At the same instant, Colonel Sothoron fired his shotgun and killed Lieutenant White. The two soldiers ran away and Colonel Sothoron again fired, wounding one of them in the back of the head.

On the same day of the shooting, October 20, 1863, there was a cipher (coded) message sent from President Lincoln to Donn C. Piatt. President Lincoln replied that he wanted to see two young men who apparently had knowledge that Lincoln wanted to know by interviewing them himself.[253] Donn C. Piatt was the Chief of Staff for Major General Schenck, who was a politician and the military administrator of the Union Middle Department in Baltimore. Donn Piatt was a journalist and in 1877 he was indicted but never prosecuted for printing an editorial that was interpreted as a threat of assassination against President Rutherford Hayes.[254] A second version about Piatt writes that he was indicted in 1876 for "conspiring to disturb the people of the country."[255] The message concerned two young men and they were from Richmond, Virginia. Lincoln requested that they be "sent over". They have not been identified.[256] The fact that the message was sent in code is intriguing.

The chief of Union secret police counter-intelligence was Colonel Lafayette C. Baker, who had his headquarters at 217 Pennsylvania Avenue in Washington, D.C. The records of his investigations are found in the Turner-Baker Papers of the National Archives and one undated document with two signatures concerns

---

[253] Basler, *Vol. VI*, page 529.
[254] *Who Was Who In America*, page 481.
[255] *The Washington Post*, November 13, 1891, page 1, accessed 10 December 2006.
[256] Basler, *Vol. VI*, page 529.

Colonel Sothoron:[257]

>Washington, D.C.
>No 217 Pa. Av.
>Col. L.C. Baker
>Sir I Take the opportunity to inform you of Colonel John H. Sothoron who has been South in arms Against the U S government then returned home & has been engaged secreting Sothoron officers & giving All information that he could gain then seeking A way open to the Potomac & then conveying them Down & Seeing them Safe Across he then had A Servant man that he carried to Virginia with him when he & his son sent To Take Arms Against U.S.A. then the Boy returned home & was ill used he then started to the seat of war he was Taken confined Severely used to sent To Richmond to since that time he has been giving All aid & information that he cold give Against the U.S.. I remain your
>Respectfully
>W.W. Goldsborough
>With the politeness of Mr.
>E. V. Johnson

Confederate army Major William W. Goldsborough of the Second Maryland Infantry had been wounded and captured at the battle of Gettysburg in July of 1863.[258] Webster and Marshall Sothoron had served with William W. Goldsborough in the First Maryland Infantry. After the Civil War, William W. Goldsborough wrote *The Maryland Line in the Confederate Army, 1861-1865*.

The National Archives Confederate military service record for William W. Goldsborough shows that in 1861 and 1862 he was a soldier. However, there is no information in the record about his capture by the Union army or any information after 1862. Some of the wounded Confederate soldiers from Gettysburg were brought to Baltimore and placed in the prison camp of Fort McHenry.[259] A wounded Major Goldsborough may have been compelled to name Colonel Sothoron by the counter-intelligence staff of Colonel Baker. There is a Fort McHenry prison record that shows Major W. W. Goldsborough as having been captured on 4 July 1863, registered at the fort on 22 April 1864 with a disposition date of 15 June 1864 at West's Building, a Union hospital.[260] Unfortunately, the statement of William W. Goldsborough has no date on it. Both signatures and the statement were written by the same person.

Unfortunately, the undated statement attributed to William W. Goldsborough lacks clarity. It is open to interpretation as to the facts mentioned. It is not clear if the "Servant" and the "Boy" are the same person or two different persons. The "Boy" could have been Marshall L. Sothoron, because he was sick in Virginia in October of 1861. The statement could be taken to confirm that the reason for Colonel Sothoron's visit to Virginia in 1861 was to visit his hospitalized son and return to The Plains with him. There is no evidence to support the allegation that Colonel Sothoron was "in Arms" against the Union government. It is not known if the statement was written before or after the shooting incident. The fact of the 1864 imprisonment (months after the Battle of Gettysburg and the shooting of White) of Goldsborough subjects the Turner-Baker file to scrutiny as a coerced confession or forgery. Additionally, the lack of a Union prisoner of war record of Goldsborough from the time of his capture at Gettysburg leads to a suggestion that there were Union Middle Department secret jails in Baltimore, possibly located in the former slave jails that Birney emptied in July of 1863.

Colonel Sothoron escaped to Virginia by the Confederate Signal Corps route that extended through

---

[257] *NARA*, Turner-Baker Papers, M797, Microfilm 126.
[258] Goldsborough, page 243.
[259] Manakee, page 85.
[260] Fort McHenry prisoners, accessed 15 December 2006.

Maryland and across the Potomac River to Mathias Point, Virginia. Shortly after his arrival in Richmond, Virginia, he was introduced to FitzGerald Ross, an English reporter, by Major William Norris of the Confederate Signal Corps. Norris was the same Confederate officer who had promoted his son Webster. FitzGerald Ross had also traveled the courier route from the North to the South. Colonel Sothoron gave an account to him of the shooting incident at The Plains. The written version by Ross agrees with most of the other reports excepting that a greater number of 'twenty-five or thirty" Black soldiers were claimed to be at The Plains on the day of the shooting. Ross called the death of Lieutenant White "justifiable" and stated the realistic fear that Colonel Sothoron would not receive a fair and impartial trial if he remained in Union territory. Colonel Sothoron was under the control of a clandestine part of the Confederate military and it would be expected that he was used for propaganda and information debriefing purposes.[261]

One of a number of Confederate Signal Corps courier routes ran through the town of Charlotte Hall, which is close to The Plains. The uniform of General Robert E. Lee, which he wore at the Confederate surrender at Appomattox, was sent to him through Charlotte Hall.[262] The courier route was part of the "Secret Line".

The fear of not being able to have an impartial and fair trial on the part of Colonel Sothoron was realistic. On 24 September 1862, the writ of Habeas Corpus was formally suspended by proclamation of President Lincoln even though there were previous illegal arrests made by the Union military authorities in Maryland.[263]

In his book published in 1887, Piatt related the events before and after 20 October 1863. Piatt stated that the Lincoln administration was against freeing the slaves of Maryland. Piatt claimed that he directed Birney to recruit slaves in Maryland, but that Birney wanted written authorization from Schenck, which was refused. Schenck refused because Birney was acting directly by order of the War Department. When Schenck traveled to Boston, Piatt saw his opportunity and ordered Birney to begin recruiting slaves.[264]

There was immediate opposition to the recruiting of Maryland slaves. Maryland Senator Reverdy Johnson and a delegation of Maryland citizens came to Middle Department army headquarters to protest. Piatt "gave them scant comfort". The delegation then went to Washington.[265]

On 21 October 1863, the day after the shooting, the delegation of Maryland slave owners met with President Lincoln at the White House. President Lincoln was advised of the presence of armed Union troops on the Patuxent and sent a telegram to Major General Robert C. Schenck, the military political administrator in Baltimore. Lincoln reported to Schenck the fact that a delegation came to him and had advised him that Black soldiers were at landings on the Patuxent River. President Lincoln asked if any order had been given to them. Lincoln communicated to Schenck that the soldiers were frightening residents and causing confusion.[266]

According to Piatt's version, a telegram was sent from the War Department to Piatt asking who was in command at the Middle Department. Piatt replied that the Chief of Staff was in command, which was evasive doublespeak because it was his position. Piatt was summoned to personally appear at the War Department. When Piatt arrived at the department he was advised that Secretary of War Stanton was at the White House and he was to go there. Piatt arrived at the White House, did not see Stanton and was sent directly to see Lincoln. Lincoln was in a rage and threatened Piatt with dismissal. Piatt was ordered by Lincoln to countermand the

---

[261] Ross, page 164-165.
[262] Bakeless, *Spies of the Confederacy*, pages 85-87.
[263] *CLNN*, Statutes at Large, Appendix, page not numbered, page 730, accessed 7 December 2006.
[264] Donn Piatt, *Memories of the Men Who Saved the Union*, pages 43 and 44, accessed 28 December 2006.
[265] Donn Piatt, ibid., pages 44 and 45, accessed 28 December 2006.
[266] *OR*, Series 1, Volume 29, Part II, 1890, October 21, 1863, A. Lincoln to Major General Schenck, page 363, accessed 15 December 2006.

order he gave to Birney to recruit slaves.[267] There is no evidence that Piatt did anything to countermand the order.

At 6:45 PM on the evening of the same day, Major General Schenck, in Baltimore, replied to President Lincoln. Schenck minimized what the delegation told Lincoln and referred to an alleged report of Birney sent that day to the Adjutant General. He said he ordered Birney to look for a "camp of instruction and rendezvous for colored troops" and to place recruiting squads at six landings on the Patuxent River with "special instructions". Schenck expressed his hope to arrest the "murderers" of Lieutenant White and demonized them as "two secessionists, named Southeron". Schenck claimed that the area was "a neighborhood of rabid secessionists", fearful of losing their slaves. According to Schenck, the residents were the problem and not his soldiers. In his communication, Major General Schenck placed Colonel Birney near the scene of the killing of Lieutenant White. Colonel Birney may have been the "young white man" who remained in the boat while Lieutenant White and the two soldiers disembarked and went to the Sothoron plantation house.[268] The allegation that Colonel Sothoron was a secessionist has no information to support it.

On the same day, the order of Union army General Gilman Marston contradicted the order of Union army Major General Schenck. Marston and his command were stationed at Point Lookout approximately twenty miles southeast of The Plains. He ordered Lieutenant John Mix of the Fifth U.S. Cavalry to take another officer and 106 of his soldiers to Leonardtown, approximately midway between Point Lookout and The Plains, and to establish headquarters there. Marston ordered Mix to "suppress the contraband trade and all disloyal practices, arresting deserters and escaped prisoners, and preserving the public peace." In addition, Mix was ordered to halt the illegal recruitment along the landings of the Patuxent River and to make the unauthorized recruiters leave. Marston cautioned Mix to ensure that no "depredations" were made by his soldiers. Apparently, there was no direct communication between the two generals concerning Birney's raid to recruit slaves.[269] It was almost as if the two generals were on opposing sides. Marston's obituary in 1890 claimed he was "a little insubordinate to his superiors", but lauded him as "honest as the sun" and well regarded by the soldiers under his command.[270] Marston was a congressman before and after the shooting incident.[271]

It is conceivable that Marston received a direct order from President Lincoln to take action to cease recruiting. If Marston did receive an order from Lincoln, it is possible that it no longer exists because of the allegation made that Robert Todd Lincoln destroyed some of his father's papers.[272] The motive for destruction of records would be to protect the hagiography that Lincoln was responsible for leading the efforts to free the slaves, when in fact he did not.

On the next day, Thursday, 22 October 1863, the death of Lieutenant White was reported on the front page of *The New York Times* in an article titled "Murder of a Negro Recruiting Officer in Maryland." The article claimed that Colonel Sothoron had two slaves "tied up" to prevent them from enlisting. It was claimed that a "heavily armed" Colonel Sothoron and his son had shot White after he demanded the release of the slaves. The article chained the body of Lieutenant White was to be "forwarded to his friends in Massachusetts." The body was actually hidden under the porch of the plantation house.[273] The same article appeared in the *National Intelligencer* on the same day. The only difference was that the article was titled "RECRUITING

---

[267] Donn Piatt, *Memories of the Men Who Saved the Union*, page 45, accessed 28 December 2006.
[268] *OR*, Series 1, Volume 29, Part II, 1890, October 21, 1863, Robt. C. Schenck to The President of the United States, page 364, accessed 6 December 2006.
[269] *OR*, Series 1, Volume 29, Part II, 1890, October 21, 1863, October 21, 1863, Gilman Marston to John Mix, page 364, accessed 6 December 2006.
[270] *The Washington Post*, July 5, 1890, "One of New Hampshire's Great Men", page 4, accessed 12 December 2006, available by subscription on the Internet.
[271] *BDUSC*, accessed 22 December 2006.
[272] Philip Van Doren Stern, *The Man Who Killed Lincoln*, page 406.
[273] Duncan Dashiel Burroughs

SLAVES IN MARYLAND, A TRAGEDY". It also was printed in the *Chicago Tribune*. The Union propaganda machine was alarming the public with phrases such as "heavily armed", as if slave owners had weapons of mass destruction. Actually, the carrying of a shotgun in Maryland was sanctioned by the Union army. On 20 September 1861, John A. Dix gave instructions to the Union army permitting shotguns used for hunting.[274] Character assassination fueled by Union political propaganda was dominating the headlines.

On the second page of the same issue of *The New York Times* appeared a news article titled "RECRUITING NEGROES IN MARYLAND" about the meeting between President Lincoln and the Maryland slave owners. The article said the "Government must have all the slaves in Maryland and the border States for military purposes."

President Lincoln sent a written communication to Major General Schenck on the same day, October 22, 1863. Lincoln asked Schenck to come to the White House. President Lincoln wrote that he wanted to avoid violence. He advocated sending whites to recruit rather than Black soldiers. Major General Schenck replied that he would arrive the next day and that he had learned that Sothoron was enlisting recruits for the Confederate army. He claimed that an arrest was about to be made when he learned of the shooting of Lieutenant White.[275] This and Major General Schenck's reply of the previous day to President Lincoln proves that he was concealing illegal recruiting activity or criminal behavior he, others above him and his subordinates had been involved in. In his book published in 1887, Donn Piatt claimed it was his responsibility for giving the order to Birney to recruit slaves during the absence of Schenck. Piatt also said his order was an act of "insubordination".[276]

It is not known if Schenck actually met with Lincoln. On a previous occasion, Schenck had abruptly left the White House on 23 July 1863 prior to a delayed meeting with Lincoln.[277]

President Lincoln used the phrase "inaugurate homicides on punctilio" in his communication to Schenck. President Lincoln could be interpreted as thinking about the political impact of the shooting on his re-election to the office of President in 1864. Also, he may have had on his mind the possibility of him as the future target of a Confederate or Union military political assassination attempt at his second inauguration after election.

Major General Robert C. Schenck, the Union army political general, later resigned as commander of the Middle Department on 5 December 1863.[278] He then occupied his seat as a Congressman in the House of Representatives. He was from Ohio, a lawyer and former Whig. In the 1850s he became a Republican and a diplomat.[279] Schenck wrote a pamphlet after the Civil War about playing the card game of poker. Schenck's communications to Lincoln about the sending of Colonel Birney to Saint Mary's County sound like the pathological behavior of a gambler who fixed the outcome of his bet.

The events in Maryland of the previous week eclipsed the military execution of a civilian. Dr. David M. Wright was hung by the Union army is Norfolk, Virginia at ten o'clock in the morning on Friday, 23 October 1863.[280] The quiet revolution was almost complete and the reign of terror was beginning. On 19 October 1863, the *Philadelphia Press* reported another delay of the execution of Wright. The article, datelined 18 October from Fortress Monroe in Virginia, reported that Lincoln had ordered the delay of "one week".[281] It may, or may not be that Wright's execution occurred two days earlier than scheduled and was a violation of Lincoln's orders.

---

[274] *OR*, Series 1, Volume 2, 1894, September 20, 1861, John A Dix to Capitan Bragg, page 597, accessed 24 December 2006
[275] Basler, *Vol. VI*, page 532.
[276] Donn Piatt, *Memories of the Men Who Saved the Union*, page 48, accessed 28 December 2006.
[277] ALPLC, ALSC, Abraham Lincoln to Robert C. Schenck, Thursday, July 23, 1863 (Schenck departed White House before meeting with Lincoln) [Copy in Nicolay's Hand], July 23, 1863.
[278] Boatner, page 725.
[279] *Biographical Directory of the United States Congress, 1774-1989*, page 1774.
[280] *OR*, Series 1, Volume 29, Part II, 1890, October 23, 1863, J. G. Foster to H. W. Halleck, page 370, accessed 6 December 2006.
[281] *Philadelphia Press*, October 19, 1863, "Fortress Monroe, A Respite to Dr. Wright", page 2, accessed 1 January 2007, available on the Internet.

The military chain of command was in shambles.

On Friday, 23 October 1863, *The New York Times* published a small article titled "The Murder of Lieut. White" giving more information. The article cited the fact that Colonel Southern was a former Maryland state legislator, labeled him "a rebel sympathizer" and claimed that he was recruiting rebels. The political sympathies of Colonel Sothoron in 1863 are not known. There is no evidence to suggest that Colonel Sothoron was recruiting for the Confederacy.

The *National Intelligencer* printed a letter to the editor titled "THE ENLISTMENT OF SLAVES IN MARYLAND, THE TRAGEDY IN SAINT MARY'S" on Friday, 23 October 1863 about the shooting incident. There were also two newspaper articles with the letter to the editor. The letter to the editor was from six "citizens of high respectability" near the area of the shooting. The letter to the editor cited the newspaper publication of President Lincoln's order on October 6 "prohibiting the abduction" of slaves in Maryland. The issue of consent was raised. White had demanded Sothoron's slaves and they refused to go. White had died because he was determined to take the slaves that Sothoron was protecting. The determination of the Union army to return and seize the plantation of Colonel Sothoron was to happen that day and the unnamed commanding officer at Benedict was to resume recruiting by force. The six predicted a winter of suffering if their able bodied slaves were taken and only women and children remained.

The letter to the editor was accompanied by the first article titled "AN ACCOUNT OF THE HOMICIDE" which was reprinted from the *Baltimore American*. The secondhand source of the story was Captain Leary of the steamboat *Cecil*. Leary stated that he had transported White and 15 or 20 soldiers on Monday to Benedict, up the river from The Plains. Leary obtained his information about the shooting from the Black soldiers he transported to Benedict. They had gone to The Plains on Tuesday, and Leary claimed that after the shooting incident he went to The Plains and recovered the body of Lieutenant White.

The story by Leary may have been financially motivated. There is a National Archives file for the transport ship *Cecil*. The *Cecil* was a privately owned vessel which was captained by Darius H. Leary. The file shows a contract signed by Colonel James L. Donaldson of the United States Quartermaster Corps and Captain Leary on 1 August 1863 for the services of the *Cecil*. The file also shows a document with a date of 21 October 1863 stating that the services of an additional assistant engineer, to commence on 1 November 1863, would be required because the *Cecil* would be running day and night. Schenck was later given an additional paymaster.

The second article was titled "INTERVIEW WITH THE PRESIDENT". Congressman Calvert and a group of prominent Maryland citizens had met with President Lincoln on Wednesday. They received assurances from Lincoln that he "thought" that "negro troops" would be withdrawn and cabinet member Montgomery Blair believed the troops would be withdrawn. A suspension of recruiting for 90 days was implied. However, it was predicted that recruitment of slaves was an inevitable future. Secretary of War Stanton was not in Washington at that time.

The article used the word "deputation". A deputation implies a delegation with authority. The use of the term implies a contemplation of an arrest. The political affiliation of Charles B. Calvert is significant. He was elected as a Unionist to Congress in 1861. In the Maryland state elections of 4 November 1863, he ran as a Conditional Unionist.[282] The Union Party was the name of the Republican Party, or a faction of it, in Maryland during the Civil War.[283] Charles Calvert was a classmate of Colonel Sothoron at the University of Virginia in 1827. Calvert died on 12 May 1864.[284]

Reverdy Johnson, also mentioned in the article, was a member of the United States Senate at the time of the shooting incident. Johnson had been a member of the peace commission in 1861 that tried to prevent the

---

[282] Scharf, *History of Baltimore City and County*, page 145.
[283] Manakee, page 60.
[284] *Biographical Directory of the United States Congress 1774-1989*, page 731.

Civil War.[285] A letter from him, on the front page of *The New York Times* on 25 May 1863, expresses his pro-Union stance. Later during the Civil War, Johnson had an allegation made against him of bribery to release prisoners incarcerated by the Union authorities.

Reverdy Johnson was a Senator at the same time that President Lincoln had been a member of the House of Representatives. Senator Reverdy Johnson had introduced the legislation that was later passed in 1848 to pay the father of Colonel Sothoron, James F. Sothoron, for damages to The Plains from the War of 1812. During his term as a member of the House of Representatives from 4 March 1847 to 3 March 1849, Abraham Lincoln had been a Whig. This was before Lincoln joined the Republican Party during the 1850s.[286] Both Colonel Sothoron and Reverdy Johnson were also Whigs. In addition, Robert C. Schenck was a Whig Congressman at the time. On 10 July 1868 Reverdy Johnson resigned from the United States Senate and became the United States minister to England in 1868 and 1869. Schenck followed Reverdy Johnson as a United States diplomat to England from 1870 to 1876.[287]

The following letter is from the National Archives pension file of Lieutenant Eben White:

> Birney Barracks, Baltimore, Maryland
> October 22 - 1863
> Mr. White;
> My dear Sir
>
> The sad duty devolves upon me of informing you of the untimely death of your son Eben White, whom we mourn as a gallant, efficient and beloved brother officer for notwithstanding the short time we had been together he had won the esteem and respect of every body. He was murdered while in the discharge of his duty as a recruiting officer by two villainous traitors, a father and son; As nearly as I have been able to learn. He started with two of men of his company to this man's place where he had heard that the best slaves were tied up to prevent their enlisting. Upon reaching the house he saw the man who told him in reply to his inquiring that & that he (the man) would not release them. When the Lieutenant not having force enough to do it himself proceeded to the field where a number over at work & while talking with them this old man and his son came down with guns and after a few angry words the son raised his piece to fire at one of the men with Lieut. White, when he pushed it aside and the old man shot him. As the old man raised his gun the Lieutenant seized the piece belonging to one of his men thus disarming him & he immediately ran while the other fired at the old man most unfortunately missing him. When this soldier ran also receiving a charge of shot in the back of his head which did not wound him dangerously - as soon as his captain Capt Weld heard of this he immediately went for him but he had been killed instantly. Capt Weld also notified the cavalry at Pt Lookout & the gunboats as the villains instantly started for Virginia - Lieutenant White's remains were immediately sent up here where they arrived last night, & his face was a little bruised on one side the main charge passed through the body near the left shoulder.
>
> The remains left here at 9:30 am. for burial in the Loudon Park burial ground situated on the Frederick town road 3 or 4 miles from town. His effects are in my possession. I hope soon to learn the disposition you wish made of them as I may not remain here more than a few days.
>
> Did I not feel that the expressed sympathy of a stranger could not be cold and possibly unwelcome at such a time I would endeavor to express the deep sympathy I feel for the Lieutenants bereaved family.
>
> I am with heartfelt sorrow for your loss, very Respectfully,

---

[285] *Biographical Directory of the United States Congress 1774-1989*, page 1270.
[286] *Biographical Directory of the United States Congress 1774-1989*, page 1372-1373.
[287] *BDUSC*, accessed 2 December 2006.

> L.F. Haskell
> Lieutenant Colonel 7th U.S.C.T.
> P.S. The letter from Miss White which I opened for the purpose of ascertaining his residence which no one here knew. I enclose all the other letters that have reached here for him. L.F.H.

There is a discrepancy between this letter and *The New York Times* and the *National Intelligencer* articles of 22 October 1863 as to the final resting place of Lieutenant Eben White. Apparently, White's body was eventually taken from under the porch of the house and interred in the Sothoron family cemetery at The Plains. The statement in the letter about not remaining in Baltimore for "more than a few days" may indicate that plans were made to reinvade Saint Mary's County.

Eben White was from Newton, Massachusetts. His survivors were his father, mother and sister. A petition was received by the United States Senate from the citizens of Newton for the relief of his relatives and it was referred to the Committee on Military Affairs and the Militia and disappeared from consideration.[288] He enlisted as a private in Company K of the 5th Massachusetts Militia for three months in 1861.[289] This appears to be from his state military record. A second military record lists him as a 2nd Lieutenant in Company B of the 7th United States Colored Troops.[290] The fact that Eben White was in the 5th Massachusetts Militia for three months in 1861 raises the idea that he was in Maryland during that time and knew about and participated in the events of that year when the state was undergoing a military coup d'état.

The Captain Weld mentioned in the letter was Lewis Ledyard Weld of Company B, Seventh United States Colored Troops. Colonel L. F. Haskell was the writer of the letter. During the siege of Richmond and Petersburg, Haskell was in command of a different regiment of United States Colored Troops and he issued an order that any soldier who had a self inflicted wound would be punished and required to continue military duty.[291] It was Haskell's method to prevent a statistical decline in the number of men "fit for duty".

Later, during the early 1870s, Colonel Sothoron wrote a statement about the shooting incident because the issue of compensation for the confiscation of The Plains by the Union army came before Congress. The following statement is from the National Archives and is written in the third person:[292]

> Washington, D.C., 187
> Statement of facts in the claim of John H. Sothoron.
> In October 1863, Col S. was on his plantation in St Mary's Co Md. & being about entering a boat with his wife to visit a sick friend, his attention was attracted by the approach toward his house of a party of soldiers. Turning to meet them at the door, Lieutenant White, in charge of Colored Soldiers, demanded to know if there were "2 colored gentlemen in irons in the house". Col S. answered that 2 of his young servants were in a room guarded by two of their relatives, - old men, without any irons or other bonds on them. Their release was demanded & an authority being demanded by Col S. Left White replied that his sword was all the authority he would show. Col S. answered that when that was drawn he would know how to meet it, but offered to give the Lieutenant a horse & servant to take him to the nearest Magistrate & procure a search warrant. Col S. avowing himself a loyal man & willing to submit to legal authority. The offer was declined & an entrance insisted upon, the result being to frighten Mrs. Sothoron & the daughters & induce the Col to order the men off the place unless they would produce

---

[288] *CLNN*, Journal of the Senate, February 11, 1864, page 144, accessed 7 December 2006.
[289] National Park Service, Soldiers and Sailors System (cited hereafter as *NPSSSS*), *NARA*, Microfilm M544, roll 43, accessed November 5, 2006, available on the Internet.
[290] *NPSSSS*, *NARA*, Microfilm M589, roll 93, accessed November 5, 2006.
[291] Berlin, Reidy and Rowland, *A Documentary History of Emancipation, 1861-1867, Series II, The Black Military Experience*, pages 456-457.
[292] *NARA*, Record Group 233.

authority for their attempted action. The Left & his men turned away, but declared they would return as soon as boat loads of soldiers approaching arrived. Lieutenant White proceeded to the fields where the Colored hands were then engaged in cutting & saving tobacco & called & ordered around him 42 men. On seeing this Col S. called his son to get two guns used the day before in hunting & they followed Lieutenant White to the field & Col S calling to his overseer directed him to send the men to him. The overseer called to the men, "do you hear your Masters orders" & thereupon every one of them came around Col S. Left White turned to his men & gave some order, whereupon they all, including White, charged at a double quick & halted with leveled bayonets, on White's order within 6 feet of Col S. & his son. White demanded the number of men on Col S's place declaring "By God I will have them all" - Col S. answered "only over my dead body," White snatched a gun from one of his men & throwing himself into position said "It is now hardest - fend off" pulling the trigger of his gun. Col S, firing at the same moment without bringing his gun above his hips in the haste of his defensive action — the colored men with White firing on Col S. at the same instant & cutting his hat with bullets. White fell dead and Col S with difficulty prevented the servants from attacking the Colored Men. Col S. set a guard over the body of Mr. White & under pressure of his friends took a horse & concealed himself in a swamp for three days, sending a friend to Washington to demand protection during a trial. His wife and daughter were there also making the same demand. Owing to the excitement it was deemed impossible to secure a fair trial.

  Col S. crossed the river into Virginia there being rewards of $30,000 offered for his arrest. He remained in Richmond in civil pursuits only until the close of the war when he went to Canada & remained there until the fall of 1867. When learning that he could have a civil trial, he returned home & the next day reported himself to the Judge of his County & demanding that notice be sent to Secretary Stanton of his trial & time granted, that the government might procure all evidence desired - he was acquitted by a jury.

  Col S. had one of the Most Valuable plantations in Maryland. It was taken possession of instantly & his wife & children in a few weeks driven from it & all his property used by the government. Nothing was left him but the ground which was restored about May 1866 to his family.

  Delay to procure proof of the amounts taken has been unavoidable & the claim is now being more fully supported by evidence daily procured.

  <u>John H. Sothoron</u>

It is not known whom Mrs. Sothoron and her daughter attempted to see in Washington, D.C. The friend of Colonel Sothoron sent to Washington to "demand protection during a trial" remains unknown. The idea of the servants of Colonel Southern attacking the Union army soldiers is believable. Colonel Sothoron also declared his loyalty.

  On 26 October 1863, Order No. 329 extended recruiting to Delaware.[293] The next day, 27 October 1863, C. W. Foster sent Schenck a copy of "Circular No. 1", which was to be published in newspapers. The circular claimed to be "in accordance with orders from the President" and it established recruiting stations for colored troops in Maryland and the Eastern Shore of Virginia. Among the stations listed was Benedict, which already was already established eight days previous. The circular stated that a "Board' would have claims of "alleged owners of slaves" to be brought before it. The "Board" was composed of Hugh L. Bond, Thomas Timmons and L. E. Straughn.[294] Piatt stated that Lincoln "ordered a commission to assess damages" caused by the recruiting of slaves in Maryland. No claims for damages were paid.[295]

---

[293] Wesley and Ronfro, *Negro American in the Civil War, from Slavery to Citizenship*, page 68.
[294] *OR*, Series 3, Volume 3, 1899, October 27, 1863, C. W. Foster to R. C. Schenck, page 937 and 938, accessed 6 December 2006.
[295] Donn Piatt, *Memories of the Men Who Saved the Union*, page 46, accessed 28 December 2006.

Sometime in late October or early November of 1863, the Union army returned to The Plains and imprisoned Mrs. Sothoron, her adult daughter and seven children,

Brigadier General Lorenzo Thomas had been assigned by Secretary of War Stanton "to duty in the West raising black troops" prior to the shooting incident at The Plains. Colonel William Birney had telegraphed General Lorenzo Thomas on 13 October 1863 advising him that he had ceased recruiting black troops upon receipt of a telegram from President Lincoln.[296] Obviously, Colonel Birney resumed recruitment activities shortly after his claim of cessation on 13 October 1863 in violation of the written orders of President Lincoln.

The illegal recruitment of Black slaves from farms and plantations on the Patuxent River continued during the days following the shooting of Lieutenant White. This was despite the "thought" of President Lincoln that was made to the six Maryland citizens and published in the *National Intelligencer* on 23 October 1863 to withdraw soldiers and a cessation of recruitment for 90 days. A letter was sent from a group of persons, other than the deputation that had seen President Lincoln on 21 October 1863, to Senator Reverdy Johnson.[297] The letter was dated 28 October 1863 and protested that the Union army was taking slaves and looting farms. A written endorsement of the letter was made by Colonel Birney on 8 November 1863 and he denied that his soldiers were continuing to recruit. Despite his claim of a temporary halt in recruitment, Colonel Birney clearly stated his intent to continue recruiting in his endorsement. On 11 November 1863 Major General Schenck also endorsed the letter with a statement that supported Colonel Birney.

There was an effort to send Colonel Birney out of the area for a period of time. Found in the National Archives Union Military service record for Colonel Birney is the following order:

SPECIAL ORDERS, } WAR DEPARTMENT
} ADJUTANT GENERAL'S OFFICE
No. 485. } Washington, October 31st, 1863.
(Extract.)

3. Colonel <u>William Birney</u>, 2d U.S. Colored troops, will proceed immediately to Camp Delaware, Ohio, and make a thorough inspection of the 5th Regiment of U.S. Colored Troops, and will forward to the Adjutant General of the Army a written report of such inspection. Colonel <u>Birney</u> is also charged with the duty of superintending the movement of this regiment from Ohio to Fort Monroe, and on its arrival at the latter place, Colonel <u>Birney</u> will return to Baltimore and resume his duties as Recruiting and Mustering Officer.

By order of the Secretary of War:
E. D. Townsend,
Assistant Adjutant General.

However, for some reason, Colonel Birney never traveled to Ohio. Another order in the file, signed by C. W. Foster, directed that the order sending Colonel Birney to Ohio be countermanded and that he was to "remain on duty in Maryland."

In occupied areas of the Confederate States, the Union army abandoned the pretense used to deceive the citizens of the Union and the Border States. From Iuka, Mississippi, Union General William T. Sherman issued General Orders No. 4 through R. M. Sawyer, an Assistant Adjutant General, for his Army of the Tennessee on 28 October 1863. He declared the area an "insurrectionary district" and made every citizen within it "liable" for military service. The service was forced and divided into two categories. The category of "conscript" was entitled to pay. The other category he classified within the concept of *posse comitatus*, which was a person taken into service by a United States marshal. A *posse comitatus* person received no compensation except food

---

[296] Basler, *Vol. VI*, page 494.
[297] Berlin, Reidy and Rowland, pages 213-215.

and clothing.[298] Shelter from the elements was not mentioned. Sherman is quoted as having said "war is hell". He was a fiend and the depredations of the army he commanded scarred the south.

The economy of the Confederacy was dependent on slavery. The news of the recruitment of slaves in Maryland and other areas negatively affected their already weak agriculturally based economy. The front page of *The New York Times* of 31 October 1863 reported the collapse of Confederate finances.

With the November elections of 1863 forthcoming, General Schenck became more intrusive in the politics of Maryland. Schenck issued a military order requiring certain voters to take a loyalty oath. On the morning of the election, a proclamation of Governor Bradford appeared in Baltimore newspapers promising protection of judges and instructing them to obey election laws.[299] On 4 November 1863, elections for state offices were held in Maryland.[300] The election was controlled by the Union army. A variety of illegal methods were used to deny citizens their right to vote. The loyalty oath order of Schenck was turned into interrogation about the voters willingness to "give up all his property" to support the Union army. Judges of the election were arrested by the Union army.[301] Unionist candidates lost because the election outcome was controlled by the "states rights" faction of the Union army political military leadership. It may be that the same form of loyalty oath that was used in Missouri, with the pledge to turn over property to the government, was used in Maryland by the Union army.

The New York Times of Sunday, 8 November 1863 carried news obtained from Richmond, Virginia newspapers in an article titled "LIFE IN RICHMOND-FROM THE RICHMOND PAPERS OF LAST WEEK". Colonel Sothoron arrived in Richmond the day before with his son. Webster Sothoron was named as the shooter of White The number of Union troops mentioned in the article at the plantation was stated to be a "battalion" and was exaggerated. A battalion of soldiers during the Civil War probably numbered about 150 to 300 troops.[302] The article is an example of Confederate propaganda.

Regardless of viewpoint taken on the innocence or guilt of Colonel Sothoron, the fact Colonel Sothoron fled from Maryland and went into Confederate territory placed him in an area where he had to conform to the opinions of the Confederate leadership. That prevailing opinion could be jaded by the cultural arrogance as expressed in the article from Richmond newspapers and republished in *The New York Times*. The fact that Norris of the Confederate Signal Corps had Colonel Sothoron interviewed in his office by FitzGerald Ross indicates that he was used by the Confederates for the purpose of propaganda. It is extremely likely that Colonel Sothoron was debriefed by Norris for military and political information about the Union. Sothoron would have little choice but to cooperate.

There was a conflict of law in regards to the recruitment of slaves for the Union army in Maryland. The Emancipation Proclamation did not apply to Maryland because the state had never seceded from the Union. Slavery was finally outlawed in the state of Maryland by a new constitution adopted in 1864, which took effect on the first of November of that year. It was illegal for slaves to be taken from their owners for any reason prior to the adoption of the new constitution. The Emancipation Proclamation did nothing to alleviate the Union troop shortage crisis during 1863.

The *Richmond Enquirer* for Friday, 13 November 1863 in an article titled "SLAVES IN THE BORDER STATES" reported the shooting incident as a "righteous slaying". The article labeled Union action in the Border States as "Lincoln's Abolition despotism". The article called Lincoln a "tyrant". The article then goes on to quote from the letter published in the *National Intelligencer* on 23 October 1863 from the "Six Respectable

---

[298] *OR*, Series 1, Volume 31, Part I, 1890, October 28, 1863, General Orders No. 4, R. M. Sawyer by order of W. T. Sherman, page 767, accessed 6 December 2006.
[299] Scharf, *History of Baltimore City and County*, page 145.
[300] Toomey, page 95.
[301] *ALPLC, ALSC,* John W. Crisfield to Montgomery Blair, Sunday, November 08, 1863 (Federal interference in Maryland election),
[302] Boatner, page 612.

Planters". After the quote the article discusses the situation in other border states. Charles Calvert, one of the "Six Respectable Planters" was a Unionist and the article refers to him in insulting terms without naming him. The legalistic viewpoint of the Confederacy is apparent in the newspaper article.

President Lincoln traveled to Gettysburg, Pennsylvania and stopped in Baltimore on 18 November 1863.[303] On 20 November 1863, President Lincoln sent a written message to Major General Robert C. Schenck, regarding two Confederate prisoners, Maynadier and Gordon. He asked that they not be executed without an order from him. It is possible that Lincoln learned about them as a result of his visit in Baltimore. No reply has been found to Lincoln's message from Schenck. The two Confederate soldiers were Private John H. Maynadier, First Virginia Cavalry, sentenced to be shot on 25 November 1863 for the accusation of spying and Private William F. Gordon of the Twentieth Virginia Cavalry, who had been commissioned as a captain to recruit within Union lines.[304] The two soldiers may have been compelled to reveal the names of others in Maryland who were on spying and recruiting missions or sympathized with the south.

Another communication was sent by President Lincoln to Major General Schenck on 20 November 1863. In his communication, Lincoln ordered Schenck to have a military trial for Union army Captain Moore because he violated General Order Number 53. Moore had two allegations against him: he had arrested the Judges of the elections in Maryland and he had interfered with the voting rights of Arthur Crisfield, who was willing to take the oath of loyalty. Lincoln also asked that the Hon. John W. Crisfield be notified of the trial.[305] In 1866, John W. Crisfield was a delegate to the Union National Convention.[306]

President Lincoln had discovered illegal election interference by the Union army in Maryland and instructed Major General Schenck to take appropriate military legal action against Capitan Charles C. Moore. This is an example of President Lincoln trying to curtail the illegal actions of the Union army in Maryland. Major General Schenck resigned about two weeks later. John W. Crisfield had run as a Conditional Unionist in the Maryland state elections of 4 November 1863 and he probably lost the election because of Union army interference.

President Lincoln communicated to Secretary of War Edwin Stanton on 22 November 1863 because Mrs. Sothoron and her children were imprisoned and under house arrest. Mrs. Sothoron and her children were guarded by soldiers and were given "starvation" rations. Lincoln politely requested Stanton to give his "attention" to the situation. The extremely diplomatic language of Lincoln in his written message reveals his dilemma of trying to curtail the excesses of the Union army political leadership while also keeping the army loyal to the government objective of winning the Civil War. He may have also been afraid of an overt military putsch of the government. The fact that Colonel Birney had participated in the revolution of 1848 in Paris, France, and his actions in Maryland establishes him as a central figure in a Radical Republican political military plot to usurp the Lincoln administration.

Lincoln sent the message to Stanton because he had seen a woman named Miss Florence Holcomb of Washington, D.C. It appears she was a friend of the family of Colonel Sothoron. She had a letter of introduction from E. W. Hazard of Chicago. There was a subsequent report from Colonel William Birney which was endorsed by him on 4 December 1863 and sent to President Lincoln regarding this communication but it has not been found.[307] Colonel William Birney became the Attorney for the District of Columbia (Washington, D.C.) sometime after the Civil War.[308] It should be noted that President Lincoln did not directly order the release of the Sothoron family, even though he had the authority to do so. The Union army was keeping Mrs. Sothoron

---

[303] Scharf, *History of Baltimore City and County*, page 146.
[304] Basler, *Vol. VII*, page 27.
[305] Basler, *Vol. VII*, page 26.
[306] *BDUSC*, accessed 22 December 2006.
[307] Basler, *Vol. VII*, page 28.
[308] Boatner, page 65.

and her children hostage to coerce the return of Colonel Sothoron.

The consolidation of Union political military power in Maryland continued. On 23 November 1863, the military draft commenced in Baltimore.[309] Maryland former Governor Thomas G. Pratt and Colonel Nicholson were deported to the Confederacy on 30 November 1863 because they refused to take the oath of allegiance.[310]

On 8 December 1863, President Lincoln issued the "Proclamation of Amnesty and Reconstruction". In the proclamation a provision was made for Confederates to sign a loyalty oath to gain amnesty. Excepted were persons who left "judicial stations under the United States to aid the rebellion".[311] Colonel Sothoron fled Maryland to escape a certain military execution for the shooting of Lieutenant White and not to aid the Confederacy. The proclamation appears to be an attempt by Lincoln to counterbalance the negative effects and publicity caused by the actions of the Union army political military leadership. A form of loyalty oath was included in the Proclamation that did not have a pledge of property by Confederates making an oath to support the Union. This may have been Lincoln's last effective act to counter the Union army political leadership. Subsequent parole forms signed by surrendered Confederate soldiers do not show pledges about property.

With the new promise of amnesty made by him, President Lincoln continued to give orders to the Union army to halt executions. On 10 December 1863, President Lincoln gave an order to Union political general Benjamin F. Butler at Fort Monroe, Virginia to cease "all and any" executions within his command until "further order".[312]

The "missing" alleged report of 21 October 1863 (that Schenck said was sent to the Adjutant General) or parts of it, endorsed by Colonel William Birney on 4 December 1863 and made to President Lincoln may have been copied and included in information later made available to Congress in 1874 in regards to a claim made by Colonel Sothoron for losses and damages to The Plains. The following report of 1874, although dated 19 December 1863, may have been based on that report:[313]

> Headquarters Camp Stanton
> December 19, 1863
> Sir: I have the honor to enclose a report made to me November 23, 1863, by Capt. Lewis L. Weld, Company B, Seventh United States Colored Troops, which gives the circumstances of the murder of Lieut. Eben White, Company B, Seventh United States Colored Troops, by John H. Sothoron and Webster Sothoron.
>
> Dr. Thomas, a respectable physician of this county, states that on the morning of the occurrence John H. Sothoron was in Benedict, and, in the hearing of said Thomas, threatened to take the life of Lieutenant White if he should ever set foot on his (Sothoron's) farm.
>
> Numerous witnesses can be produced to substantiate the following charges:
>
> That John H. Sothoron was an avowed sympathizer with the rebels; That he had visited Richmond since the beginning of the rebellion; and That he had repeatedly entertained rebel officers at his house; especially Lieutenant Countee, and Captains Lemon and White, formerly residents of this neighborhood.
>
> Your obedient servant,
> William Birney
> Colonel Second United States Colored Troops, Recruiting and Mustering Officer.

---

[309] Scharf, *History of Baltimore City and County*, page 146.
[310] Scharf, *History of Baltimore City and County*, page 146.
[311] *OR*, Series 2, Volume 6, 1899, December 8, 1863, A Proclamation, Abraham Lincoln, pages 680 to 682, accessed 16 December 2006, also see *The New York Times*, December 10, 1863, page 4, column 2.
[312] *OR*, Series 2, Volume 6, 1899, December 10, 1863, A. Lincoln to Major General Butler, page 683, accessed 6 December 2006.
[313] *NARA*, Record Group 233, House Executive Document 281, 43rd Congress, 1st Session, June 12, 1874.

The Adjutant-General United States Army.
Adjutant-General's Office
June 6, 1874
Official:
Thomas M. Vincent,
Assistant Adjutant-General

Seventh Regiment United States Colored Troops,
Camp Stanton, November 23, 1863.

Colonel: In reply to a request from you to examine the two witnesses of the murder of Second Lieut. Eben White, of Company B, of this regiment, and to report their statements, together with the facts relating to the said murder after it occurred, as they fell under my own observation, I have the honor respectfully to report:

Of the two privates who accompanied Lieutenant White to the house of Colonel Sothoron, near Benedict, I first called and examined John W. Bantum, a private of Company B, Seventh United States Colored Troops. I took down his statement as he delivered it, excepting that, in matters of grammar and dialect, I have endeavored to render it into good English. The statement is as follows:

We were twenty men of Company B, who were put off from the steamer John Tracy under the charge of Lieutenant White, on the 19th day of October, 1863, Monday. (The witness has no memory of the exact date, but this date is correct.) On Monday afternoon, the day of the landing, we moved the rations and tools under shelter, and spent the rest of the day cleaning our guns and making ourselves comfortable for the night. We posted guards that night. The next day we called in the guards and staid about till afternoon. The lieutenant was part of the time down with us and apart of the time up in the town.

Question. Did he have any particular conversation with any one that morning? If so, with whom? - Answer. I do not know. He talked with a good many, but I do not know whom in particular. About 3 o'clock that afternoon (Tuesday, October 20) Lieutenant White, with Benjamin Black and myself, together with a young white man, whose name I do not know, went into a boat off the wharf and went across the mouth of the creek to Sothoron's plantation. As soon as we landed Lieutenant White told Black and myself to put caps on our guns. We then went up over the bank toward some colored men and women whom we saw working in the field. When we had come within about fifteen rods of them the lieutenant told us to halt, and he went on to them and talked with them. He then went off toward the house and called to us to come up to him. We joined him at once. I was on the right side of him and Black on the left. When we got to the house he sent Black to the back, and I went up to the porch door with him. Colonel Sothoron and a young man, said to be his son, were standing on the porch. Lieutenant White went up to them and said, "Is this Mr. Sothoron?" and he answered, "Yes, that's my name." The lieutenant said, "I heard that you have some of your servants tied up." Sothoron answered "Yes, sir; I have them tied." The lieutenant said, "I want them." Sothoron answered, "You can't get'em." The lieutenant, "You say I can't get get'em?" Sothoron, "No, sir; you can't get'em." The lieutenant, "Well, sir, you know the law." Sothoron, "Yes, sir; I know it." As soon as he said that the lieutenant turned and called me, and we went by the side of the house. He told Black to come on. We started right down to the fence to the barn. There we met a young colored man. The lieutenant asked him if he wanted to enlist He answered, "Yes, sir." The lieutenant told him to come on, then, and go with him. We went on further and found another colored man piling up tobacco. Lieutenant White asked him the same question, and he answered, "Yes, sir." The lieutenant told him to come on and go with him, when the boy looked behind and saw Colonel Sothoron and his son coming with guns in their hands; and I said, "Lieutenant, let's shoot'em," at the same time bringing my gun down from my shoulder. The lieutenant looked around in my face and said, "O, no; don't shoot them." We walked on a few steps and I looked back again, and again said, "Lieutenant, let's shoot'em; they are going to kill us." He said again, "No, don't shoot." Colonel Sothoron then called out to an old colored man and said, "Tell all them niggers to come to me; every one of them." Then he called out to another further back and said, "Tell that nigger woman to come to me," and called to the old man to catch hold of Lieutenant White. The lieutenant said, "My man, don't you touch me." Then Sothoron cursed the lieutenant, and called him a "damned nigger-stealing son of a bitch." At this the lieutenant turned and walked right back toward Sothoron, and I was by his side. He said, "Mr. Sothoron, I am attending to my business, as I was sent to do." Sothoron answered, "Business? Hell and damnation I know right from wrong as well as you do." Then Sothoron's son jumped out in front of the lieutenant and shook his revolver in his face, calling out, "Don't you talk to me about business, you damned son of a bitch." Then, after some more words, all of which I do not remember, he (the young man) stepped up to the lieutenant, and spit in his face. At the same time the old man said, "How dare you bring your men on my premises with their guns half-cocked?" and the young man said, "God damn you, I have a mind to blow you down." The lieutenant answered, "You might get yourself into trouble by it." At the same time, both father and son fired - one at his head, the other at his breast At the time they fired they were, I should think, about 12 feet apart. As soon as I saw Lieutenant White falling, I aimed my gun and fired at the old man. Then I knew there was no use in staying there, and turned to run. Black had already started. As I turned, the old man fired at me, striking me in the back of the head, and knocked off my cap. As I ran I looked back, and saw Lieutenant White lying on the ground and the young man beating him over the head with the butt of his gun. When I got to the creek, I found Black already in the boat, and the white man who came with us, pushing from the shore. They came back for me, and we all went over to Benedict. When we got to Benedict, I changed my bloody coat for my blouse, and came down to the wharf, where I saw the steamboat Cecil coming in. As soon as it came, two of us went on board, and told the captain that Lieutenant White was killed, and we did not know what to do unless we went with him. The captain asked about the circumstances, and, when I told him, we all went on board. When I went on the boat I lay down, for my head was full of shot, and was bleeding and sore. Others went and brought down the body.

This statement having been read over slowly to the witness, he reaffirmed the whole, not wishing to add to or subtract from it.

Benjamin Black, a private in Company B, who was not present when the foregoing statement was made, was then called. His statement was so entirely confirmatory of that made by his comrade that I have not thought it necessary to reproduce it here. Suffice to say that his account was identical with that of Bantum in every important particular.

On the evening of the same day the steamer Cecil arrived at Town Creek, near the mouth of the Patuxent River, where a camp had been established, of which I was then in command. The captain of the Cecil at once reported to me, stating the facts so far as he knew them, and asked for further instructions. I immediately ordered Second Lieutenant Ryder to proceed without delay, with a proper escort, on board the Cecil, and, with the body, to report to you at Baltimore. I also ordered First Lieutenant Edgerton to start at once on horseback, with a guide, to the headquarters of the district of Saint Mary's, at Point Lookout, and report the fact of the murder to the commanding officer at that post, and that the murderers were said to be endeavoring to escape into Virginia, through those lines. Unprovided as I was with any force which would have been efficient in such a pursuit, this was my only recourse.

This, so far as I am able to give it, is a full statement of this most unfortunate and terrible murder, which took from the Army and from our own immediate corps one than whom there was none more brave, generous, or devoted.

>I have the honor to be, colonel, with great respect, your obedient servant,
>Lewis Ledyard Weld,
>Captain Seventh United States Colored Troops.
>Col. Wm. Birney,
>Commanding Post at Benedict, Md.
>Adjutant-General's Office, June 6, 1874
>Official:
>Thomas M. Vincent
>Assistant Adjutant-General

The above statement by deceased witness John W. Bantum essentially disagrees with other accounts. Of interest is the "young white man" who was in the boat with Lieutenant White and the two Black soldiers and remains unidentified. He could have been a higher-ranking Union army officer such as Captain Weld, Colonel Haskell or Colonel Birney or a political operative. The Confederate officers mentioned as being "entertained" by Colonel Sothoron are named as soldiers in *The Maryland Line in the Confederate Army, 1861-1865*. Weld states the transport steamship was named the *John Tracy* while another source named it as the *Cecil*.

Obviously, the above statement establishes that Private Bantum was criminally facilitating Lieutenant White to shoot Colonel Sothoron. Unfortunately, according to his National Archives Union military record, Private Bantum, a witness, died in the camp hospital at Benedict on 1 March 1864 of "consumption". According to his National Archives Union military record, Captain Weld later became a military court judge. The National Archives Union military record of Private Black reveals that he survived the war and was discharged in 1866. Union army General McDowell had been given a show trial on the evidence of a dead witness and the Union army was using the same repressive method to illegally cause Colonel Sothoron to appear guilty.

The "charges" made by Colonel Birney against Colonel Sothoron were that he was a rebel "sympathizer", had "visited Richmond" and that he was "entertaining" rebel officers. To have sympathy for his sons who fought for the Confederacy is not a crime. He visited Richmond to visit his son who was sick in the hospital. To have friends visit for dinner is not a crime.

Col. Birney applied for permission to visit Washington. This letter was found in his National Archives Union army military record:

>Headquarters Camp Stanton
>near Bryantown, Md.
>December 20, 1863
>To the Adjutant General U.S.A.
>Sir,
>I have the honor to apply for permission to visit Washington City, taking with me one officer of this command, for a period not exceeding three days.
>
>There is a variety of business growing out of my duties as Mustering Officer and connected with this command, which I must attend to. A missing muster-roll is to be searched for in the Department; I need instruction on several points from the Ordinance office and to settle up an old account with it; I wish to have blanks for reports of drills and other blanks printed; and to get various public documents. My personal attention is necessary.
>
>The distance is but thirty six or seven miles.
>Your obedient servant,
>Capt. L.L. Weld   William Birney
>7th U.S.C.T.   Colonel 2nd U.S.C.T.,

Mustering Officer

Two days later, Colonel Birney remained at Camp Stanton. He wrote a letter of resignation from the 2nd U.S.C.T. because he had accepted the appointment of Brigadier General of Volunteers for Colored Troops. On 24 December 1863, his resignation was accepted by E. D. Townsend "to enable him to accept promotion". Colonel Birney's statement that he wanted to "settle up an old account" with the Ordinance office supports the fact that the gun of the Black soldier taken by Lieutenant White misfired and that Birney was angry because of being supplied with defective equipment. The missing muster roll, a list of soldiers, remains a mystery.

The status of the military resignation of Major General Schenck is not clear as reflected by a message from President Lincoln to Secretary of War Stanton on 23 December 1863. In that message, Lincoln directed Secretary Stanton to see General Schenck and appoint for Schenck an "Additional Pay Master".[314]

The *Civil War Dictionary* gives his date of resignation as commander of the Union Middle Department as 5 December 1863 while the *Biographical Directory of the United States Congress, 1774-1989* gives the date as 3 December 1863. It would be interesting to discover the name of the Additional Pay Master, the reason for his appointment, and the need for additional payment. However, the allegation that some of the papers of President Lincoln were destroyed by his son, Robert Todd Lincoln, may prevent this knowledge from being discovered.[315]

From 21 December 1863 to 21 June 1864, Saint Mary's County was under the jurisdiction of the Union Department of Virginia and North Carolina.[316] Saint Mary's County was removed from the control of Schenck of the Middle Department and placed under command of Benjamin F. Butler, known for his atrocities in New Orleans and his vile behavior against women.

The most odious day of United States history was on 26 December 1863. The Civil War had produced the need for a new class of ships. The new ships were called "ironclads". They were ships made of iron and powered by steam engines. The iron armor protected the crew from injury by their opponents. John Ericsson was the designer of Union ironclad ships. The ominous name of an ironclad he designed was launched on 26 December 1863. It was named the *U.S.S. Dictator*.[317]

Months later, on 26 June 1864 Congress passed a joint resolution concerning the ironclad ships. The *U.S.S. Dictator* had been contracted for by the Navy Department on 28 July 1862 along with a second ironclad named *Puritan*. Congress made payment for the *Dictator* contingent on completion of the *Puritan*.[318] The *Dictator* was commissioned as a Navy ship on 11 November 1864.[319]

The origin of the concept of dictator is found in the Civil War that existed in England during the 1640s. Oliver Cromwell, without a military background, led an army that fought in the English Civil War. After the monarch Charles I was beheaded in 1649, it is generally recognized that Cromwell became the Puritan dictator of the English empire. The names of the United States ships *Puritan* and *Dictator* suggest New England theocratic and fascist military dominance of Union politics. After the restoration of the monarchy in 1661, a number of Cromwell's major generals were executed.

On the same day as the launching of the *Dictator*, 26 December 1863, President Lincoln sent Secretary of War Stanton a message inviting him to take a voyage down the Potomac River the next day. He pressed

---

[314] Basler, *Vol. VII*, page 88.
[315] Stern, page 406.
[316] Phisterer, Frederick, *Statistical Record of the armies of the United States*, page 28, accessed 28 December 2006.
[317] *ORN*, Series II, Volume 1, 1921, Statistical Data of U.S. Ships, U.S.S. Dictator, page 74, accessed 6 December 2006.
[318] *CLNN*, Statutes at Large, 38th Congress, 1st Session, Joint resolution authorizing the Secretary of the Navy to amend the Contract with John Ericsson for the Construction of two impregnable Floating Batteries, the "Dictator" and the "Puritan", page 409 and 410, accessed 7 December 2006.
[319] *ALPLC, ALSC*, John Ericsson to Abraham Lincoln, Friday, December 09, 1864 (U. S. S. Dictator) [With Endorsement by Lincoln],

Stanton for details of when and where to leave from.[320] The language and tone of his message was humble and condescending. It implies that President Lincoln was afraid of Secretary of War Stanton. Given the actions of Colonel Birney, Major General Schenck and Secretary of War Stanton, President Lincoln may have been afraid of a Union army military coup d'état. Colonel Birney, with his background of participation in the revolution of 1848, in Paris, France, was the central figure in plotting the illegal recruitment of slaves in Maryland.

A day later, President Lincoln and Secretary of War Stanton visited the prison camp for Confederate soldiers and civilian rebel sympathizers at Point Lookout in Saint Mary's County, Maryland. They departed from Washington on Sunday, 27 December 1863.[321]

The return of President Lincoln and Secretary of War Stanton from Point Lookout on the evening of 28 December 1863 was reported in the New York *Tribune* on 29 December 1863. The *Tribune* also reported that the President and Secretary of War had determined that about one thousand of the Confederate prisoners there were ready to "enter the service of the United States".[322] A search of *The New York Times* for an article about the journey failed to reveal any mention of it. Union army regiments composed of former Confederates were created and protected the western frontier of the United States from Indians. A number of Indian tribes sided with the Confederacy.

It is obvious that Colonel Sothoron and his son would have faced a military tribunal or commission composed of Union army political officers if they stayed in Maryland. His flight to the Confederacy was to save his life. If Colonel Sothoron brought his entire family with him, he would have risked their lives besides his own. The fate of his wife, adult daughter and seven children were in the unclean hands of Colonel William Birney and the Union army. Because of the change in administration of military zones Birney may have been the puppet of "Beast" Butler.

One year to the day exactly after the death of Lieutenant Eben White, President Lincoln issued a proclamation. On 20 October 1864, Lincoln proclaimed that the last Thursday of November be a day of "thanksgiving and praise to Almighty God". He recommended that "my fellow-citizens . . . humble themselves in the dust" and pray to the "Great Disposer of events".[323] It may, or may not, be that our national holiday of Thanksgiving was created by a mourning Lincoln appealing to his religious supporters and emotionally flagellating himself before the nation. His message was a pontificating edict of obfuscation.

*   *   *

The Radical Republican quiet revolution was complete but their political leadership was unwilling to reward the soldiers who had been their vanguard. Colonel William Birney was promoted to the rank of Brigadier General. On 11 January 1864, he presented a "memorial" to Congress through Representative Abel Carter Wilder of Kansas to increase the pay of Union army Black soldiers to thirteen dollars per month to equalize it with white soldiers. His proposal was referred to the Committee on Military Affairs and disappeared from consideration.[324]

In New Jersey, the legislature was taking action. In either a pre-emptive action or an action to redress a previous event, the legislature passed "An Act to provide for compensating parties whose property may be injured or destroyed as a consequence of mobs or riots." A requirement of the act was that a corporation or person had to use "all reasonable diligence" to prevent damage and notify the mayor or sheriff of any threat by

---

[320] Basler, *Vol. VI*, page 95.
[321] King and Long, *The Civil War Day By Day, An Almanac, 1861-1865*, page 449.
[322] Basler, *Vol. VII*, page 95.
[323] *CLNN*, Statutes at Large, 38th Congress, Appendix, page 749, accessed 7 December 2006.
[324] *CLNN*, Journal of the House, January 11, 1864, page 121, accessed 7 December 2006.

any mob or riot. The act was approved on 11 March 1864.[325] The issue of mobs and riots in New Jersey during the Civil War deserves future research.

On 28 June 1864, in what appears to have been an afterthought, the United States Congress ended the "rendition" of escaped fugitive slaves. Sections of the legislation, commonly known as the Fugitive Slave Act of 1793, were repealed and the 1850 fugitive act was entirely repealed.[326]

* * *

A subplot of the drama of the shooting of Lieutenant White was the conflict between the regular officers of the United States army and politicians who had become the generals of Lincoln. On 4 August 1863, Special Orders No. 346 was issued by the Adjutant General's office of the Union army War Department. The orders, written by E. D. Townsend, were to convene a court of inquiry. The court was convened "By direction of the President of the United States". The purpose of the court was to investigate the evacuation of Winchester and Martinsburg by the Union army. The Union army court specifically was to investigate if Major General Robert H. Milroy and Brigadier General Dan Tyler had disobeyed the orders of the General in Chief, who was Henry W. Halleck.

Milroy had been arrested on the orders of President Lincoln. Milroy was in command of the Union forces at the Battle of Winchester from 13 to 15 June 1863, an embarrassing and humiliating Union defeat. Tyler, in command at Martinsburg, had sent a message on 14 June 1863 at 3 PM to both Schenck and Lincoln. Part of his message stated: "I imagine our rebel friends are waiting for grub and artillery." By his use of the words "rebel friends", Tyler expressed a prohibited heretical expression of sympathy for the Confederacy. Grub is a word for food. Lincoln had communicated directly to Schenck on 14 June 1863 and told him to have Milroy move his forces to Harper's Ferry. Politician Lincoln was giving military command orders to politician Schenck.

The court convened on 7 August 1863. It was composed of Major General E. A. Hitchcock, Brigadier General W. F. Barry, Brigadier General J. J. Abercrombie and Captain Capitan Robert N. Scott, judge advocate. On 10 August 1863, Hitchcock was "relieved from duty" as a member of the court and replaced by Brigadier General G. A. De Russy.

Testimony in the case revealed the interplay of orders and communications between Halleck, Schenck, Piatt and Lincoln. Schenck was summoned to the court on 3 September 1863 but instead sent Piatt, his chief of staff. Schenck appeared on 4 September 1863 and submitted a request to the court. In his request he stated that the testimony in the case was to be personally considered by Lincoln. He asked for the "right" to summon as witnesses Major Generals Henry W. Halleck, General in Chief, and Joseph Hooker. Part of his "right" was for him to cross examine them. The court denied his request. Schenck was acting as if he was a defendant rather than a witness.

The communications presented to the court as evidence revealed that Halleck repeatedly told Schenck that Winchester was an outpost for the Union army and the soldiers there should be withdrawn to Harper's Ferry. In a communication of 30 April 1863, Halleck said the town of Winchester "is no place to fight a battle." Schenck and Piatt chronically and repeatedly failed to heed Halleck's messages. The Union army lost the Battle of Winchester. There were significant Union losses of men and equipment.

On 7 September 1863 Schenck sent the court a communication accusing an unnamed person at the headquarters of the Union army of giving information to *The New York Times*. A newspaper article had been published which criticized Schenck and Milroy in connection with their actions that led to the Union defeat at

---

[325] *Acts of the Eighty-eighth Legislature of the State of New Jersey, and Twentieth Under the New Constitution*, Session of 1864, Chapter CL, page 237 to 239.
[326] *CLNN*, Statutes at Large, June 28, 1864, 38th Congress, 1st Session, page 200, accessed 6 December 2006.

Winchester. On 7 September 1863, Robert N. Scott, judge advocate of the court, returned the communication to Schenck, saying it had nothing to do with the matter before the court. The court of inquiry was turning into a public show trial and a kangaroo court. Schenck's boneheaded actions were being deservingly known to the readers of newspapers.

The court proceeding exposed the serious defects about Union army command structure and the politicization of the command process. Politicians Lincoln, Schenck and Piatt, all with no formal military training, were making unintelligent military decisions. Tyler had directly communicated to politicians Schenck and Lincoln and had bypassed military Commander in Chief Halleck. The duplicity of the military trial had been guided by Lincoln. Lincoln's reliance on Schenck and Piatt, who had campaigned for him in 1860 in Illinois, blinded him to the fact that he needed to listen to Union army commanders with formal military training. Because of his own duplicity, Lincoln was as blind to the coming of the Civil War in 1860 and 1861 as he was blind in 1863 to the machinations of his close political associates who were appointed as military officers in the now politicized Union army.

Having initiated and manipulated the military court of inquiry, Lincoln fixed the outcome. On 27 October 1863, President Lincoln wrote an endorsement to the findings of the court of inquiry. He absolved everyone involved of blame including Schenck. Lincoln was unable to truthfully admit to the deficiency of Union army command problems caused by the fact that his own sponsorship of close political associates to positions of power within the Union army had caused defeat, failure and needless death.[327] "Honest Abe" covered up his own failings.

Behind the drama in Maryland and the doors of the White House, years later in 1887, Piatt revealed his communications with President Lincoln during September of 1863 about the trial of Milroy. Piatt, Schenck's minion, met with Lincoln because Schenck was "to be put under arrest for disobedience." During the conversation with Piatt, Lincoln said "Halleck's act is mine". Lincoln was admitting that he was the decider and originator of the action against Milroy. Lincoln gave Piatt a written order that suspended the court action against Milroy, probably to retain the political support of Schenck and avoid public embarrassment the show trial was beginning to produce. Piatt delivered the message the next day and the court of inquiry immediately closed.[328] The shooting incident at The Plains may have been related to Piatt exploiting a political crisis caused by a Schenck facing the possibility that Milroy's court martial would show him to be destructively unintelligent in Union military matters. In October of 1863, Schenck and Piatt were trying to preserve their diminished power while Birney was looking for opportunities to pursue his revolutionary goal. On 14 September 1865, a newspaper article quoted Piatt as saying the Lincoln assassination was "a God send".[329]

The quiet revolution had achieved its preliminary goals and was to unleash and extend its new found power by looting and ravaging the Confederacy.

---

[327] *OR*, Series 1, Volume 27, Part II, 1889, No 400 Record of a Court of Inquiry convened to investigate the evacuation of Winchester and Martinsburg, pages 88 to 204, accessed 30 December 2006.
[328] Donn Piatt, *Memories of the Men Who Saved the Union*, page 39 to 42, accessed 28 December 2006, available on the Internet.
[329] *The Erie Observer*, September 14, 1865, "Political Items", page 1, accessed 1 January 2007, available on the Internet.

Chapter 5

HOSTAGES AT THE PLAINS

The issue of the treatment of prisoners of war and non-combatants during the Civil War was and remains the subject of moral examination and argument. However, no person may argue that an infant should be held hostage. Mrs. Sothoron and her children were held hostage in their home at The Plains. The youngest of her children was an infant under one year of age. Catherine (Kate) Lansdale Sothoron was born on 25 January 1862.

The Civil War created problems that caused difficulty for the ability of ordinary citizens in Union controlled territory to distinguish between authentic government agents and imposters. On 2 December 1862, the United States Congress passed Joint Resolution S. R. 103. The Joint Resolution, introduced by Senator Lazarus Whitehead Powell of Kentucky, identified the problem of imposters "pretending" to have the authority of the United States. Imposters of government agents falsely arrested citizens and placed them in "military prisons and camps" without due process. The resolution called the false arrests "a usurpation of power never given by the people to the President". Congress "demanded" that the arrests cease and that the prisoners be immediately freed or tried.[330]

Hostages are taken for a variety of reasons. Among those reasons is the kidnapping or abduction of a hostage to be held as ransom for money, property or the exchange of a person held by the other side. Sometimes persons are kept hostage by the government to intimidate the public into quiet submission.

On 3 November 1863, J. Holt, the Judge Advocate General of the Union army reported to Secretary of War Stanton the number of records he had of trials held by the Union army, from 1 September 1862 to 1 November 1863, during the previous fourteen months. It was 17,357. To accommodate the workload, Holt wanted a separate bureau. Defendants facing trials before the Union army were both soldiers and civilians.[331]

During the Civil War, at least 13,000 civilian prisoners were held by Union authorities.[332] Prisoner lists from that time use the category of "political prisoner". The legislation the United States Congress passed on 3 March 1863, titled "An Act relating to Habeas Corpus and Regulating Judicial Proceedings in Certain Cases" used the phrase "state or political prisoner" to describe civilians imprisoned by the Union army and government. The legislation required the Secretary of State and the Secretary of War to provide to the courts lists of state and political prisoners.[333]

The "state or political prisoners" category included hostages. Throughout the records of the Civil War, there are found numerous references to prisoners being kept for "safe-keeping" to ensure their future exchange

---

[330] *CLNN*, Joint Resolutions, December 2, 1862. S. R. 103, The resolution may have been secret because it does not appear in Statutes at Large, accessed 16 December 2006.
[331] *OR*, Series 3, Volume 3, 1899, November 3, 1863, J. Holt to Hon. E. M. Stanton, page 988, accessed 6 December 2006.
[332] Lee, *Mr. Lincoln's City*, page 85.
[333] *CLNN*, Statutes at Large, 37th Congress, 3rd Session, pages 755 to 758, accessed 16 December 2006.

for a prisoner kept by the other side. "Safe-keeping" also appears to have used to describe incarceration for other reasons. Both sides, Union and Confederate, engaged in the practice of hostage taking. However, there is no known precedent during the Civil War about the taking of a mother and her children prisoner or hostage except the case of Rose O'Neill Greenhow and her daughter.

Mrs. Sothoron, with her adult daughter and her seven other children, the youngest an infant, remained imprisoned at the main house of The Plains under the guard of the Black troops of General Birney. They were insulted and humiliated by the soldiers and appealed to the Union officers without result. All removable property was taken from the plantation. At the end of January 1864 all the slaves, about 100, were removed from the plantation by a government ship. It is not known where they were moved to.

General William Birney told Mrs. Sothoron to leave the house because it was to be used as a smallpox hospital for soldiers. Birney told Mrs. Sothoron that if she did not leave the sick would be moved in anyway. The true pestilence was the Union army. Mrs. Sothoron, her adult daughter and her seven children left their home on 4 February 1864. Birney was a pathological blackmailer and a hostage taker.

On 7 March 1863, Mrs. Sothoron wrote to President Lincoln and described the circumstances of the incarceration. She asked to be allowed to return to her home and she set the value of movable property stolen by the Union army at $30,000.[334] There is no known direct reply by Lincoln. The letter of Mrs. Sothoron was delivered to Montgomery Blair by Representative Edwin Hanson Webster of Congress and apparently forwarded to Lincoln. Congressman Webster was a member of the Unionist and later Unconditional Unionist political party.[335] Webster stated that he knew John H. Sothoron from serving in the Maryland Senate with him and he expressed the hope that the "helpless family certainly should not be oppressed" by the government.[336]

On 18 March 1864, a written communication was sent from President Lincoln to Secretary of War Stanton. Lincoln stated that the Sothoron family did not reside in their home at The Plains. Lincoln wrote that the homeless Sothoron family was "without a shelter or crumb" and "burthening our friends". Lincoln admitted that Lieutenant White was killed because he did not follow instructions agreed upon by Lincoln, Stanton and Governor Bradford of Maryland. Lincoln advocated that the Sothoron family be returned home to quiet opposition against the government, unless the house was needed for "public service" or the ownership of the house was transferred. The letter was a declaration of guilt and plea by President Lincoln in regards to the Sothoron family for Stanton to help his political reputation.[337] President Lincoln's comment about Colonel Sothoron's family "burthening our friends" suggests that Mrs. Sothoron and most of her children remained in Union controlled territory.

On the same day of the written communication from Lincoln to Stanton, 18 March 1864, the last of the four regiments of Black soldiers raised in the area, the 30th United States Colored Troops, departed from the area. They had been organized at Camp Stanton at Benedict from 12 February to 18 March 1864.[338]

While President Lincoln's comment to Stanton that Lieutenant White was killed because he did not follow instructions ("the temper and manner agreed by yourself"), this does not confirm his giving direct orders that led to the arrival of Union troops at The Plains on 20 October 1863. It does implicate him as having planned the illegal recruitment of Maryland slaves into the Union army. Because President Lincoln was also the Commander in Chief of the Union army, the ultimate responsibility for decisions and actions was his onus.

A few months later, on 5 May 1864, Mrs. Sothoron was given notice that The Plains was seized by the Union army. The following letter is from the National Archives Records of the U.S. House of

---

[334] *ALPLC, ALSC*, E. M. Sothoron to Abraham Lincoln, Monday, March 07, 1864, accessed 16 December 2006.
[335] *BDUSC*, accessed 16 December 2006.
[336] *ALPLC, ALSC*, From Edwin H. Webster to Montgomery Blair, Monday, March 7, 1864, (Cover Letter, Endorsed by Lincoln), accessed 16 December 2006.
[337] *ALPLC, ALSC*, Abraham Lincoln to Edwin M. Stanton, Friday, March 18, 1864, (Prisoners of War) (Draft), accessed 16 December 2006; see also Basler, *Vol. VII*, page 255.
[338] Dyer, page 1728.

Representatives:[339]

> Head Quarters District Saint Mary's
> Point Lookout Maryland
> May 5th 1864
> Mrs. E.M. Sothoron is hereby notified that the estate belonging to her Husband John H Sothoron in Saint Mary's Co Md. is seized in the name of the United States under the Confiscation Act.
> H.W. Weymouth
> Major and Provost Marshall
> Saint Mary's District Maryland

It is not known from where Major Weymouth obtained his instructions to issue the order for the seizure of The Plains.

Major Weymouth cited the "Confiscation Act" as his legal authority for seizure. There were two acts passed by Congress regarding confiscation.

* * *

The first confiscation act was passed on 6 August 1861. It was titled "An Act to confiscate property used for Insurrectionary Purposes". The legislation of the United States Congress set the requirement that the President make a proclamation "that the laws of the United States are opposed, and the execution thereof obstructed, by combinations too powerful to be suppressed by the ordinary course of judicial proceedings, or by the power vested in the marshals by law".

The key part of the first confiscation act of 6 August 1861 centered on property. Property used to aid an insurrection could be confiscated. The legislation made it the "duty" of the President to cause property "to be seized, confiscated and condemned." The legislation required that the expropriated property, called "prizes and capture" be the subject of a condemnation proceeding in a district or circuit court of the United States. Section 3 of the legislation allowed that "any person may file an information" with the Attorney General or a district attorney. The "informer" would receive half of the property confiscated.[340]

The second confiscation act was passed on 17 July 1862. It was titled "An Act to suppress Treason and Rebellion, to seize and Confiscate the Property of Rebels, and for other Purposes." The legislation said it was "the duty" of the President to "cause the seizure of all the estate and property . . . for the support of the army".

Section 6 of the second confiscation act set a time limit of 60 days after a "public warning and proclamation" made by President Lincoln persons to return their allegiance to the United States and to cease aid, countenance and abetting of the rebellion. Excluded from the group were Confederate government officials, seceded state government officials, army and navy officers and property owners is loyal states who "assist and give aid and comfort" to the rebellion.

For persons living in loyal states of the Union, such as Maryland, their property could be subject to confiscation. As in the first confiscation act, condemnation proceedings had to be initiated in a court of law regarding confiscated property in Section 7. Section 13 gave Lincoln the power to grant pardon and amnesty.[341]

There is no found condemnation proceeding for the property of Colonel Sothoron. Lincoln, in his message to Congress about the second confiscation act objected to it "becoming a law."[342]

---

[339] *NARA*, Record Group 233, U.S. House of Representatives.
[340] *CLNN*, Statutes at Large, 37th Congress, 1st Session, page 319, accessed 16 December 2006.
[341] *CLNN*, Statutes at Large, 37th Congress, 2nd Session, page 589 to 592, accessed 16 December 2006.
[342] *CLNN*, Journal of the Senate, July 17, 1862, pages 871 to 874, accessed 16 December 2006.

Within congressional[343] and military records[344] there is a copy of a proclamation by President Lincoln made on 25 July 1862, but his language differs somewhat from the language of the second confiscation act. Lincoln called for the return of the allegiance of persons to the United States or they would suffer "pain of the forfeitures and seizures".[345] Lincoln added the word of forfeiture, which is to give something up. He omitted mention of the sixty day requirement.

Both the congressional and military copy of Lincoln's proclamation of 25 July 1862 used the same language within them about the "joint resolution explanatory thereof". The Joint Resolution regarded the construction of the second confiscation act. The act was not to be "construed to work a forfeiture of the real estate of the offender beyond his natural life."[346] This was the "joint resolution thereof" which Lincoln referred to and it addressed his objection, of many others, that the legislation could violate Article III, Section 3 of the Constitution regarding "corruption of blood", which is a prohibition against forfeiture beyond the life of the accused.[347]

There was an additional resolution made or the same day. Joint Resolution S. R. 102 was made on 17 July 1862, the day of the passage of the second confiscation act. The preamble of the joint resolution is "For the relief of the present owners and holders of drafts or bills of exchange drawn by Russell, Majors and Waddell, and accepted by John B. Floyd, late Secretary of War." John B. Floyd was the Secretary of War under the predecessor of Lincoln, President James Buchanan. Floyd resigned his position in late December of 1860. John B. Floyd became a Confederate general and died in 1863. The issue of Russell, Majors and Waddell may, or may not, have been a potential source of embarrassment to the Lincoln administration.

In the *Journal of the Senate* of 17 July 1862 are found three messages from President Lincoln. The third message was addressed to "Fellow-citizens of the Senate and House of Representatives". In the third message Lincoln said that he had "inadvertently" failed to inform Congress about a merchant ship. The ship President Lincoln did not tell Congress about was the *Vanderbilt*, owned by Cornelius Vanderbilt of New York. Lincoln stated that the Vanderbilt had been in government service since March of 1861, which was the month of his first inauguration.[348] Vanderbilt was extremely wealthy from his business ventures, including transportation services, which were much needed by the Union army.

After the three messages of Lincoln, reports of the Judiciary Committee from Mr. Foster were read. Among the documents read was a report from the Secretary of War in regards to the Russell, Majors and Waddell case.[349] The case of Russell, Majors and Waddell was also known as the "Floyd acceptances". Years later, on 9 March 1874, Benjamin F. Butler of the House of Representatives introduced legislation for the indemnification of Pierce & Bacon of Boston, Massachusetts in regards to the drafts made by Majors, Russell and Waddell.[350]

* * *

On 9 April 1864, there was a political purge in the United States House of Representatives. Alexander Long, a congressman from Ohio, advocated that the United States recognize the Confederate States as independent. A motion was made to expel Long from the house. During the debate congressman Benjamin Gwinn Harris of Maryland said that "the south" had asked to "be left in peace". Harris said the Union answer to

---

[343] *CLNN*, Statutes at Large, 37th Congress, Appendix, No. 15, page 1266, accessed 16 December 2006.
[344] *OR*, Series 3, Volume 2, 1899, July 25, 1862, A Proclamation, Abraham Lincoln, page 274, accessed 6 December 2006.
[345] *OR*, Series 3, Volume 2, 1899, July 25, 1862, A Proclamation, Abraham Lincoln, page 274, accessed 6 December 2006.
[346] *CLNN*, Statutes at Large, 37th Congress, 2nd Session, Res. 63, page 627, accessed 16 December 2006.
[347] *CLNN*, July 17, 1862, Journal of the Senate, pages 873 and 874, accessed 16 December 2006.
[348] *CLNN*, July 17, 1862, Journal of the Senate, page 874, accessed 14 December 2006.
[349] *CLNN*, July 17, 1862, Journal of the Senate, pages 874 and 875, accessed 14 December 2006.
[350] *CLNN*, March 9, 1874, Journal of the House, page 576, accessed 14 December 2006.

peace request of the south was that the Union would "subjugate" them. Long was expelled and Harris was censured. The originator of the motion to censure Harris was Robert C. Schenck.[351]

In the month of March or April of 1864, after the communication of 18 March between President Lincoln and Secretary Stanton regarding the Sothoron family, the command structure of the Middle Department was again changed. General Lockwood was replaced by General Lew Wallace on 22 March 1864.[352] Again, there are discrepancies as to the date of the command change. Scharf gives the date of appointment as 12 March 1864 with the assumption of command on 22 March.[353] In addition to the two dates given above, a third date of 19 April 1864 is given by Boatner for General Lew Wallace assuming command of the Union army Middle Department.[354] General Lew Wallace later wrote *Ben Hur A Tale of the Christ*.

A pattern appears to emerge surrounding events in Maryland. On at least two occasions, about one month after a communication from President Lincoln in regards to the Sothoron family, a command change occurs in the Union army Middle Department. In addition, the date of the command change varies according to different sources of information.

There is also a question of the jurisdiction of the Union army Middle Department. Saint Mary's County does not appear to have been a part of the Middle Department.[355] It does not appear to have been included in the Washington, D.C. Department of the Union army until later.[356] Saint Mary's County could have been considered an administrative plum or nightmare due the wealthy property or extent of opposition to Union army political interference in the county. The fact that both General Marston and Schenck gave orders on 21 October 1863 which conflicted with each other tends to suggest this idea.

Because Mrs. Sothoron stated that her seven children were with her during her imprisonment at The Plains, it is possible that Robert Bowie Sothoron, age 17, was also imprisoned. Robert Bowie Sothoron was later able to flee south to Virginia.

Mrs. Sothoron and her children became homeless refugees from the Union army quiet revolution.

---

[351] *CLNN*, April 9, 1864, Journal of the House, pages 505 to 510, accessed 14 December 2006.
[352] Boatner, page 549.
[353] Scharf, *History of Baltimore City and County*, page 146.
[354] Boatner, page 887.
[355] Boatner, page 549.
[356] Boatner, pages 549 and 893.

Chapter 6

FATHER AND SONS IN THE CONFEDERACY

Colonel Sothoron apparently remained in Richmond Virginia, after he escaped from a certain death by the unclean hands of the politicized Union army in Maryland. A search of many books regarding Confederate military activities and wartime politics have failed to reveal any mention of a formal association between him and the Confederate government. Jefferson Davis, in *The Rise and Fall of the Confederate Government, Vol. II*, mentions a few persons by name and many incidents to illustrate the Union oppression of Maryland.[357] There is no mention of Colonel Sothoron or the shooting incident at The Plains. However, Colonel Sothoron was peripherally associated with the Confederate government and did personally meet with Confederate President Jefferson Davis.

There was an effort by members of the Confederate army and government to have Colonel Sothoron appointed as a military court judge in late February and March of 1864. Nine letters of recommendation were sent on his behalf. The first letter had two endorsements written on it. The following letters are from National Archives records for Confederate Papers Relating to Citizens or Business Firms:[358]

Richmond
Feb 24th '64
Hon. James A. Seddon
Secretary of War
    It gives me great pleasure to give your favorable notice and attention to Colonel J.H. Sothoron of Maryland. You are aware of the circumstances under which he left his State, after having given two of his Sons to the cause of the South. Since his departure all of his slaves have been taken from his estate, and a proposition is now before the Yankee Government to appropriate his land for the benefit of the robbers whom he slew. Colonel Sothoron is applying for a position on one of the Military Courts. I have known him for a long time and can bear the fullest testimony to his admirable fitness for such a place. He is eminently qualified by temper, patience, nerve and talent for the important duties of that office. I hopefully trust he will not be disappointed.
Very respectfully
Your obedient servant
Robert Ould
    From the known character of Colonel Sothoron & the exertions he has ever displayed in favor of the Confederate cause, I take great pleasure in adding my recommendation & urging his appointment to

---

[357] Davis, *The Rise and Fall of the Confederate Government, Vol. II*, pages 460-468.
[358] *NARA*, Confederate Papers Relating to Citizens or Business Firms, M346, Microfilm 964.

the favorable consideration of the President & Secretary of War
S. Cooper
A. & I. Gen.
[Author's note: there is another faded and illegible endorsement; however, it appears to have been made by Maryland Confederate General John H. Winder]

Robert Ould (1820-1882) held various appointed positions in the Confederate government. In his letter of recommendation for Colonel Sothoron, Robert Ould stated that he had known "him a long time". Robert Ould was in charge of the Confederate Secret Service.[359] Ould's name appears frequently in *The War of the Rebellion: a Compilation of the Official Records of the Union and Confederate Armies* because of his position in the Confederate government as a negotiator for the exchange of prisoners. The second and third letters of recommendation from the National Archives file are:

26 February 1864 - Letter from Colonel Bradley T. Johnson at his headquarters in Staunton, Virginia to General Samuel Cooper.
26 February 1864 - Letter from T. B. Barton in Richmond to Secretary of War Seddon. Barton indicates that he was a schoolmate of Colonel Sothoron at Charlotte Hall. T. B. Barton was the father of two Confederate officers, General Seth Barton and Major William S. Barton.[360]

The fourth letter in the National Archives file was from a member of the Confederate government:

28[?] February 1864 - Letter from George W. Randolph in Richmond to Secretary of War Seddon.

George W. Randolph (1818-1867) served in the Confederate army as a major and later was a member of the cabinet of Jefferson Davis.[361] The fifth letter in the National Archives file was from an elected member of the Confederate government:

29 February 1864 - Letter from Thos. S. Gholson in Petersburg to Secretary of War Seddon. Gholson indicates he knew Colonel Sothoron from college.

Thomas S. Gholson (1809-1868) was an attorney and an elected member of the Confederate government. He also served as a judge. Colonel Sothoron and Thomas Gholson had attended the University of Virginia together in the 1820s.[362] The sixth letter in the National Archives file was from another elected member of the Confederate government:

5 March 1864 - Letter from A. T. Caperton in Union, Monroe County to Secretary of War Seddon.

Allen T. Caperton (1810-1876) was an elected member of the Virginia legislature prior to the Civil War. He was a Confederate Senator and opposed President Jefferson Davis. It is out of the ordinary that Allen Caperton was not a secessionist but had voted for it. Allen Caperton also attended the University of Virginia and probably was a classmate of Colonel Sothoron.[363] After the Civil War Caperton was a Democrat Senator.[364]

---

[359] Wakelyn, *Biographical Dictionary of the Confederacy*, page 336.
[360] Tidwell, Hall and Gaddy, page 350.
[361] Wakelyn, pages 362-363.
[362] Wakelyn, page 201.
[363] Wakelyn, pages 124-125.

The seventh and eighth letters of the National archives file were from two persons who have not been identified:

9 March 1864 - Letter from Frank G. Ruffin Richmond to Secretary of War Seddon.
15 March 1864 - Letter from Lewis G. Harris [or Hanson?] of the Richmond and Danville Railroad to Secretary of War Seddon.

The ninth and last letter in the archives file was from a Confederate general from Maryland:

30 March 1864 - Letter written from General Arnold Elzey in Richmond to General Braxton Bragg.

In 1861, General Elzey had also written a previous letter of recommendation for Colonel Sothoron's son, Webster. In all, the nine letters and two endorsements indicate that Colonel Sothoron had influential friends within the Confederate government. Colonel Sothoron was also associated with moderate and Unionist elements within the Confederate States.

Apparently there was a problem with the legality of appointing a citizen of Maryland to the position of Judge of the Military Court. The following is from the same National Archives file:

Richmond June 15, 1864
His Excellency the President
Sir
Understanding that the recent legislation of Congress has removed the difficulties attending the appointment of Judges for the Military Courts, I beg leave very respectfully to again bring my name to the attention of your Excellency - You are already familiar with the facts of my case. May I not indulge the hope that I am justified in drawing a favorable gauging from the kindness both of speech and manner which your Excellency showed towards me in a former interview? I should have greatly preferred a personal interview but for my unwillingness to trespass upon your more valuable time — I have the honor to be most
Respectfully Yours
John H. Sothoron

It is not known if Colonel Sothoron was appointed to the position of Judge of the Military Court. The National Archives file contains a memo from Secretary of War Seddon to President Davis on 18 June 1864 which indicates that General Robert E. Lee had sent a letter outlining the Constitutional difficulties of appointing Colonel Sothoron to the military court as a judge. The above letter indicates that at some prior time, President Davis had personally met with Colonel Sothoron. The letter implies that there were others present because of the statement of Colonel Sothoron that he would have "preferred a personal interview".

In April, about two months prior to the above letter, Colonel Sothoron completed a form recommending the transfer of Private William Howard from Company G, Second South Carolina Regiment, Kershaw's Brigade, McLaw's Division of Longstreet's Corps in the Army of Northern Virginia to the Maryland Line, Camp Howard, Hanover Junction, commanded by Colonel Bradley T. Johnson. The document was signed at Richmond, Virginia on 16 April 1864 and Colonel Sothoron stated that he knew William Howard as a resident of Saint Mary's County, Maryland. The form also had a provision for a soldier to transfer to the Maryland Line at Camp Maryland, Staunton, commanded by Major General Elzey. The document was also signed by [H?] M. Owen, Major of Artillery, P.A.C.S.

---

[364] *BDUSC*, accessed 22 December 2006.

About one month prior to his letter written to President Jefferson Davis, Colonel Sothoron and M. Miller were the recipients of weapons and military equipment. National Archives records show that they each received from Captain O. W. Edwards Austrian rifles and military accouterments while in Richmond.[365] The day they received the military equipment was one of the most desperate for the Confederate army. On that day, 12 May 1864, during the Battle of Spotsylvania, Union troops under General Grant broke through the Confederate lines at a place called the "Bloody Angle" or the "Mule Shoe Salient". About 2,000 to 4,000 Confederate troops were killed, captured or wounded on that day. Confederate soldiers had to restrain General Lee from personally going to the front lines in his effort to contain the breach in the lines from the massive Union attack.

Colonel Sothoron is mentioned in the personal papers of Alexander R. Boteler. His name appears on a list of "Miscellaneous Applications for Military Court Appointments". He was one of eight candidates:[366]

> Military Court Cavalry Army N. Va.
> 7. Sothoron, John Recommended by General Fitz Lee – See Maryland memorandum of Colonel Lubbock enclosed in General Fitz Lee's letter of November 11, 1864.

The home of Alexander R. Boteler in Shepherdstown, Virginia was burned down by the troops of Union General Hunter.[367] Alexander Boteler was a United States and a Confederate Congressman. He later became a pardon clerk in the United States Department of Justice.[368] He was a Unionist.

In *Volume XV (1887)* of the *Southern Historical Society Papers* there is a listing for a J. H. Southern. The volume is a roster of all the Confederates who surrendered with General Robert E. Lee at Appomattox Court House on 9 April 1865. There is a "List of Unattached Non-Commissioned Officers and Privates Cut off from their Commands, Paroled by Major D. B. Bridgford, Provost Marshall". J. H. Southern is on the list and his rank is given as Private while his unit is listed as Company D, 21st North Carolina Infantry.[369] There is no National Archives Confederate military service record for a J. H. Southern of the 21st North Carolina Infantry.

This is Colonel Sothoron who left Richmond with the retreating Confederate army. It is not likely that it is someone with a similar name. A signed parole document would have been essential for Colonel Sothoron to return to Maryland or flee to Canada. On 12 April 1865, the first of the Confederates who surrendered at Appomattox returned to Richmond, Virginia.[370] With the assassination of President Lincoln on 14 April 1865, Colonel Sothoron may have felt that he would have been treated harshly if caught, and determined to escape to Canada.

The Major David B. Bridgford who paroled the above soldier was the commander of the Confederate Provost Guard which was the personal guard for General Robert E. Lee and also had responsibility for the processing of Union prisoners.[371]

*　　*　　*

The Confederate authorities may have transferred S. Webster Sothoron to the city of Mobile, Alabama in an effort to protect him from retaliation. Another Marylander assigned to Mobile was Admiral Franklin Buchanan of the Confederate navy.[372]

---

[365] *NARA*, Unfiled Slips and Papers of the Confederate Government, M347, Microfilm 373.
[366] *NARA*, Personal Papers of Alex R. Boteler.
[367] Goldsborough, page 245.
[368] *Biographical Directory of the United States Congress, 1774-1989*, pages 645-646.
[369] *Southern Historical Society Papers, Vol. XV (1887)*, page 462.
[370] Lee, *General Lee's City*, page 179.
[371] Tidwell, Hall and Gaddy, pages 110-111.
[372] Manakee, page 148-149.

The National Archives military record for S. Webster Sothoron shows that on 28 December 1863 he was appointed "Drill Master with rank of 2 Lieutenant" and the appointment was effective from 25 December 1863. He was to report to "Lieutenant Colonel J.R.C. Lewis". The first indication of him detailed to Mobile is a signed requisition for two cords of wood for the month of March 1864. The requisition is dated 2 March 1864 and shows the fuel was received from the Confederate quartermaster. Webster Sothoron signed the requisition twice and put after his name "2nd Lt P.A.C.S.". The initials "P.A.C.S." were an acronym for the Provisional Army Confederate States.

Webster Sothoron next appears on a Roster of General and Staff Officers of Artillery Brigade at Mobile dated 27 April 1864 as a Lieutenant and Acting A.D.C. (aide-de-camp) to Colonel Charles A. Fuller. The next document in the Archives file is a "Requisition for Forage" for the private horse of Lieutenant Sothoron, A.D.C. for the month of June. The 180 pounds of corn and the 270 pounds of fodder were received from M. L. Strong, Q.M.C.S. Army. Sothoron's name is on a list of officers at the Military Post of Mobile, Alabama for the month of July 1864 as an A.D.C. to Brigadier General Higgins. Also, there is a form for "commutation of quarters" indicating that Webster Sothoron was reimbursed for living quarters from July to September of 1864. During the fighting in August of 1864, Admiral Franklin Buchanan was wounded and captured; he was later exchanged back to the Confederates.[373]

Webster Sothoron may have participated in the defense of the port of Mobile when Union naval forces attacked it on 5 August 1864. This was the battle where Union navy Admiral Farragut is reported to have said "Damn the Torpedoes". During the Civil War a torpedo was a manufactured explosive device that was not self-propelled to its target, which is what a modern naval submarine torpedo does. A civil war torpedo included devices that were underwater anti-shipping mines. The Confederates may have had a technologically advanced underwater electrically operated minefield to protect the port of Mobile from the Union navy.[374] During the battle, the Union navy ironclad "*Tecumseh*" suffered a massive explosion and sank within a minute.[375]

On 5 February 1865, a unit of Maryland Confederate artillery was assigned to Mobile after having participated in the defense of Georgia. The Third Maryland Artillery, also known as Stephen's Light Artillery, was commanded by Captain Ritter. Mobile was evacuated by the Confederates on 11 April 1865.[376] Mobile finally fell and the city was entered by Union troops the next day on 12 April 1865.[377] The retreating Confederate troops traveled by boat and land to Demopolis, Alabama and then by rail to Meridian, Mississippi. On 4 May 1865, the Confederate troops at Meridian under General Richard Taylor surrendered to Union forces under General Canby. The Third Maryland Artillery was paroled on 10 May 1865.[378]

Also in his archives file is a card indicating that Lieutenant Sothoron was a prisoner, but there are no further details regarding this such as the date of incarceration. The card appears to be for a person who was a prisoner of the Confederate authorities as it follows their practice of an inventory of personal items for each prisoner.

Webster Sothoron received his parole from Union authorities on 12 May 1865 at Meridian, Mississippi:

No. 560

I, the undersigned, Prisoner of War, belonging to the Army of the Department of Alabama, Mississippi

---

[373] Manakee, page 140.
[374] *ORN*, Series I, Volume 16, 1903, June 1, 1865, Detailed report of Rear Admiral Dahlgren, U.S. Navy, transmitting drawings and reports of torpedoes, torpedo boat, and obstructions., report pages 380 to 403, page 387, accessed 6 December 2006.
[375] *ORN*, Series I, Volume 21, 1906, August 6, 1864, Report of Capitan Drayton, U.S. Navy, commanding U.S. flagship Hartford, with enclosures, page 425 to 428, page 425, accessed 6 December 2006. See also June 1, 1865, Detailed report of Rear Admiral Dahlgren, U.S. Navy, transmitting drawings and reports of torpedoes, torpedo boat, and obstructions., page 386.
[376] Goldsborough, pages 314-315.
[377] Boatner, page 550.
[378] Goldsborough, page 315.

and East Louisiana, having been surrendered by Lieutenant Gen R. Taylor, C.S.A., Commanding said Department, to Maj. Gen E.R.S. Canby, U.S.A., Commanding Army and Division of West Mississippi, do hereby give my solemn PAROLE of HONOR that I will not hereafter serve in the Armies of the Confederate States, or in any military capacity whatever, against the United States of America, or render aid to the enemies of the latter until properly exchanged in such manner as shall be mutually approved by the respective authorities.

Done at <u>Meridian Miss</u>

this <u>12</u> day of May, 1865 <u>W. Sothoron</u>

2d Lt Co "D" Virginia Art

Approved:

<u>R.L. Gibson</u>, Brig. General, C.S.A.}

Commissioners

<u>G.L. Andrews</u>, Brigadier General, U.S.A.}

The above named officer will not be disturbed by United States authorities, as long as he observes his parole, and the laws in force where he resides.

It is intriguing to note that Webster Sothoron's burial record in the *All Faith Church Parish Register* for 11 October 1883 gave him the military rank of major. Tidwell, Hall and Gaddy in their book *Come Retribution, the Confederate Secret Service and the Assassination of Lincoln* mention a person using the name and rank of "Minor Major", "Major" or "Majors" as an alias or nom de guerre. Major was part of a group of Confederates who engaged in covert warfare in the Mississippi Valley and was organized in 1863 by Judge Joseph W. Tucker, a former Missouri editor. Major was mistakenly arrested by the Confederate authorities.[379]

At the beginning of the Civil War, Webster Sothoron was under 21 years old and he was an underage minor. Tidwell, Hall and Gaddy mention more of him and the covert Confederate action group. The purpose of the group was to destroy Union ships by placing explosives in them. Six of the group left Richmond and were arrested by Confederate authorities in Mobile but released as a result of General Richard Taylor communicating with President Davis. A Union informant, William Murphy, gave information that led to the arrest of another ten of the group. One of the members of the covert action group identified Minor Majors as leader of the group. Minor Major also was in Canada seeking financial assistance from a Confederate government representative there. Robert Loudon was a member of the group.[380]

Ship explosions at that time could also have been from mechanical design defects. The development of "superheated" steam engines was new and may have resulted in inexplicable catastrophic failures. The fuel used to heat steam engines was also a factor. Wood was a traditional source of fuel. A newer source of fuel was coal. Coal was mined from under the surface of the earth. The primary industrial energy source changed from wood to coal.

There is enough factual evidence to establish that S. Webster Sothoron was doubtless a Confederate known as "Major". Because the word "Major" was used in the plural it is possible that there were others with the rank or alias. Given his level of skill and ability it is conceivable that he may have been used in covert operations in different locations as needed.

The operations of individual members of the above covert action group continued after the surrender of the Confederate Army of Northern Virginia at Appomattox on 9 April 1865. On 26 April 1865 the transport ship *Sultana* left Vicksburg, Mississippi with a large number of released Union soldiers who had been prisoners of the Confederates.[381] On 27 April 1865, the *Sultana* refueled at Memphis, Tennessee and departed from the

---

[379] Tidwell, Hall and Gaddy, page 164.

[380] Tidwell, Hall and Gaddy, page 167.

[381] Eliot, *Transport to Disaster*, page 83.

dock at 1:00 AM.[382] A few miles down the river, the ship exploded at 2:00 AM with the loss of at least 1,200 lives. Union authorities at the time claimed it was a defective boiler but years later a different version of events appeared.

A person by the name of William Streeter claimed that a torpedo had been taken aboard the *Sultana* by Robert Lowden (or Louden). Robert Lowden also used the alias of Charles Dale.[383] Tidwell, Hall and Gaddy mention Lowden as a member of the covert team led by Major.

A Confederate group responsible for the destruction of ships by explosion or arson may have also operated in Baltimore, Maryland. In Baltimore on 28 September 1863, the Union transport steamboat *City of Albany* was damaged by fire while docked.[384]

The use of a torpedo as a military weapon was known to the Union navy operating in tidewater region of Maryland and Virginia on 9 February 1864. Rear Admiral Porter gave an order to execute "anyone" found placing a torpedo by being "shot on the spot".[385] If captured, Webster Sothoron and any member of the covert action team would have faced summary military execution.

*　*　*

Marshall Lyles Sothoron may have also been transferred by the Confederate government away from the Virginia area to protect him from capture and identification as a member of the Sothoron family. Found in the National Archives records of letters received by the Adjutant and Inspector General's office are two letters concerning his transfer to the Confederate navy:[386]

> Confederate States of America
> Navy Department
> Richmond, February 13th, 1864
> Marshall L. Sothoron Esquire
> Richmond Va.
> Sir:
> Herewith you will receive a bond which you will have executed and returned to this department. Two or more sureties are required and each will make oath on the back of the bond that he is worth over and above his debts and liabilities the amount he may subscribe as surety to the bond. The Judge or District Attorney of the Confederate States for the District in which you reside will also certify to the sufficiency of the security.
> Upon the reception of your bond executed to the satisfaction of the Department, you will be appointed an assistant Paymaster in the Navy, and your compensation will commence.
> I am respectfully
> Your Obedient Servant
> S. Mallory
> Secretary of the Navy

---

[382] Elliot, page 93-95.
[383] Elliot, page 212.
[384] Scharf, *History of the Confederate States Navy*, page 145.
[385] *Civil War Naval Chronology, 1861-1865*, page IV-16.
[386] *NARA*, M474, Microfilm 141, letters 344-S-1864.

Stephen Russell Mallory was the Confederates Secretary of the Navy and a former Senator.[387] Because Marshall L. Sothoron was to handle money, the Confederate navy required that he be bonded. The other letter in the file is from Colonel Sothoron:

Richmond February 16th 1864
Hon Jas. A. Seddon
Secretary of War
Sir
I have respectfully to ask the discharge of Private Marshall L. Sothoron of Capt. Dements Battery, Pranctons Battalion, Army of Northern Virginia, he having received the appointment of Asst Paymaster in the C S Navy –
John H. Sothoron

The order for his transfer was issued by the office of General Samuel C. Cooper, the Adjutant and Inspector General of the Confederate army. The following is from the National Archives Confederate military naval service file of Marshall L. Sothoron:

Adjutant & Inspector Generals Office
Richmond March 1 1864
S. O. No. 50
I. Private Marshall L. Sothoron of the 1st Maryland Battery having received the appointment of Assistant Paymaster C.S. Navy will be discharged his former service. S 344

The First Maryland Battery was also known as the Maryland Flying Artillery.[388] Marshall Sothoron also served on the *C.S.S. Chattahoochee* in 1864 and was later assigned to the Savannah, Georgia naval station in the same year

Marshall Sothoron and J. Thomas Scharf (Scharf later wrote the *History of the Confederate States Navy*) were participants in a Confederate boat raid against Union ships in the Gulf of Mexico blockading the Apalachicola River near the panhandle section of Florida. The raid was led by Lieutenant George W. Gift. About ninety Confederate sailors and soldiers in seven row boats were to attempt to capture the Union steamers *Somerset* and *Adela*. Marshall L. Sothoron and J. Thomas Scharf both appear on a list of persons having receiving pistols on 4 May 1864 for the attempted capture of the *Somerset* and *Adela*.[389]

There was a problem because the weather was too clear for the Confederates to surreptitiously approach the Union ships. The Confederates attempted to return to the mainland. The weather became bad and the boat that Gift, Sothoron and Scharf were in became separated from the others. They were shipwrecked on Saint George's Island and survived by eating vegetation and alligators. It was providential they were shipwrecked because the Confederates in the other boats were captured by the Union navy.

After the raid, the Confederates retreated from Columbus, Georgia and destroyed the navy yard there along with the steamship *Chattahoochee*, the iron-clad gunboat *Columbus*, an uncompleted torpedo boat and machine shops.[390] Paymaster Marshall L. Sothoron and Lieutenant George Gift traveled from Columbus,

---

[387] *BDUSC*, accessed 22 December 2006.
[388] Amann, page 96.
[389] *ORN*, Part I, Volume 17, 1903, May 3, 1864, S. P. Blanc's Diary, C.S.S. Chattahoochee, pages 700 to 702, list on page 702, accessed 6 December 2006.
[390] Scharf, *History of the Confederate States Navy*, pages 618-622.

Georgia down the Chattahoochee River to Eufaula, Alabama on 21 May 1864.[391] Sothoron and Scharf appear on a list of officers attached to the *C. S.S. Chattahoochee* on 1 June 1864.[392]

John Thomas Scharf was born in Baltimore on 1 May 1843. J. Thomas Scharf also served with the First Maryland Artillery and fought at the Second Battle of Bull Run and at Chancellorville. In 1863, he was a commanding midshipman in the Confederate navy. During the winter of 1864, he was sent on a mission to Canada by the Confederate government and captured. He was pardoned by President Johnson in 1865. He served on the editorial staffs of three Baltimore newspapers and wrote a number of history books. He held various elected and appointed Maryland and federal positions. Scharf died in New York City on 28 February 1898.[393]

J. Thomas Scharf served in the First Maryland Artillery and his own writing shows that he and Marshall Lyles Sothoron served with the Confederate Navy on the same mission against a Union ship. Their military careers parallel each other with service in the same units of both the Confederate army and navy during the same time.

In August of 1864 the Confederate city of Atlanta fell to the Union army. Union General William T. Sherman marched with his army across Georgia in the fall of 1864 and captured the city of Savannah in late December of that year. During the march, the countryside of Georgia between the cities of Atlanta and Savannah were ravaged by the depredations of the Union army.

In the National Archives records concerning citizens and business firms that had a financial association with the Confederate government are found copies of checks drawn by Assistant Paymaster Marshall L. Sothoron. The four checks were drawn from the C.S. Depository at The Mechanic's Bank in Augusta, Georgia:[394]

Check Number	Date	Amount
1	December 20, 1864	$977.00
none	January 3, 1865	$500.00
3	January 4, 1865	$200.00
none	January 6, 1865	$5,000.00
none	January 28, 1865	$4,123.00

The total amount in the account was $10,800 and the last withdrawal on 28 January 1865 was for the remaining balance. The money was used to obtain a crew and supplies for the Confederate ships on the Savannah River.

In January of 1864, Marshall Sothoron was in Augusta, Georgia. He was a paymaster and he provided the pay and clothing for the crews of two Confederate steamboats named *Macon* and *Sampson*, on the Savannah River. The purpose of the steamboats was to defend the upper Savannah River from a contemplated attack from Savannah city, which was taken by Union General Sherman in December.[395]

Marshall Lyles Sothoron was paroled on 9 May 1865 in Augusta, Georgia.[396]

* * *

---

[391] Turner, *Navy Gray, A Story of the Confederate Navy on the Chattahoochee and Appalachia Rivers*, page 194.
[392] *ORN*, Series I, Volume 17, 1903, June 1, 1864, Monthly list of officers attached to the C.C.S. Chattahoochee, at Eufaula, Ala., on June 1, 1864, page 874, accessed 6 December 2006.
[393] *Who Was Who In America*, page 38.
[394] *NARA*, M346, Microfilm 964.
[395] *ORN*, Part I, Volume 16, 1893, January 9, 1865, Report of Flag Officer Hunter, C.S. Navy, regarding repairs to steamers Macon and Sampson, and their services in the Savannah River, pages 498-499, accessed 6 December 2006.
[396] Carroll, *Register of Officers of the Confederate States Navy, 1861-1865*, page 186.

Another son of Colonel Southern, Robert Bowie Sothoron, entered the Virginia Military Academy at Staunton, Virginia on 24 December 1864.[397] Cadets from the military academy were stationed in Richmond. They were disbanded on 2 April 1865.[398]

* * *

At the end of the Civil War, Colonel Sothoron fled to Canada. It is possible he may have found his son in Richmond or Staunton, Virginia and they both went to Canada. The activities and whereabouts of Colonel Sothoron in Canada have not been established.

They were no longer refugees from the quiet revolution; they were political exiles.

---

[397] Alumni Records of the Virginia Military Institute, accessed, available on the Internet.
[398] Jennings C. Wise, *The Military History of the Virginia military Institute, from 1839 to 1865*, page 418, accessed 28 December 2006.

Chapter 7

THE OCCUPATION OF THE PLAINS

After the Union army forcibly evicted the Sothoron family and their slaves from The Plains, the plantation was used as a "contraband" camp. The plantation was described as "Government farms" in Union army records. The occupied areas were also described as "contraband farms" and "contraband settlements".

Located about twenty-five miles south east of The Plains was the Union army post at Point Lookout, Maryland. Point Lookout is a sandy peninsula which extends into the confluence of the Potomac River and the Chesapeake Bay. A prison camp for Confederates soldiers was located there. Because the Union army had looted The Plains of everything, spring planting was impossible at the farm. To solve the problem they originally caused, the Union army marauded into Confederate territory in Virginia from Point Lookout.

Brigadier General Edward W. Hinks was the Union army officer commanding at Point Lookout. On 12 April 1864, he embarked on a raid across the Potomac River and into Virginia. Three hundred soldiers of the 36th United States Colored Infantry under Colonel Draper and 50 cavalrymen under Lieutenant John Mix were loaded into the transport steamboat *Long Branch*. They were escorted by three gunboats of the Potomac flotilla commanded by Captain Eastman. Once ashore is Virginia, Draper and his men seized 177 boxes of "superior Gravely tobacco, probably worth $40,000 U.S. currency."

The owner of the tobacco was Joseph H. Maddox, who claimed to be an emissary of the "Federal Government". Maddox, arrested previously for blockade running, said that he paid a bribe of $1,000 to Senator Reverdy Johnson to be released. Hinks, in his report of the raid, said that the brother of Maddox had previously confirmed his story. The claim by Maddox to be a federal emissary raises a question about him or Johnson being a licensee of Lincoln who was exempted from the blockade and allowed to engage in economic trade with the Confederacy.

Confederate cavalry was sighted and chased. Hinks reported that a few buildings were burned because his troops were fired upon by occupants of them. The raiders returned on 14 April 1864 with 50 "contrabands" (i.e., former slaves) and the tobacco looted from Maddox.[399] On 20 April 1864, Hinks was relieved of his command by Major General Benjamin F. Butler and replaced by Colonel Draper.[400] Butler was again involved with depredations in Maryland. It is likely that some of the slaves were impressed into the Union army while the others were sent to The Plains. Hinks may, or may not, have been removed because he documented bribery in his report.

---

[399] *OR*. Series 1, Volume 33, 1891, April 15, 1864, April 12-14, 1864.–Expedition from Point Lookout, Md. to Westmoreland County, Va., Report of Brig. Gen. Edward W. Hinks, U.S. Army, commanding Saint Mary's District, page 268 and 269, accessed 6 December 2006.

[400] *OR*. Series 1, Volume 33, 1891, April 20, 1864, Special Orders No. 110, R. S. Davis by order of Major General Butler, page 930 and 931, accessed 6 December 2006.

On 11 May 1864, Colonel Draper again raided into Virginia. Draper with 300 soldiers of the 36th United States Colored Troops and thirteen cavalrymen were transported to Virginia by the transport steamboat *Star*, which was escorted by the gunboat *Yankee*. Part of their mission was to remove underwater mines, but they also committed depredations. Henry Barrack was accused of helping the Confederates and his mill was burned. They skirmished with a small detachment of Confederate marines and cavalry. The Union raiders stole 33 cattle along with 22 horses and mules. They also captured "vehicles", which were probably carts and wagons. On 14 May they returned to their base in Maryland.[401]

On 28 May 1864 Colonel Alonzo G. Draper of the 36th United States Colored Troops wrote to Major R. S. Davis, the Assistant Adjutant General of the Department of Virginia and North Carolina, at Fort Monroe, and asked for permission to "make another raid" into Virginia with 300 men. The Department of Virginia and North Carolina was the territory of Major General Butler. The reasons he gave for his proposed raid into Virginia was "to procure horses and other property much needed in the quartermaster's department here, and on our contraband farms on the Patuxent." He also asked for permission to make future raids.[402] On 1 June 1864 Draper again wrote to Davis. Draper stated "We are greatly in need of horses for the quartermaster's department, and of farming implements for our contraband settlements on the Patuxent." The contraband settlements on the Patuxent River were the Sothoron, Forrest and Coles property. Draper signed his communication as "Colonel, Commanding District".[403]

On 11 June 1864, Draper again raided into Virginia. Draper, in his report of the raid, specifically stated that the objective was "to obtain horses for the quartermaster's department, and farming implements, transportation &c., for the contraband settlement on the Patuxent River." It appears that the 50 former slaves (i.e., contrabands) that he took during his April raid into Virginia were at The Plains and waiting for farming supplies to begin spring planting. Draper's raid into Virginia lasted 10 days.

Draper left with 475 soldiers of the 36th United States Colored Troops and 49 cavalrymen of the 2nd and 5th United States Cavalry. They disembarked from Point Lookout in the transport steamboats *Georgia*, *Charleston*, *Long Branch* and *Favorite*. At the nautical rendezvous with gunboats near Saint Mary's River there was an accident. The gunboat *Resolute* rammed the *Long Branch*. Troops on the *Long Branch* were transferred to the *Georgia*.

They crossed the Potomac River and the next morning the raiding party landed in Virginia. The area near where they landed into offered little booty for their pillaging and they moved farther south. During the raid Second Lieutenant O'Brien disobeyed orders. On 16 June he sent three of his men to a house about one mile away from the columns of troops. Only one of the men returned alive. Draper covered for O'Brien, writing that he performed his other duties well. O'Brien's violation of orders may have alerted Confederates in the area to attack the Union army plunderers. Confederates composed of regular soldiers and the home guard harassed the Union raiders. During a skirmish, Draper was isolated and in danger because many of his soldiers retreated.

After burning the mill of Robert M. T. Hunter, Draper and his soldiers loaded transport steamers at Layton's Wharf. In his report of 22 June 1864, Draper recapitulated the pillage stolen by the Union army: 375 cattle, 160 horses and mules, 600 former slaves (i.e., contrabands), farm machines, carts, carriages and harnesses. Of the 600, Draper thought about 60 to 70 would be suitable recruits for the Union army and navy.[404]

---

[401] *OR*, Series 1, Volume 37, Part I, 1891, May 15, 1864, May 11-41, 1864, Expedition from Point Lookout, Md. to the Rappahannock River, Va., Report of Col. Alonzo G. Draper, Thirty-sixth U.S. Colored Infantry, commanding expedition., page 71 to 73, accessed 6 December 2006.

[402] *OR*, Series 1, Volume 36, Part III, 1891, May 28, 1864, A. G. Draper to R. S. Davis, page 278, accessed 6 December 2006.

[403] *OR*, Series 1, Volume 36, Part III, 1891, June 1, 1864, A.G. Draper to R. S. Davis, page 472, accessed 6 December 2006.

[404] *OR*, Series 1, Volume 37, Part I, 1891, June 22, 1864, June 11-21, 1864.-Expedition from Point Lookout to Pope's Creek, Va., Report of Col. Alonzo G. Draper, Thirty–sixth U.S. Colored Troops., page 163 to 167, accessed 6 December 2006. Robert Mercer Taliaferro Hunter was a congressman.

The 600, less the number of recruits taken by the Union army, were probably taken to The Plains and the other government farms on the Patuxent River or transported north to become servants or factory workers..

On 21 June 1864, by Order Number 214 of E. D. Townsend, Assistant Adjutant General, the area including Saint Mary's County, Maryland was added to the Department of Washington.[405] Union army Colonel Alonzo G. Draper, in an organizational listing of the Department of Washington of 30 June 1864, appears as the chief of the District of Saint Mary's.[406] The action removed Saint Mary's County from the tentacles of Major General Benjamin F. Butler and into the morass of a Washington based government bureau.

Creditors of Colonel Sothoron were initiating civil court action. On 26 July 1864, Union army War Department Solicitor William Whiting wrote an opinion about the property of Colonel Sothoron. Benjamin Adams and others had filed suit in the Circuit Court of Saint May's County for debts owed to them by Colonel Sothoron. Whiting labeled the expropriation of The Plains by the Union army as a "sequestration". Whiting claimed that one of the plaintiffs was "disloyal, if not an active enemy." He said the "sequestration" was a prior lien and that the Union army would not pay the debt because it would benefit Sothoron.[407] The truth of the raid and looting of The Plains was being lost in a turbulent sea of the semantics of usury to avoid describing the harsh reality of the Union army seizure and occupation. The final answer from the Union government and army to all questions regarding The Plains was that they would not tolerate any idea except that it was theirs and they would charge excessive interests rates to anyone who questioned their illegal seizure.

On 8 November 1865, Brevet General M. C. Meigs of the Union Quartermaster General wrote a report about the activities of the Quartermasters Department to Secretary of War Stanton. The Sixth Division of the Quartermasters Department had the responsibility for the records and reports of registered graves. The total number of registered graves was 116,148. Counted by race, there were 95,803 whites and 20,345 colored. Counted by other categories, there were 98,827 loyal, 12,596 disloyal, 600 refugees and 4,125 contrabands.[408] Included in the total of 116,148 were 14,412 reinterments of Union army deaths, leaving the remainder of 101,036 as most likely civilian deaths. There were no registered graves included in the statistics for Maryland. It is not known if any of the contrabands taken to The Plains died during the time they were there.[409]

* * *

Second Lieutenant Edward F. O'Brien, the disobedient officer who accompanied Draper on at least one of the raids into Virginia, was the Union army officer who was the superintendent of the government farm at The Plains. His commanding officer beginning in November 1864 was Captain James M. Brown. Brown was the "Chief" of the Bureau of Government Farms and his headquarters was at 132 Pennsylvania Avenue, Washington, District of Columbia. There was a mysterious "Mr. Byron" associated with the Bureau.[410] Apparently, O'Brien was formerly a private in the 14th Pennsylvania Cavalry.[411] There is also a Union record

---

[405] *OR*, Series 1, Volume 37, Part I, 1891, June 21, 1864, General Orders No. 214, E. D. Townsend by order of the Secretary of War, page 659, accessed 6 December 2006.

[406] *OR*, Series 1, Volume 37, Part I, 1891, June 30, 1864, Troops in the Department of Washington (Twenty-second Army Corps), Maj. Gen. Christopher C. Augur, U. S. Army, commanding, June 30, 1864, page 698, accessed 6 December 2006.

[407] William Whiting, *War Powers Under the Constitution of The United States*, 43rd Edition, (Boston, Lee and Shepard, Publishers; New York, Lee, Shepard and Dillingham, 1871), Opinion No. 730, John H. Sothoron's Creditors, page 386, accessed 29 December 2006, available on the Internet. .

[408] *OR*, Series 3, Volume 5, 1900, November 8, 1865, M. C. Meigs to Hon. Edwin M. Stanton, report from page 212 to 249, page 241, accessed 6 December 2006.

[409] *OR*, Series 3, Volume 5, 1900, Statement of the number of interments registered during the war, white and black, loyal and disloyal, so far as reports received at this office under General Orders, No. 40, Quartermaster General's Office, 1865., page 317, accessed 6 December 2006.

[410] *OR*, Series 1, Volume 46, Part III, 1895, April 16, 1865, Edwd. F. O'Brien to J. M. Brown, page 801, accessed 6 December 2006.

[411] *NPSSSS, NARA*, M554, roll 92, accessed 11 November 2006.

for him being in Company G of the 18th Veteran's Reserve Corps as a First Lieutenant.[412]

In April 1865, two ships were captured by Confederate naval raiders in the Chesapeake Bay, which the Patuxent River flows into. On 1 April 1865, the *St. Mary's* was captured at the mouth of the Patuxent River. The *Harriet De Ford*, a ship with one mast and powered by a propeller, was captured in Herring Bay at 2 AM on 5 April 1865.[413]

On 9 April 1865, Confederate General Robert E. Lee and his army surrendered to General U.S. Grant at Appomattox, Virginia. Confederate soldiers paroled there began to return to their homes. Colonel Sothoron was among the surrendered soldiers and most likely was either headed home to Maryland or to join his son Robert B. Sothoron. Robert B. Sothoron was at Virginia Military Academy or some other place.

After the surrender of Lee and the Confederate army on 12 April 1865, a group of thirty Confederate soldiers was seen moving in the direction towards the "Government farms" in Saint Mary's County. It was presumed that their objective was to capture a steamboat on the Patuxent River. Union cavalry was dispatched from Point Lookout to search for them.[414] The Confederates true objective may have been to meet the ships captured in early April.

On 14 April 1865, President Lincoln was assassinated at Ford's Theater in Washington, D.C. Communications were quickly transmitted from Union headquarters in Washington alerting outposts to the assassination. Apparently, the communications were made both by telegraph and courier.

The Confederate unit the Union cavalry was looking for was a company of the 43rd Battalion, Mosby's Rangers, under the command of Garland Smith. On 15 April 1865, near Mechanicsville, the Confederate and Union forces fought a skirmish. Captain F. F. Buckley, the Union commander, reported losing one man.[415]

O'Brien made a report to Brown in Washington with different facts than Buckley. O'Brien said that no Union cavalryman was lost and that one prisoner was captured. O'Brien stated that the skirmish took place at the "edge of the farms."

In his report to Brown in Washington, O'Brien requested a guard for his horses and men "when they start for the farms." O'Brien requested that if Brown was not able to obtain a guard, he should "arm the men who are with Mr. Byron and telegraph me when they start."[416] The Rangers may have been waiting in the vicinity of The Plains or Benedict for the objective of meeting a steamboat captured by Confederates.

On 17 April 1865, the Commander of the Potomac flotilla, Foxhall A. Parker, reported the capture of Thomas Nelson Conrad, who was a Confederate chaplain, spy and scout. Conrad was captured by the Union ship *U. S.S. Jacob Bell* and he was a prisoner on the *U.S.S. Don*.[417]

In his erudite book *April '65, Confederate Covert Action in the American Civil War*, William A. Tidwell connected elements of the Confederate government to the assassination of President Lincoln. The presence of Confederate military operations, both of the army and navy in and near Saint Mary's County, support Tidwell's contention that the escape of Booth from Washington was connected to and expected by Confederate intelligence units. One of the findings of Tidwell is that John Wilkes Booth, the assassin of Lincoln and co-conspirator David E. Herod were moving in an easterly direction to a rendezvous point with a Confederate military unit in Saint Mary's County but changed their direction south to the Potomac River at the house of Dr. Samuel A. Mudd in Charles County. Herod was familiar with the geography of the area because he had attended

---

[412] *NPSSSS, NARA*, M636, roll 29/30, accessed 11 November 2006.
[413] *ORN*, Series I, Volume 5, 1897, April 5, 1865, T. A. Dornin to Washington, page 542, accessed 6 December 2006.
[414] *OR*, Series 1, Volume 46, Part III, 1895, April 15, 1865, S. G. Willauer and J. Barnes to Major General Auger, page 769, accessed 6 December 2006.
[415] *OR*, Series 1, Volume 46, Part III, 1895, April 16, 1865, F. F. Buckley to Captain Willauer, page 801, accessed 6 December 2006.
[416] *OR*, Series 1, Volume 46, Part III, 1895, April 16, 1865, Edwd. F. O'Brien to J. M. Brown, page 801, accessed 6 December 2006.
[417] *ORN*, Series I, Volume 5, 1897, April 17, 1865, Report of Commander Parker, U.S. Navy, commanding Potomac Flotilla, of the arrest of noted guerilla and spy Thomas N. Conrad, Foxhall A. Parker, page 555, accessed 6 December 2006.

Charlotte Hall Academy.[418] He may have known the Sothoron sons who also went there. At that time, mere former association with one of the conspirators would have resulted in at least arrest.

The surrender of Confederate armies did not end secret arrests and imprisonment. On 15 June 1865, a prisoner was admitted to the Old Capitol Prison and placed in a cell next to Dick Taylor. No one knew anything about him, including his name. The only thing known was that he was in prison because Secretary of War Stanton had ordered it. The newspaper published the article about the anonymous prisoner with the title "Stantonism".[419]

On 26 April 1865, as a result of the assassination of President Lincoln, the zones of military occupation in Saint Mary's County changed. The District of Saint Mary's was discontinued. In its place, the District of the Patuxent was created. The new district included parts of Charles County and all of Saint Mary's except Point Lookout. The military units of the district were led by Colonel Wells, Twenty-sixth Michigan Volunteers, headquartered near or at Port Tobacco.[420] On 28 April 1865, Wells reported that Captains Pettit and Krebs, leading cavalry detachments, were in Saint Mary's County investigating the possibility that Booth and Herod had passed through the area.[421]

After the assassination of Lincoln, the events in Saint Mary's County were investigated by Union authorities to establish the possibility that the Confederate naval and land actions were part of an escape plan for the assassin of Lincoln and his accomplices. This possibility, combined with the fact that Colonel Sothoron remained wanted by the Union army for shooting Lieutenant White necessitated his traveling to exile in Canada.

*   *   *

Troubles continued for other residents of Saint Mary's County. A Union military court martial accused Congressman Benjamin Gwinn Harris of giving two Confederate soldiers money, food and shelter on or about 26 April 1865. The soldiers were Sergeant Richard Chapman and Private William Read of Company K, 32nd Regiment Virginia Infantry. Harris was sentenced to three years in prison. On 31 May 1865, President Andrew Johnson "remitted" his sentence and ordered him released.[422] Harris had been the victim of the political purge by censure, on 9 April 1864 in the United States House of Representatives. The Representatives making the motion to censure Harris was Robert C. Schenck.[423]

*   *   *

While Colonel Sothoron was in Canada, his wife and friends in Saint Mary's County continued to press Union military and civilian authorities for the return of The Plains. The following letter is from a National Archives file.[424]

---

[418] Wikipedia, accessed 1 January 2007.
[419] *The Erie Observer*, September 14, 1865, page 1, "Stantonism", accessed 1 January 2007, available on the Internet.
[420] OR, Series 1, Volume 46, Part III, 1895, April 26, 1865, April 26, 1865, General Orders No. 56, J. H. Taylor, page 962, accessed 6 December 2006.
[421] OR, Series 1, Volume 46, Part III, April 28, 1865, H. H. Wells, to J. H. Taylor, page 1002 and 1003, accessed 6 December 2006.
[422] OR, Series 2, Volume 8, 1899, June 1, 1865, General Court Martial Orders No. 260, E. D. Townsend, page 632 and 633, accessed 6 December 2006.
[423] CLNN, Journal of the House, April 9, 1864, page 507, accessed 14 December 2006.
[424] NARA, Records Group 233, Miscellaneous Papers, 43rd Congress, Accompanying Papers, Sothern, J.H.

(Copy)
Leonardtown Oct 4th 1865
To General Fullerton
Dear Sir

I was incidentally mentioned between us in our conversation relative to the real Estate to be restored to Mrs. Elizabeth Sothoron & her children, that the United States had put some improvements on the farms, which might be taken account of, with a view to the reimbursement of the Government

I beg leave to say that when the family was ousted by military authority, there was left behind a most sumptuously furnished house & Estate, with far more than was necessary for their comfort & much to be spared for the cedatives & now, without the generous indisposition of the Government, they will reoccupy, without a bed to sleep on, an ear of corn, a mulch cow, or a pound of meat, except by the charity of their friends, & neighbors, the personality & crops, then might with justice be left them for their use, and I beg leave to say that the family will at any time, immediately, if deemed proper, enter into a settlement for any real improvements that the Government may have put upon the Estate.

They do not desire the government should lose one cent on account of any improvements they may have put on the property. I however beg leave to say that they suppose that while the Government does not desire to lose, (and it is proper that they should not) any thing by this property, that they also suppose the Government does not desire to make any thing, except what they may have made by the cultivation of the farm. That nothing would give the wife & children greater pleasure than to Enter into & investigation & account with the Government, In which account the Estate may be charged with real improvements put there by the Government, & at the same time credited with the amount and value of the personal property crops & c. taken from the farm & used there by the government, That the family are perfectly willing that the investigation should be made by some Government agent, the Evidence reduced to writing & laid before the Department. That the account by made out on the principles of impartial justice, such as should govern individuals, in their transactions with each other & should characterize a great Government in its transactions with its own citizens. The undersigned only mentions this, as the subject was incidentally mentioned at our late interview & not as keeping the matter of the settlement of the account at this time.

That the undersigned hopes that nothing will impede the issue of the order for the restitution of the farms, as a shelter in the coming winter to a helpless and very destitute woman and children and only wishes this for fear that some obstacle may be prevented on account of some claim of the Government may have for improvements. I have the honor to be most Respectfully yrs H G S Key

Rather than having improved Colonel Sothoron's farm, the Union army removed items from it, including buildings.

Prom the same National Archives file, a letter from Mrs. Sothoron to President Andrew Johnson is found. The letter appears to have been received on 9 September 1865 and turned over to President Johnson's military secretary:

To his Excellency
President Johnson,
Sir

Suffer me to impose upon your notice in behalf of myself and my seven suffering, innocent and unoffending children. I have observed you magnanimous pardon to prominent Rebels in the Border States, the Army, and Navy and amnesty to all. I see reason why the same should be denied me and my helpless family. My husband has never held a position in the rebel service. I therefore Mr. President implore your mercy and justice. For months I was guarded by the military, a part of the time held as a prisoner in my own house. I received all kinds of taunts and indignities, was not allowed even the necessaries of life. I lived upon the bounty of my neighbors. Knowing there was no cause for deserting my home and having none other to seek, I bore all uncomplainingly, before being ordered to leave, my servants were all taken and in mid winter I was left without a living soul to provide me even a stick of wood, but for the timely succor of friends I know not what would have been my fate. Every thing has been taken from me to give you all the particulars would be beyond the limits of a letter. For nearly two years I have been a homeless wanderer without means of support, y children scattered and living upon the charity of the world and my life a living death. I have friend to whom I can apply for aid in this my hour of need and great destitution. I now crave Mr. President your clemency and humbly ask the restoration of my home and property & you will ever have the grateful thanks and prayers of a miserable & suffering woman. I have always been unerring & do now faithfully promise to abide by and sustain the government. Praying this may meet your approval & sanction. May God in Heaven bless you, very respectfully

  E.M. Sothoron

No reply has been found to the above letter.

  Mrs. Sothoron was allowed to return to The Plains on 27 February 1866.[425] Barnes Compton, the son-in-law of Colonel and Mrs. Sothoron had written to President Andrew Johnson on behalf of his Sothoron relatives. His letter, from the National Archives file, had a date of 15 February 1866. In the letter, he indicated that the return of The Plains had been ordered by President Johnson five months previously. The letter also indicates that the Sothoron children were living in different places.[426] The letter was endorsed by General Grant and he recommended that the estate be restored on 10 March because that date was projected by General Fullerton as achievable.[427]

  On 19 February 1866 President Johnson also endorsed the letter: The first endorsement was from General Grant who ordered General Oliver O. Howard to return the Sothoron property unless there was some "reason" to keep it. President Andrew Johnson then signed it and Ketcham signed it below.[428] When congress had passed the bill to pay compensation to James F. Sothoron for the damages to The Plains from the War of 1812, Andrew Johnson had been a representative in Congress. Taught by his wife how to read and write. Andrew Johnson was a President who courageously met the responsibilities of his office.

  On 3 March 1865 the United States Congress enacted legislation titled "An Act to establish a Bureau for the Relief of Freedmen and Refugees." The bureau was to cease to exist one year after the cease of the present war of rebellion". The bureau also was assigned the responsibility for abandoned lands. It was to be led by a commissioner appointed by the President with the "advice and consent" of the Senate. The bureau could distribute ford, clothing and fuel. It was also empowered to give "temporary shelter". The legislation established the sharecropper tenant farm system. After three years of paying rent, 40 acres of property could be purchased by the lessee.[429] Because The Plains had not been abandoned, it was to be returned to its rightful owners.

  General Howard, chief of the Bureau of Refugees, Freedmen and Abandoned Lands, then issued an order for the restoration of The Plains to the Sothoron family:[430]

---

[425] Hammett, page 150.
[426] *NARA*, Records Group 105, Records of the Bureau of Refugees, Freedman and Abandoned Lands, Headquarters Office, Washington.
[427] *The Papers of Ulysses S. Grant, Volume 16: 1866*, page 462.
[428] *NARA*, M345, Microfilm 253.
[429] *CLNN*, Statutes at Large, 38th Congress, 2nd Session, pages 507 to 509.
[430] *NARA*, M345, Microfilm 253.

>War Department
>Bureau of Refugees, Freedmen and Abandoned Lands,
>Washington, February 21st, 1866
>
>Special Orders}
>In accordance with instructions from the President of the United States the property of John H. Sothoron situated in Saint Mary's Co. Md. will be turned over immediately to the claimants thereof proper care being taken to secure the public property on the place and provisions being made elsewhere for any indigent Freedmen now resident on the estate.
>By order of Major General O.O. Howard Commanding
>Signed Max Woodhull
>Assistant Adjutant. General
>Official
>A.P. Ketcham
>Acting Assistant Adjutant General

It is not known where the Freedmen were moved to, but the order gave about six days for the army to arrange for Mrs. Sothoron to return to The Plains. Another date given for the restoration of The Plains to Mrs. Sothoron is May of 1866, as stated in a Congressional Report of 1874.

Coincidentally, Mrs. Mosby, the wife of Colonel John Singleton Mosby had seen President Johnson around that time. She obtained a parole document signed by General Grant on 4 February 1866 for her husband.[431] In Saint Mary's County, there was resentment and violence directed towards the now free Blacks who occupied The Plains under the auspices of the Freedmen's Bureau. A letter was written by Lieutenant Edward F. O'Brien about three week prior to Mrs. Sothoron returning to The Plains.[432] He was in charge of The Plains and the letter concerned the maltreatment and assault of a discharged Black soldier. The victim of the assault, Isaac Barbour, had served with the 30th Regiment of the United States Colored Troops which had been organized at Camp Stanton in Benedict during 1864. His name does not appear in the Census of 1870 for Saint Mary's County. It is likely that he left the area because of abusive acts against him. Also, he may have no longer had a home when the Quartermaster Corps returned The Plains to the Sothoron family.

Some of the free Blacks at The Plains may have remained there until May of 1866 to process the tobacco crop from the previous year. The following letter is from the Accompanying Papers File of John H. Sothoron from the 43rd Congress:[433]

>Copy
>Headquarters, U.S. Government Farms.
>Charlotte Hall, St Mary's County Maryland.
>February 25th 1866
>Lieutenant S.A. Clark
>Assistant Acting Adjutant General
>Lieut. (Extract)
>
>Since the receipt of your first notification I have strained every man to accomplish removal from this farm.
>
>I shall have removed, tomorrow, all the people except those who are to care for, and strip the

---

[431] Jones, *Ranger Mosby*, pages 278-279.
[432] Berlin, Reidy and Rowland, *Freedom, A Documentary History of Emancipation, 1861-1867*, pages 802-804.
[433] *NARA*, Record Group 233, Accompanying Papers File of John H. Sothoron from the 43rd Congress.

tobacco. The school house and barrack are already torn down and ready for transportation.

Yesterday I removed many tons of manure, some corn &c. Tomorrow morning I begin removing my Head Qrs. and shall be ready to give up the occupancy of the mansion house the day after (27th instant)

To do all this I have pressed into service, the lighter, (on which the file drawer was placed) the 2 confiscated and a number of borrowed boats, and worked the people unremittingly, even this Sabbath day. Requiring the help of the lighter and boats I can do about double what I can by wagon hauling, and shall be able to get everything off sooner that I expected. The teams are also kept hauling.

I shall have the barracks at the Sand Gates in a few days.

On the 28th inst. Lieut. Purdy will be ready to turn over the "Sothoron Estate" and take receipt therefore in my name. After 28th inst. please direct communication to "Leonardtown".

I am Lieutenant,
Very Respectfully,
Your Obedient Servant,
(Signed) Edward F. O'Brien
1st Lieutenant Veterans Reserve Corps Superintendent & etcetera

This letter reveals the final looting of The Plains, along with the possibility that boats used to transport stolen movable property were also stolen. Furthermore, the extent of the confiscation of riverfront plantations is also shown. In addition to The Plains, the Forrest, Coles and Sand Gates (Sandgate) plantations were also confiscated, probably by Colonel Birney in 1863. O'Brien moved a barrack building, which is a house for military personnel, from The Plains to Sandgate, located farther down the Patuxent River.

However, Lieutenant O'Brien was accused of stealing money from the sale of items from The Plains.[434] The fact that he mentioned a "file drawer" in intriguing, because one of the charges against him were that on 18 April 1866 he refused to turn over to Captain E. B. Gates the files for the "government farms". He was also accused of stealing from neighborhood forms in the vicinity of The Plains. The last page of the charges lists 36 witnesses.

※ ※ ※

On 16 April 1865, the day after President Lincoln died from the wounds of his assassination, Secretary of War Stanton issued an order by direction of the President. He ordered General Gordon at Norfolk, Virginia "that the confiscation sales be postponed indefinitely". The reason given was so that the Freedmen's Bureau could be organized.[435] However, it may be that President Johnson took immediate action to halt the Union army from confiscation sales because the sales would inhibit peace and reconstruction. It was a complete reversal of policy.

On 20 August 1866 President Andrew Johnson made a proclamation in which he declared the "insurrection" was ended. In the same proclamation, Johnson said that "standing armies, military occupation, martial law, military tribunals and the suspension of the writ of habeas corpus" were threats to liberty, commerce and individual rights is times of peace but needed during invasion, rebellion or insurrection.[436] The Civil War began by proclamation and ended by proclamation. The effect of Johnson's proclamation was to end the possibility that Colonel Sothoron would be tried by a military tribunal.

---

[434] *NARA*, Records of the Freedman's Bureau, M1055, Microfilm 21, frames 0664 to 0674.
[435] *OR*, Series 1, Volume 46, Part III, 1895, April 16, 1865, Edwin M. Stanton to General Gordon, page 799, accessed 6 December 2006.
[436] *CLNN*, Statutes at Large, Appendix, August 20, 1866, Proclamation 4, page 814 to 817, accessed 14 December 2006.

After the war Colonel Sothoron went to Canada. It is probable that he returned after President Johnson's proclamation ending the conflict. In November of 1866 he was indicted by the Grand Jury of Saint Mary's County because of the death of Lieutenant White. The Presentment of the Grand Jury dated 24 November 1866 is as follows:[437]

> November Term 1866
> State of Maryland Saint Mary's County to wit
> The Grand Jurors for the body of Saint Mary's County do upon their oath present John H. Sothoron for killing Eben White on or about the twenty first of October eighteen hundred and sixty three on the evidence of Miss Mary Sothoron
> John C. Herbert
> Foreman

It is remarkable that Mary Sothoron was the person providing the evidence against Colonel Sothoron. Colonel Sothoron may have wanted the issue of him shooting Lieutenant White resolved so that he could legalize his return to Saint Mary's County.

The Indictment dated 27 November 1866 is as follows:[438]

> State of Maryland
> Saint Mary's County to wit the Grand Jurors of the State of Maryland for the body of Saint Mary's County on their oaths present, that John H. Sothoron, late of said County and said State (farmer) on the twenty first day of October in the year of our Lord eighteen hundred and sixty three, with force and arms at the County aforesaid, in and upon one Eben White in the peace of God and the said state then and there being, an officer in the Army of the United States fulminous and willfully did make an assault; and that the said John H. Sothoron, a certain <u>shotgun</u> of the value of ten dollars, then and there loaded and charged with gunpowder and leaden shot, which said gun, loaded and charged as aforesaid, he the said John H. Sothoron, in both his hands then and there had and held, to, against and upon the said Eben White, then and there fulminous and willfully did shoot and discharge, and that the said John H. Sothoron with leaden shot aforesaid, out of the gun aforesaid, then and there by force of the gunpowder shot and sent forth aforesaid, the said Eben White, in and upon the front parts of the head, neck and body of him the said Eben White, then and there fulminously and willfully did strike, puncture and wound, thereby giving to the said Eben White, then and there, with the leaden shot aforesaid, so as aforesaid shot, discharged and sent forth out of the gun aforesaid, by the said John H. Sothoron in and upon the front parts of the head, neck and body of him the said Eben White three mortal wounds of the depth of three inches, <u>each</u> of which said mortal wounds, the said Eben White then and there instantly died; and so the Grand Jurors aforesaid upon their oaths aforesaid do say, that the said John H. Sothoron the said Eben White in manner and form aforesaid, fulminously and willfully did kill, contrary to the acts of Assembly, in such cases Made and provided, and against the peace Government and dignity of the State of Maryland
> James T. Blakistone
> States Attorney for
> Saint Mary's County

It appears that Blakistone, the writer of the above, was actually using the word fulminous which is defined as of

---

[437] *MSA*, Saint Mary's County Grand Jury Papers, SM 1602, 1866, November term (MSA: 20,280-11, Location 1/57/7/28).
[438] *MSA*, Saint Mary's County Grand Jury Papers, SM 1602, 1866, November term (MSA: 20, 280-11, Location 1/57/7/28)

or pertaining to thunder and lightning or violently denunciatory. Fulminate was the chemical used in percussion caps which ignited the gunpowder of Civil War era firearms.

The Thursday 29 November 1866 issue of the *Saint Mary's Gazette* gave the result of the case of State vs. John H. Sothoron. Colonel Sothoron was indicted for manslaughter. The trial was by jury and the verdict was not guilty. Blakistone was the attorney for the State of Maryland. Thomas, Ford and Stone were the attorneys for the defense of Colonel Sothoron. Blakistone was most likely the James T. Blackiston who had been "unnecessarily" arrested by the Union authorities three or four years earlier.[439]

The verdict of not guilty vindicated Colonel Sothoron and allowed his free presence in Saint Mary's County. One of the three attorneys representing Colonel Sothoron was probably John Lewis Thomas, Jr., who later represented him for his claim against the Quartermaster Corps of the United States army. It may be that one of the three was Frederick Stone, an attorney from Charles County who also was a congressman. Stone had been the associate counsel for David E. Herod, an accessory in the assassination of Lincoln and the chief counsel for Dr. Samuel A. Mudd.[440]

Col. Sothoron had other legal problems. A newspaper advertised the sale of his farm. The sale was to satisfy a lawsuit by Walter Mitchell against Colonel Sothoron.[441] Apparently The Plains was not sold because Colonel Sothoron still owned it up until his death in 1893.

---

[439] *OR*, Series 2 Volume 2, 1897, January 31, 1862, A. V. Colburn to Joseph Hooker, page 201, accessed 6 December 2006.
[440] *The Washington Post*, October 18, 1899, article "Death of Judge Fred Stone", page 9, accessed 10 December 2006.
[441] Wearmouth, *Abstracts from the Port Tobacco Times and the Charles County Advertiser, Vol. II, 1855-1869*, page 160.

Chapter 8

THE CLAIM AGAINST THE QUARTERMASTER CORPS

On 4 July 1864, Congress passed legislation compensating "loyal citizens" for property seized and occupied during the Civil War. The legislation was titled "An Act to restrict the Jurisdiction of the Court of Claims, and to provide for the Payment of certain Demands for Quartermasters' Stores and Subsistence Supplies furnished to the Army of the United States."

The legislation removed the Court of Claims from hearing cases of claims about property destroyed or taken by the United States Army or Navy. The claimant had to be loyal and not from a state in rebellion.[442] This was the legislation under which Colonel Sothoron filed his claim. However, his loyalty was an issue.

John Lewis Thomas, Jr. was the attorney who filed the claim of Colonel Sothoron against the Quartermaster's Corps. Thomas had been a member of the House of Representatives from 1865 to 1867. He was elected as an Unconditional Unionist and lost reelection when he became a Republican.[443] Colonel Sothoron had an attorney who had been elected to Congress as an Unconditional Unionist and later ran as a Republican to represent him for the claim.

The claim amounted to $98,638 against the United States army Quartermaster Corps for losses and damages sustained to The Plains during the war. The following is a letter from the National Archives file for the claim to Secretary of War Stanton from John L. Thomas:

Baltimore Feb 6/68
Hon. E. M. Stanton
Secretary of War
Dear Sir
Sometime in the latter part of the year 1863 the Government troops took possession of the Plantation of Colonel John H. Sothoron of Saint Mary's County in this State, located on the Patuxent River. The Government troops remained in the possession of Colonel Sothoron's plantation from Nov. 1863 m. l. to May 1866 and during that time foraged immense quantities or numbers of Government horses and cattle and other stock on his farms - took possession and sold all of his growing crops including Tobacco, wheat, corn, hay, straw and other provender, besides cutting off and using an immense quantity of wood and timber, destroying a large amount of property, including Barnes outhouses & c, taking away and selling his household and other furniture - We have so far succeeded in tracing the sales of about 59 hogsheads of tobacco taken from his plantations and sold in January 1865 by Colonel R.M. Newport (then Q.M. at Baltimore) to W.W. Berry for and on account James M. Brown, then Q.M. for the District in which his farm is located, but at present Q.M. in the Freedman's Bureau - This Tobacco brought

---

[442] *Appendix to the Congressional Globe*, 38th Congress, 1st Session, July 4, 1864, page 258, accessed 6 December 2006.
[443] *Biographical Directory of the United States Congress, 1774-1989*, page 1928.

5,228.27, also the sale of another lot of Tobacco July 19, 1865 by order of Colonel R.M. Newport of 22 hogsheads of Tobacco sold to & Wilkins for $680.50 and supposed to be per order of said Brown.

We are satisfied that some 1500 bushels of wheat and 1500 bushels of corn besides other provender was taken and sold during the time our troops were in the occupancy of his plantations.

You will do me an especial favor as the counsel of Colonel Sothoron to furnish me with the following information:

1. The number of Hogsheads of Tobacco taken and sold by the Government during or after its occupancy by the government - The price it was sold for, and whether the proceeds have been turned over to the War or Treasury Departments.

2. The number of bushels of Wheat and the number of bushels of Corn taken and sold by the Government - what part of the same was sold and what part was used or turned over the Q.M. Department and the value of the same.

3. The number of cords of wood and the value of the same taken and used by the Government.

4. What disposition was made of his furniture, What part was sold and for how much and whether the proceeds were turned over to the War Dept. or Treasury.

5. Also an account of the number of horses, mules cattle hogs and other stock, including poultry taken and used for the Q.M. department for the same period.

6. Also an account of the number and value of Wheat machines, thrashing machines - ploughs, harrows - cultivators hoes and axes and other farming implements - boats and seines taken and used by the Q.M. Dept. for the same period.

7. Also a copy of any order from the War Department or any General in command of U.S. Troops at the time directing the seizure and sale of any or all the above enumerated items. Our object in asking for this information is to apply for relief and payment of the losses sustained by Col Sothoron in the seizure and sale of said property Maryland being a loyal state - the Confiscation Act of Congress could not in any way apply to any other citizens, not in rebellion, or to any property in its limits not used for insurrectionary purposes. I am satisfied from your honorable and upright character - your reputation as a lawyer and your goodness of heart that you will not refuse to give us the information we seek in relation to this property which if wrongly taken would tend to vindicate the bona fides of the officers employed in the transaction.

I would suggest that Col James H. Brown, at present in the Q.M. Department (Freedman's Bureau) can furnish much of the information asked for in this communication, especially in relation to the Tobacco.

Very Respectfully
Your Obedient Servant
John L Thomas Jr.
Late MC from MD

Colonel R. M. Newport was the chief of the Quartermaster depot in Baltimore. He assumed the position on 24 September 1864 from Major C. W. Thomas.[444]

The list of items taken from The Plains is revealing. Besides taking movable property, the Union army also attacked the ecology of the plantation. An immense quantity of timber (i.e. trees) were cut down and taken. The problem of cutting down trees is that the ability of the soil in the forest and surrounding fields is negatively affected. Erosion of soil used for farming crops which becomes food to sustain humans occurs. The forest was inhabited by animals, which were also food for humans. A question remains as to who the Union army

---

[444] *OR*, Series 3, Volume 5, 1900, November 8, 1865, M. C. Meigs to Hon. Edwin M. Stanton, report from page 212 to 249, page 219 accessed 6 December 2006.

exploited to cut down the trees. Who were the tree cutters? Former slaves? Confederate prisoners of war? Political prisoners?

The date of the filing of the claim, 6 February 1868, is significant. President Johnson had survived a vote to be tried for impeachment on 7 December 1867. However, after the claim was filed, Congress voted again to try him for impeachment on 24 February 1868 and the motion passed.[445]

The political atmosphere in Washington, D.C. in February of 1868 was filled with turmoil. On 5 February 1868 the front page of *The New York Times* carried a headline with an article relating that President Johnson had directed General Grant to disregard Secretary of War Stanton. *The New York Times* front page headline of 22 February 1868 reported the removal of Secretary of War Stanton and the appointment of Adjutant General Lorenzo Thomas as Secretary ad interim. Then, *The New York Times* of 23 February 1868 reported the arrest of Adjutant General Thomas as being caused by Secretary Stanton. Finally, *The New York Times* of 28 February 1868 reported that General Thomas was suing Secretary Stanton for $150,000 in damages.

The claim may have been filed during that time because of a perception that a more favorable political climate was emerging in Washington, D.C. Edwin M. Stanton, the Secretary of War under Presidents Lincoln and Johnson, had refused to resign. Secretary of War Stanton said that it would take armed troops to remove him from office. He finally did resign on 26 May 1868. Stanton died in 1869.[446]

On 10 March 1868, a report was received by General Grant from Major General Oliver O. Howard about the activities of Colonel John S. Mosby in Virginia and Maryland. Colonel Mosby was in Baltimore, Maryland for seven days in the first half of February of 1868.[447] John L. Thomas wrote the letter filing the claim for Colonel Sothoron from Baltimore around the same time that Colonel Mosby was in the city. Mosby was under surveillance by government agents.

Within the next year, General Grant would be elected President of the United States. General Grant's wife, Julia Boggs (nee Dent) Grant had ancestry from Saint Mary's County, Maryland. She was a descendant of Thomas Dent who settled in Maryland in the 17th century. Mrs. Grant stated in her memoirs that her ancestors were three brothers who came to Maryland in 1643.[448]

A letter responding to most of the issues raised by John L. Thomas from James M. Brown is within the Archives file:

Washington D.C. February 24th 1868
Brevet Brigadier General B. Whittlesey
Acting Assistant Adjutant General
General,
    I have the honor to submit the following being all the facts in my possession on a request of Hon. John L. Thomas Jr. counsel for Col John H. Sothoron dated Baltimore Feb 6, 1868 directed to Hon. E.M. Stanton, Secretary of War referred by the Quartermaster General there the Commissioner to furnish "all the information in my possession relative to the occupation, seizure and sale of property belonging to Col Sothoron Saint Mary's County Md.
    I know nothing of the alleged occupation of Col Sothoron's property by Government troops in November 1863.
    I have been informed, that the farm of Col Sothoron being one of the Government Farms (so called comprising the John H. Sothoron Joseph Forrest and Cole farms which had been used (how long I

---

[445] *Burke's Presidential Families of the United States of America*, page 312-313.
[446] Sifakis, pages 616-617.
[447] Simon, *The Papers of Ulysses S. Grant, Volume 18, October 1, 1867 to June 30, 1868*, pages 524-525.
[448] Grant, *The Personal Memoirs of Julia Dent Grant*, page 40.

cannot state) as a place of refuge for Freedmen, were in the summer of 1864 by a change in the limits of the military Department of Washington included in this Department. In November 1864 (one year after the alleged occupation by the government troops) the supervision of these farms was given to me. My office and duty as a Captain and A.Q.M. being in Washington D.C. Lieutenant E.F. O'Brien then and late an Officer of the Veteran Reserve Corps was at this time placed by the Commanding General in immediate charge as Superintendent of the farms.

At this date (November 1864) there were on the (3) farms about (500) Five Hundred Freedmen mostly women and children supported by the Government a portion being employed in cultivating land.

On the upper or Sothoron farm there were 40,000 forty thousand pounds estimated of Tobacco. I was informed that this Tobacco had been shipped some time before to Point Lookout and reshipped to the farm by whom I never learned.

There was no household furniture on either of the farms. A small number of horses, cattle and wagons used in cultivating the farms were property of the United States Quartermaster's Department.

There were bills then due for farm implements purchased early in the season. I directed the Tobacco, 60 Hogsheads, which was liable to be destroyed by fire to be packed and shipped to Baltimore for sale at public auction, in accordance with the orders of the Department Commissioner dated Washington D.C. November 15, 1864 (copy herewith).

Statement of Sale
530 lbs 1 Hogshead Tobacco @ 13.25 per 100 lbs $70.22
41100 lbs 59 do @ 12.55 "100" 5158.05
149 lbs beef hides @ 13.50c per lb 20.12
11 lbs calf hides @ 11 5/lic per lb 1.27
dollars 5249.66
Auctioneers Commissions $264.45
Advertising in "American" $4.80, in "Wecker" $4.37 in
"Clipper" $3.75 275.37
*probably the hides of slaughtered government cattle $4974.29 The proceeds of sale will be found properly accounted for on my Account Current for the month of January 1865.

The sale of (22) twenty two Hogsheads of Tobacco referred to in the letter of Mr. Thomas were packed and shipped by Lieutenant E.F. O'Brien from Government Farms to Baltimore in July 1865 and sold by public auction in accordance with authority given.

Statement of Sale
22 Hogsheads Tobacco 13610 pounds 5 per 100 lbs $680.50
auctioneers Commissions $34
Advertising in "Clipper" $2.00 "American" 2.50 "Wecker" $2.25
40.75
$639.35

The proceeds of sale will be found properly accounted for on my Account Current for the month of July 1865. - what portion of these two lots (60 and 22 Hogsheads of Tobacco) were raised by Col Sothoron I have no means of ascertaining.

To the 1st 2nd 3rd 5th & 6th enquiries proposed by Mr. Thomas I have and can give no information except as above.

During the time Lieutenant O'Brien was in charge of the Farms cultivated by Freedman supported by the Government no separate or distinct returns were made with Sothoron, Forrest or Coles farms in fact they were known only as Government farms, embracing the (3) three articles were accounted for on the returns of Lieutenant O'Brien as property "Government Farms".

To the 4th enquiry I have no knowledge whatever except as before stated of the sale or other disposition of the household furniture, horses, cattle, farm implements, or any other articles belonging to the Sothoron estate.

To the 7th Enquiry, I have given the only order in my possession in reference to the subject.
Very Respectfully
Your Obedient Servant
J.M. Brown
late Captain & Acting Quartermaster

An intriguing aspect of the letter is the statement that the tobacco had been shipped to Point Lookout and then returned to the farm. It may be that Point Lookout was to be used as a shipment area and that the prisoners were to be used to process and pack the tobacco. Point Lookout was a Union prisoner of war camp for Confederate soldiers and civilian sympathizers. Also located at Point Lookout were a military hospital and a fort. Point Lookout was officially known as Camp Hoffman but in most records it is referred to as Point Lookout.[449]

The statement in Brown's letter that there were bills due for "farm implements purchased" deserves special attention. Union army records document the theft of farm implements from Virginia by army officers Draper and O'Brien. It may be that O'Brien was also illegally submitting false bills to the Quartermaster Corps for farm implements he stole on raids into Virginia.

A copy of the 1864 letter, which Capitan Brown referred to in his letter to Whittlesey, ordering the sale of movable property from The Plains is included the Archives file:

Head Quarters Department of Washington
22nd Army Corps
Washington, DC. Nov: 15, 1864
Capt J.M. Brown Acting Quarter Master
in charge of Bureau of Freedmen and Government Farms
Captain:
    The Major General Commanding directs in accordance with instructions from the War Department that the necessary clothing be provided to the contrabands on the farms in your charge and the requisite repairs be made to their quarters, that the specified property recommended by you to be sold. be so disposed of, and for the purposes indicated; that the unpaid bills for articles "used during the season" be liquidated; that the wages due contrabands from July 1st to Oct 31st inclusive be paid; that twenty five ($25) dollars be paid Mrs. Shaw for the rent of her farm, and that the requisite repairs be made to place in operation the steam saw and grist mill. These expenditures are to be made from funds accruing by sale of Crops from the farms. The guard will be increased as recommended and a Commissioned Officer of the V.R.C. will be ordered to report to you to take charge of the farms under your direction on the Patuxent River.
I am Captain
Very Respectfully
Your Most Obedient Servant
(signed) J.H. Taylor
Chief of Staff A.A.G.
L. B. 434
a true copy
J. A. Fladeu

---

[449] Manakee, page 88-89.

(1ˢᵗ Lieutenant) Acting Capt 26 infantry

"Contrabands" was the word used by the Union army to describe former slaves who had fled plantations and sought refuge within Union lines. The date of the above letter is significant. Congress did not enact legislation for the Bureau of Freedmen until March of 1865, later than the letter was written. The anachronism "V.R.C." represents the Veteran's Reserve Corps which was for disabled soldiers to continue service in a non-combat status.[450] The providing of clothing, wages and shelter to the contrabands possibly represents one of the first known uses of federal funds for the support and welfare of non-military persons. Again, the issue of illegal false billing appears in this letter.

On 4 July 1868, President Johnson made a proclamation giving full pardon and amnesty to Confederates who were accused of treason and other felonies with the right to restoration of property except for two categories. First, slaves could not be returned to their owners. The second category was "any property of which any person may have been legally divested under the laws of the United States."[451] Because of the lack of a condemnation proceeding in a court of law, as required by both of the two confiscation acts of Congress, the legal basis for the Union army occupation of and theft of movable property from The Plains was nonexistent.

Another letter in the National Archives claim file is from an "agent" in the Quartermaster Corps of Baltimore and is humorous in regard to the portrayal of Colonel Sothoron's loyalty:

Office Deputy Q.M. General
Baltimore, Maryland
July 30, 1868
Brevet Major General
Stewart Van Vliet
Deputy Q.M. General U.S.A.
General

With reference to the case of Col John H. Sothoron of Saint Mary's Co. Maryland, referred to this Office for investigation by the Q.M. General, by letter dated February 27, 1868. I have the honor to submit for your consideration the following statement.

That there is not on file in this office any record, to show that there was ever any thing coming from the farm of Col Sothoron, sold in this City, for and on account of the United States.

Mr. Thomas of the firm Adreou, Thomas & Co., Auctioneers in this City, stated to me, that his firm in 1864 and 1865 sold in the City of Baltimore by direction of Col R.M. Newport U.S.Q.M. for and on account of Capt J.M. Brown A.Q.M. stationed in Saint Mary's Co., some 60 or 70 hogsheads of tobacco, and that the a/c sales contained in the report of Capt Brown accompanying these papers, are correct. He also further stated, that he remembers of having heard at that time, that many of the articles taken from Col Sothoron's farm were shipped to New York and sold there but that neither he or any other Auctioneer in this City ever sold during the war or since its close for and on account of the U. States any other article coming from the farm of Col Sothoron was the tobacco above referred to.

With regard to the "loyalty" of Col Sothoron there seems to be in the community in which he resides but one opinion, and that is "that he was thoroughly Southern in his feelings during the entire war". Colonel J.M. Blakistone, stated to me in Leonardtown, "that he as U.S. Prosecuting Attorney, had Col Sothoron indicted and tried before the Civil Court of Saint Mary's Co. Md. for the 'murder' of Lieutenant E.F. O'Brien U.S.A. and that he was acquitted by the said court on the ground of 'justifiable Homicide' - and that immediately after the rendition of the verdict, Colonel Sothoron went South and

---

[450] Boatner, page 870.
[451] Statutes at Large, 40ᵗʰ Congress, Appendix, Proclamation No. 6, pages 702 and 703, accessed 14 December 2006.

> remained there during the entire war."
> I am
> General
> very respectfully
> your obedient servant
> Th. P. Chiffelle
> Agent

The letter mistakenly identifies the shooting victim as Lieutenant O'Brien and states the Colonel Sothoron went south after the "verdict" rather than the shooting incident. James T. Blackiston (also spelled Blakistone) had been falsely arrested by the Union authorities. In a report of 31 January 1862, A. V. Colburn wrote to Brigadier General Joseph Hooker that Blackiston, of Leonardtown, had been "unnecessarily arrested" and subsequently released.[452]

The shipping of articles to New York and their sale occurred prior to the Quartermaster Corps occupation of The Plains. The interior paneling of The Plains was removed by Union troops.[453] The person to whom the letter was addressed, Stewart Van Vliet, was stationed in New York City with the Quartermaster Corps during the time of the removal of items from The Plains.[454] It is possible that the Quartermaster Corps in New York City may have acted in the capacity of a dealer for the stolen items looted from The Plains.

There may have been a concern among the neighbors of Colonel Sothoron that the plantation house would be completely destroyed by the occupying Union troops. The following was written by Lieutenant O'Brien:[455]

> The small farms of the Forrest Estate occupied by the various tenants were taken possession of as a part and parcel of Joseph Forrest's' Estate after he had abandoned them.
>
> Some of them are occupied by Freedmen and some by Loyal Union men.
>
> No data nor authentic record can be found of the property. And in all cases where I have found men occupying any portion of the estate and were inimical to the Government of the U.S., I have ejected them, taking possession thereof of all I found and which could be proven as belonging to the Estate of Joseph Forrest
>
> I have caused repairs to be made on the various buildings of the farms and would respectfully suggest that while the property remains in the possession of the U.S. that the tenants be allowed to receive pay in some Shape for what improvements they make.
>
> The Sothoron property was abandoned by the Sothoron family, the afternoon of the murder of Lieut. White, leaving behind them their people, telling them that farming must stop now and that they could leave. The day following some of the neighbors removed the furniture across Burroughs Creek to the house of Dr. Thomas when the family had fled to while Colonel Sothoron and his son Webster were conveyed by Thomas' carriage away, reaching the city of Richmond eight days later.
>
> Mrs. Sothoron has been in constant communication with the murderers of Lieutenant White, and is justly entitled to be considered as an accessory after the fact.
> Edward F. O'Brien
> 1st Lieutenant Veteran Reserve Corps

---

[452] *OR*, Series 2: Volume 2, 1897, January 31, 1862, A. V. Colburn to Joseph Hooker, page 201, accessed 6 December 2006.
[453] Forman, page 48.
[454] Boatner, page 867-868.
[455] *NARA*, Records of the Freedman's Bureau, M1055, Microfilm 17, frame 0395.

O'Brien made no mention of his theft from Virginians to replace the items looted by the Union army before he arrived at The Plains. He ignored the fact that Mrs. Sothoron and her children remained at The Plains for three months until their illegal eviction by the blackmail of Birney.

In May of 1873, eight documents from the claim file were removed and placed in the Auditors Office of Treasury Department for "safe-keeping". "Safe-keeping" was fascist propaganda terminology used during the Civil War by the Union army to imprison political prisoners. In June of 1886 a thirteen page letter summarizing the claim was returned from the Treasury Department to the Quartermaster Corps. The envelope for the group of documents lists ten enclosures while the letter inside lists eight enclosures.

It appears that the claim remained in an inactive status up until February of 1874. Rather than attempt to have the Quartermaster Corps pay the claim, legislation was introduced to have Congress honor the claim. The following is from the *Congressional Record* of Monday, 16 February 1874:[456]

> John H. Sothoron
> Mr. Albert introduced a bill (H. R. No. 1975) for the relief of John H. Sotheron, of Saint Mary's County, Maryland; which was read a first and second time, referred to the Committee on War Claims, and ordered to be printed.

The hopes of Colonel Sothoron were now placed with Congress. The Representative who introduced the bill was William Julian Albert. He was a Republican and had worked against the secession of Maryland at the beginning of the Civil War.[457] From the National Archives, a copy of the proposed bill is as follows:[458]

> [Printer's No., 2023.
> 43d Congress,
> 1st Session H.R. 1975.
> IN THE HOUSE OF REPRESENTATIVES.
> February 16, 1874.
> Read twice, referred to the Committee on War Claims, and ordered to be printed. Mr. Albert, on leave, introduced the following bill:
> A BILL
> For the relief of John H. Sotheron, of Saint Mary's County, Maryland.
>
> > Be it enacted by the Senate and House of Representatives of the United States of America in Congress assembled. That the proper accounting officers of the Treasury be, and they are hereby, authorized and required to pay, out of any money in the Treasury not otherwise appropriated, to Colonel John H. Sothoron the sum of ninety-eight thousand six hundred and thirty-eight dollars, in full satisfaction for two hundred and forty thousand pounds of tobacco, one thousand five hundred bushels of corn, one thousand one hundred and fifty bushels of wheat, twenty-two head of horses and mules, sixty-four head of cattle, and other articles of personal property, more fully set forth in the schedule hereto attached marked A; also, for use and occupation of farming-lands, and so forth, appertaining thereon, situated in the above-named county and State, from November first, eighteen hundred and sixty-three, to May first, eighteen hundred and sixty-six, used as a home for freedmen, and so forth, as will appear from the schedule hereto attached marked A; all taken and used by the proper military authorities of the United States during the late war.

---

[456] *CLNN, Congressional Record*, House of Representatives, 43rd Congress, 1st Session, February 16, 1874, page 1524, accessed 14 December 2006.
[457] *Biographical Directory of the United States Congress, 1774-1989*, page 517.
[458] *NARA*, Record Group 233, H.R. 1975, February 16, 1874, 43rd Congress, 1st Session.

Based on information supplied by the American Tobacco Company, 240,000 pounds of tobacco would make 133,333,000 regular size cigarettes.

Col. Sothoron replaced John L. Thomas and retained different legal counsel. The day after the above legislation was introduced in the House of Representatives a letter was sent from a different law firm. This letter is from the National Archives claim file of the Quartermaster Corps:

Offices of Bartley & Jenner
Attorneys-At-Law
May Building, N.E. corner of 7th and E streets
T.W. Bartley L.E. Jenner
residence 216 I street residence 1520 G P1 N.W.
Washington D.C. February 17th, 1874
General M.C. Meigs
Q.M.G. U.S.A.
Washington D.C.
Sir
    We have the honor to request the return of the papers filed by us Dec 10/73 in the case of John H. Sothoron of Saint Mary's County Md.
Very respectfully your
Obedient Servants
Bartley & Jenner
of Attorneys for Sothoron

William Green, Colonel Sothoron's foreman and another person named John Dotson gave statements to Robert Lyon Rogers, a United States Commissioner on 18 March 1874. Both were former slaves of Colonel Sothoron. Their statements told of their being at the Sothoron farm during its occupation by the Union army and of the removal of goods from it. In addition, they identified the headquarters of Colonel Birney as being in Camp Stanton at Benedict. William Green stated that he was born on Colonel Sothoron's plantation while John Dotson said that he came there in 1832.[459] The arrival of John Dotson at The Plains in 1832 may have been a result of the Chancery Court proceeding during that year.

On 3 June 1874, Colonel Sothoron wrote a letter asking that Congress delay action on his case until the next term.[460]

Baltimore, Md. June 3, 1874
Hon William Lawrence
Chairman of the Committee of War Claims
House of Representatives, Wash. D.C.
Sir:
    Being convinced that this session of Congress is too near its close for me to expect to obtain relief by it — and acting upon the suggestion of my Attorney as well as several members of Congress. I have the honor to request that my case may be acted upon by your Honorable Committee at an early day with a view to its <u>being sent</u> to the <u>Court</u> of <u>Claims</u>.
    I most earnestly hope, that after a careful consideration of my case the committee will report

---

[459] *NARA*, Record Group 233, Miscellaneous papers, 43rd Congress, Accompanying Papers, John H. Sothern.
[460] *NARA*, Record Group 233, Miscellaneous papers, 43rd Congress, Accompanying Papers, John H. Sothern.

favorably — and grant me this privilege and report to the House giving me the enabling Act to go to said Court.
Very Respectfully,
Your Obedient Servant
John H. Sothoron

Because the legislation passed in 1864 prohibited the Court of Claims from hearing cases about military confiscation legislation to enable the claim being heard was needed.

In 1875 the claim was rejected by the Congressional Committee on War Claims. A "Letter from the Chief Clerk of the War Department" (Executive Document Number 281) had been printed and provided to the committee. The letter contained Colonel Birney's report of 19 December 1863, which was previously mentioned and had his statement and the report by Captain Weld along with the statement of the deceased Black soldier, John W. Bantum.

The letter also had the statement by W. W. Goldsborough, the captured Confederate army Major, which was given to Colonel Lafayette C. Baker, the head of the Union secret police. Incredibly, J. Holt, a Judge Advocate General, mistakenly identified W. W. Goldsborough as a slave of Colonel Sothoron. In the portion of the letter that he wrote, he was "without information as to the writer" of the statement (who was W. W. Goldsborough) but that "he is supposed to have been one of the slaves of John H. Sothoron".[461]

As a result of Executive Document Number 281, Report Number 47 was issued by the Committee of War Claims and recommended that the matter be tabled by the House of Representatives.[462] The following is from the *Congressional Record* of 8 January 1875:[463]

John H. Sothoron
Mr. Hazelton, of Wisconsin, from the same committee, reported back, with the recommendation that it do not pass the bill (H. R. No. 1975) for the relief of John H. Sothron, of Saint Mary's County, Maryland; which was laid on the table, and the accompanying report ordered to be printed.

Representative Gerry Whiting Hazelton had been a delegate to the Republican National Convention of 1860 where Abraham Lincoln was nominated for the election to be President. In 1866, Hazelton had been removed from his position as collector of internal revenue by President Andrew Johnson.[464]

The report that was ordered to be printed was Number 47. It stated that Colonel Sothoron was "notoriously and persistently disloyal to the Government during the war". The fact that Colonel Sothoron had been found innocent of the manslaughter of Lieutenant White by a jury in Maryland was not mentioned in either Executive Document Number 281 or in Report Number 47 of the Congressional Committee of War Claims.

The political atmosphere and the presence in Washington, D.C. of William Birney as prosecutor may have made consideration of pursuing the matter of the unpaid claim through the court system entirely impractical.[465] In addition, Hugh L. Bond, whose advocacy in 1863 probably had encouraged the Union army to engage in illegal actions in Maryland was a Judge with the 4th U.S. Circuit Court and later became a chief justice.

*   *   *

---

[461] *NARA*, Record Group 233, House Executive Document 281, 43rd Congress, 1st Session, June 12, 1874.
[462] *NARA*, Record Group 287.
[463] *CLNN, Congressional Record*, House of Representatives, 43rd Congress, 2nd Session, January 8, 1875, page 347.
[464] *Biographical Directory of the United States Congress, 1774-1989*, page 1162.
[465] *The Washington Post*, August 18, 1907, "Birney Reached Goal", page E1, accessed 10 December 2006.

In 1878, the *Record of the Services of the Seventh Regiment, U.S. Colored Troops from September, 1863 to November, 1866* was published. It was written by an anonymous and unidentified officer of the regiment. In the book, the anonymous author admitted to having committed illegal acts besides the recruitment of slaves. He made an admission of the taking of supplies from farmers in Maryland for military purposes. He stated that Colonel Birney rarely gave orders in writing. To add to the mystery of the final resting place of Lieutenant White, the anonymous author stated that his body was placed in a "vault" in Baltimore.[466]

In all, there were four regiments of the United States Colored Troops that were stationed or organized at Camp Stanton:

7th U.S.C.T. - organized at Baltimore from 26 September to 12 November 1863[467]
9th U.S.C.T. - organized at Camp Stanton 11 to 30 November 1863[468]
19th U.S.C.T. - organized at Camp Stanton 25 December 1863 to 16 January 1864 and sent to Camp Birney[469]
30th U.S.C.T. - organized at Camp Stanton 12 February to 18 March 1864[470]

Two of the above regiments, the 19th and the 30th, had participated in the Petersburg Mine Assault on 30 July 1864. Explosives had been detonated in a tunnel dug beneath the Confederate lines and Union forces suffered 3,798 casualties attempting to exploit the breach. Union General Grant called the assault "a stupendous failure".[471] The Union army called it the "Petersburg Mine Assault" while the Confederates called it "The Battle of the Crater".

Most of the soldiers of the above four regiments must have been former Maryland slaves. By their illegal recruitment into the Union army, their condition of slavery was changed into involuntary paid servitude with the possibility of death from disease or combat. However, at the end of the Civil War, the surviving members of the regiments did obtain their freedom by being discharged from the army. The regiments could have also had Black freemen within their ranks.

By late March of 1864, the recruiting and training camps for Black soldiers at Benedict had ceased their activities and moved on. On their march through Prince Georges County, a recruiting squad found an incarcerated slave allegedly owned by Colonel Sothoron. He was held in the county jail.[472] The departure of troops from Camp Stanton may have been a result of the communication from President Lincoln to Secretary of War Edwin Stanton on 18 March 1864.

Colonel William Birney was promoted to the rank of Brigadier General. On 11 June 1864, he presented a "memorial" to Congress to increase the pay of Black soldiers to thirteen dollars per month. His proposal referred to the Committee on Military Affairs.[473] Congress rewarded the vanguard of the quiet revolution with a pay raise retroactive to 1 January 1864 in an appropriations bill.[474]

---

[466] Anonymous, *Record of the Services of the Seventh Regiment, U.S. Colored Troops from September, 1863 to November, 1866*, pages 7-14.
[467] Dyer, *A Compendium of the War of Rebellion, Vol. III, Regimental Histories*, page 1724.
[468] Dyer, *ibid.*, page 1725.
[469] Dyer, *ibid.*, page 1726.
[470] Dyer, *ibid.*, page 1728.
[471] Boatner, pages 647-649.
[472] Berlin, Reidy and Rowland, *Freedom, A Documentary History of Emancipation, 1861-1867, Series II, The Black Military Experience*, page 217-219.
[473] *CLNN*, Journal of the House, page 121, accessed 14 December 2006.
[474] *CLNN*, Statutes at Large, 38th Congress, 1st Session, June 15, 1864, An Act making Appropriations for the Support of the Army for the Year ending the thirtieth of June, eighteen hundred and sixty-five, and for other Purposes, page 129, accessed 3 February 2007.

Chapter 9

AFTER THE CIVIL WAR

The Federal Census of 1870 for Saint Mary's County reflects the loss of personal property for Colonel Sothoron. He gave the value of his real estate as $40,000 and the value of his personal property as $1,500. His household composition is as follows:

Name	Age	Sex	Occupation	Birthplace
Sothoron, John H.	62	Male	Farmer	Maryland
Sothoron, Elizabeth	50	Female	Keeps House	Maryland
Sothoron, Mary E.	30	Female	at home	Maryland
Sothoron, Faney	18	Female	at home	Maryland
Sothoron, Amelia	17	Female	at home	Maryland
Sothoron, Hellen	15	Female	at home	Maryland
Sothoron, James F.	10	Male	at home	Maryland
Sothoron, Kate L.	8	Female	at home	Maryland
South, Mosses	30	Male	Farm Laborer	Maryland
Pilkinton, Benn	32	Male	Farm Laborer	Maryland
Huntington, Louis	17	Male	Farm Laborer	Maryland

The possibility of the three farm laborers listed above being the three sons of Colonel Sothoron (S. Webster Sothoron, Marshall Lyles Sothoron and Robert Bowie Sothoron) using aliases is entirely conceivable. Their ages approximately correspond to those of the three Sothoron sons. Given his covert activities during the Civil War, Webster Sothoron would have been a candidate for the hangman's noose if he had been discovered. Colonel Sothoron's other son, John H. Sothoron Jr., age 14, is listed in the census among classmates at Charlotte Hall Academy.[474]

An example of a person filing a will and in the process revealing an alias is found for Saint Mary's County in courthouse will records:[475]

Barnes, Thomas, alias Jordan   Feb. 1892   JBA 1 245

The name Thomas Jordan is of a Confederate spy. Thomas Jordan also used the name Thomas John Rayford.[476]

The Agricultural Census of 1870 of Colonel Sothoron's farm is as follows:

---

[474] page 632.
[475] *Maryland Index to the Wills of Saint Mary's County, 1662-1960*, page 6.
[476] Tidwell, Hall and Gaddy, pages 10, 67, 68-70, 73, 75.

Line 17, Sothoron, John H.

Improved acres of land	700
Acres of woodland	500
Cash value of farm	30,000
Value of farm implements and machinery	350
Wages paid during the year including board	1,500
Horses	6
Mules and asses	2
Mulch cows	10
Working oxen	2
Other cattle	14
Sheep	16
Swine	2
Value of all livestock	1,696
Winter wheat, bushels of	1,600
Indian corn, bushels of	2,500
Tobacco, lbs. of	1,400
Wool, lbs. of	50
Irish potatoes, bushels of	300
Sweet potatoes, bushels of	45
Butter, lbs. of	720
Value of animals slaughtered or sold for slaughter	461
Estimated value of all farm production	6,031

There are categories for other farm products similar to the 1860 census and there are no entries for them. The agricultural census clearly shows the decline in productivity due to the Civil War occupation of the farm.

The Census of 1880 for Saint Mary's County in the Fifth Election District reveals that Webster, Marshall and Robert Sothoron had returned to their father's household:

Name	Sex	Age	Relationship	Occupation
Sothoron, John H.	M	72		Farmer
E.M.	F	64	Wife	Keeps House
Mary E.	F	42	Daughter	
Webster	M	38	Son	
Marshall	M	34	Son	Laborer
Robert	M	32	Son	Laborer
Fannie	F	25	Daughter	
Amelia	F	22	Daughter	
Ellen	F	21	Daughter	
Kate	F	17	Daughter	School
James F.	M	20	Son	School

The marital status for all the above except John H. and E.M. (Elizabeth) Sothoron is single. The census also states that Colonel Sothoron's wife Elizabeth suffered front partial paralysis. John H. Sothoron, Jr., born in 1856, does not appear with his family.

The Agricultural Census for 1880 shows the following:

<u>Line 4, Sothoron, John H., Owner</u>

Acres of improved tilled land	180
Acres of permanent meadows	90
Acres of woodland and forest	150
Farm value	20,000
Value of farming implements and machinery	340
Value of live stock	1,300
Cost of building and repairing fences	40
Cost of fertilizers	160
Amount paid for wages	920
Weeks of hired labor	60
Estimated value of farm production	5,000
Horses	6
Mules and asses	2
Working oxen	6
Mulch cows	5
Other neat cattle	18
Cattle sold	2
Butter, pounds	260
Sheep and lambs	112
Lambs dropped	25
Purchased	1
Sold living	40
Slaughtered	15
Killed by dogs	6
Died of disease	4
Died of stress of weather	3
Fleeces	56
Weight of fleeces, pounds	275
Swine	35
Poultry, barnyard	55
Poultry, other	44
Eggs produced	100
Acres of Indian corn	125
Indian corn, bushels of	4,000
Acres of wheat	150
Wheat, bushels of	1,700
Acres of tobacco	20
Tobacco, lbs. of	15,000
Acres of apples	5
Apples, bearing trees	115
Apples, bushels of	300
Peaches, acres of	2
Value of orchard products	60

Honey, pounds of	240
Cords of wood cut	30
Value of forest products	60

The census appears to show more diversity in farm products and an increase in overall productivity for Colonel Sothoron's farm compared to the census of 1870. However, there appears to be a decline in the monetary value of the farm, its products and wages paid.

Major Webster Sothoron died on 9 October 1883. He was buried at All Faith Church on 11 October 1883. His tombstone gives his name as "S. P. Webster Sothoron" and inscribed on the tombstone is the epitaph:

His will was done

The full name of S. Webster Sothoron remains elusive.

Col. Sothoron's wife, Elizabeth M. Sothoron died on 4 August 1888 and was buried at All Faith Church. Inscribed on her tombstone is:

Her children will rise up & call her blessed

On 11 November 1891, Catherine (Kate) Lansdale Sothoron married Dr. Lloyd Woolley Curtis, U.S.N., Assistant Surgeon. The marriage was performed at the Dent Memorial Chapel in Charlotte Hall, Maryland. Lloyd Curtis was from New Jersey and his age was given as 30.[477] The marriage was reported in the Saint Mary's County *Beacon* of 12 November 1891.

After the Civil War, Colonel Sothoron was a tobacco inspector. He died on 12 April 1893 at the Hotel Ebbit in Washington, D.C. *The Washington Post* on Thursday, 13 April 1893 reported his passing in an article titled "DEATH WITHOUT WARNING, Col. John Henry Sothoron, of Maryland, Suddenly Stricken, LONG AND NOTED CAREER". The article stated Col. Sothoron had been staying in Washington, D.C. with Charles H. Fickling for several weeks. He was with a group of Maryland friends at the Hotel Ebbit to promote the "foreign consulship" of one of the group and preparing for a visit to the White House. The group consisted of Maryland state attorney Benjamin Camillier, F. F. King, editor of the *Saint Mary's Beacon*; Marshall Dent, and Edward Harrison. The article described his legislative political career.[478]

An obituary for Colonel Sothoron also appeared is the Saint Mary's County *Beacon* of 20 April 1893 in an article titled "Colonel Sothoron Dead". The article said that just prior to his death, Colonel Sothoron and friends were visiting Vice President Stevenson in regards to a "proposed visit to the President in the interest of Colonel J. Marshall Dent." The funeral was attended by the "former servants" who had been slaves of Colonel Sothoron. William Green, described as a "foreman" of Colonel Southern was at the funeral. In the Census of 1870 for Saint Mary's County, William Green and his family lived near the Sothoron family. William Green was a Black man.

Benjamin Gwinn Harris, mentioned in the *Beacon* obituary, had been a Democrat member of the United States House of Representatives from 4 March 1863 to 3 March 1867 and also had trouble with Union authorities during the Civil War.[479] During the 1850's, the name of Benjamin Gwinn Harris appears frequently in Saint Mary's County Court records in regards to the freeing of slaves. For the Maryland state elections of 4 November 1863, Benjamin G. Harris ran as a Conditional Unionist.[480]

---

[477] Fresco, page 74.
[478] *The Washington Post*, April 13, 1893, page 5 accessed 10 December 2006.
[479] *Biographical Directory of the United States Congress, 1774-1989*, page 1137.
[480] Scharf, *History of Baltimore City and County*, page 145.

Col. J. Marshall Dent, also mentioned in the obituary, was a Confederate veteran of the Civil War. He appears on a list of Confederates with the rank of Private in Company B, First Maryland Cavalry.[481] The First Maryland Cavalry was the only Confederate unit that broke through Union lines at Appomattox and did not surrender with General Lee on 9 April 1865.[482] Dent probably went to North Carolina to notify the Confederate army of Joseph Johnson of the surrender. The National Archives Confederate military service file for John M. Dent shows a parole document signed by him on 28 April 1865 at Mechanicsville, Virginia.

Colonel Sothoron was buried at All Faith Church, Charlotte Hall, Maryland. Inscribed on his tombstone is a quote from the Bible:

> For he is faithful that promised
> Hebrews X chapter 23 verse 2

---

[481] Hammett, page 131, Goldsborough, page 231.
[482] Goldsborough, pages 225-227.

Chapter 10

CONCLUSION

Colonel John Henry Sothoron (1807-1893) of Saint Mary's County, Maryland was a wealthy owner of slaves and land prior to the American Civil War. His attitudes towards Blacks indicate toleration and acceptance. A number of his slaves lived surprisingly long lives. Colonel Sothoron inherited money from a claim for damages from the War of 1812. He was a Maryland state elected politician. Colonel Sothoron, with other citizens of the Border States, must have had a great fear that the terrorist raid on Harper's Ferry, supported by northern interests known as the "Secret Six", was to be repeated. Prior to the Civil War in 1860, he was against emancipation.

Slavery is a leftist economic system. In a planned socialist system, the welfare of the workers is controlled from birth to death. Slave owners controlled almost every aspect of the life of slaves. The parentage of slave children could be decided by the slave owner. Where and who lived with who was decided by the slave owner. Medical treatment or a lack of it was decided by the slave owner. Who worked where and how long was a decision made by the slave owner. Slavery was based on the scientific organization of labor, family and plantation. The economic success or decline of a plantation and the happiness or misery of the slaves depended on the attitude and actions of the slave owner. While economically exploited, the slaves did receive the basic necessities of life such as food, clothing and shelter.

It may be said that the Civil War ended a socialist system of slavery. It was not complicated for the Union army to replace economic slavery with involuntary military servitude. After the Civil War, the agricultural economic system of the south became an impoverished system of sharecropping and tenant farming. The Civil War was fought not to end slavery, but to decide who would profit from the labor of workers. The Emancipation Proclamation of 1 January 1863 was made because of "military necessity" and was not made because of any munificent philanthropic policy. A question that remains to be answered is about the war motives of northern business interests: Did they covet the slaves of the south because they had a labor shortage in the north, the existence of which was confirmed by President Lincoln on 8 December 1863?

In 1861, to secure Washington and break the siege of it, President Lincoln allied himself with extremist Union elements and northern business interests. Lincoln used secret midnight arrests to respond to the secession crisis. The arrival and deployment of Union militias in Maryland constituted a coup d'état against the lawful government of the state of Maryland. Saint Mary's County suffered from the pillaging and depredations of the Union army as early as September of 1861. The fact that President Lincoln had an exclusive economic monopoly of exceptions to the economic blockade of the Confederacy casts a dark shadow on the hagiolatry about his life. The financial issue of Russell, Majors and Waddell and its connection to the Civil War and Benjamin F. Butler, which was given the alias of the "Floyd acceptances" by Congress, deserves research. To secure their gains, the Union army needed a quiet revolution with a subsequent reign of terror.

Prior to the death of Lieutenant White on 20 October 1863, Union politicians in Congress passed laws of confiscation, emancipated compensation and the military draft. President Lincoln made proclamations required by laws and also to clarify some aspects of his policy direction. The combined effect of the laws and proclamations did nothing to stop the Union army from atrocities, depredations and excesses. In 1863, the Union army demanded a written pledge of personal property to enforce allegiance to it in Missouri. There are is credible evidence that the pledge of personal property was also used by the Union army in Maryland during their interference with the November elections of 1863. The Union army was more interested in seizing private property to support itself than to enforce loyalty.

This was the conspiracy of the quiet revolution of political and military events led to the death of Union army Lieutenant Eben White on 20 October 1863. His shooting was possibly the last act of civilian resistance in Union controlled Border States against the recruitment of slaves into the Union army. Lincoln had previously countermanded the Union army and ordered the cessation of recruitment of Maryland slaves. There is no known written order by Lincoln to resume recruitments. The idea and possibility of compensated emancipation ended on that day. The conspiracy of events was the maneuverings of the Union political and military leadership to increase the numbers and power of the Union army, which had a significant decline in enlistments beginning in June of 1862. Union laws were draconian and the implementation of them by the Union army was illegal and brutal. It was fascism before the word was commonly used.

There were verbal and written communications among President Abraham Lincoln, Secretary of War Edwin McMasters Stanton, Major General Robert Cummings Schenck and Colonel William Birney about the recruitment slaves into the Union army in the months prior to the shooting incident. Clearly, there was a planned fascist subversion against the law by the Union army Middle Department in Maryland and in other Union army controlled states and areas.

Colonel Birney, with his background of participation in the revolution of 1848 in Paris, France, seems to have been the "loose cannon" whose actions were not stopped by President Lincoln and others. Donn C. Piatt, the minion of Schenck, lit the fuse of the loose cannon. Blimey was the central promoter of a quiet revolution to militarize the Union government. Major General Schenck speciously justified the actions of Birney in his communications to Lincoln. Schenck guarded the lies of the conspiracy. Stanton, Schenck, Piatt and Birney were Radical Republicans with a hidden agenda to seize the Union government with the goal of installing a dictatorship. Benjamin F. Butler, Schenck and Birney acted like feudal warlords with their own personal fiefdoms.

After the shooting incident, President Lincoln was able to do little to prevent and moderate the actions of the Union political militarists. Lincoln was able to halt or delay a number of executions by the Union army in a futile attempt to stop a widespread reign of terror. It appears that the allegation that Robert Todd Lincoln, the son of a verbose and pontificating President Lincoln, destroyed some of his father's writings is true and his motive was to protect the hagiographic propaganda about the actions of his father. The complete story may never be known.[483] It is conceivable that the actions of President Lincoln averted his ouster by putsch from the government by a Union political military clique.

Colonel Sothoron, a member of an economic class that was demonized, was involved at a political level in Maryland against emancipation. He was in the capitol of the Confederacy at Richmond, Virginia in October of 1861, but returned to his plantation in Maryland prior to October of 1862. His son S. Webster Sothoron participated in covert Confederate military actions. Both Colonel Sothoron and his son may have been the target of a Union counter-intelligence action. Subsequent to the shooting incident, when he fled to and resided in Richmond, Virginia, Colonel Sothoron may have unwittingly or knowingly helped the Confederates. After the surrendering with Confederate General Robert E. Lee and the remnants of the Army of Northern Virginia at Appomattox in April of 1865, Colonel Sothoron fled in exile to Canada, possibly with one or more of his sons.

The wife and children of Colonel Sothoron were held as hostages by the Union army for more than three

---

[483] Stern, page 406.

months. They were evicted from The Plains by the pathological subterfuge of Colonel Birney. After release, they were "without a shelter or crumb" according to the writing of President Lincoln. Mrs. Sothoron communicated through a member of Congress to President Lincoln after her eviction from The Plains.

The shooting incident may have tended to prolong the Civil War by outraging Abolitionist elements and frightening Confederates about losing their slaves and other property without compensation. The possibility also exists that the events surrounding the shooting incident were considered by President Lincoln when he wrote the Proclamation of Amnesty and Reconstruction because he referred specifically to persons who had left jurisdictions, which was what Colonel Sothoron had done. After the shooting incident, the Civil War became more of a personal battle for the leadership. The homes of the leadership of both the Union and Confederacy were burned and destroyed.

One year exactly to the day after the death of Lieutenant Eben White President Lincoln issued a proclamation. On 20 October 1864, Lincoln proclaimed that the last Thursday of November be a day of "thanksgiving and praise to Almighty God". He recommended that "my fellow-citizens . . . humble themselves in the dust" and pray to the "Great Disposer of events".[484] It may, or may not be, that our national holiday of Thanksgiving was created by Lincoln mourning the death of White.

The Plains was occupied and used as a "contraband" camp for freed slaves by the Union army. From November 1863 to the summer of 1866, The Plains was ransacked and looted. Buildings, furniture, timber, livestock and crops were sold for the personal profit of persons unknown. The thieves appear to have been kleptocratic military government employees. The claim for monetary damages filed by Colonel Sothoron was rejected by the United States government. During the occupation time, no case for condemnation of the Sothoron property was filed because it was stolen by the Union army and looted.

After the end of the war, Colonel Sothoron returned from Canada and was declared innocent by a court of law of the allegation of the murder of Lieutenant White in 1866. Evidence against him collected by Union authorities was criminally obtained at least under duress, if not by forgery and bribery. He remained politically involved until his death in 1893 and was a Maryland state tobacco inspector. The shooting of Lieutenant White by Colonel Sothoron was an act of justifiable homicide. The culpability for his death is a burden on the shoulders of a Republican group of politically radical militarists.

The extent of the actions of repression by the Union army remains unknown. It is estimated that there were 360,000 Union and 250,000 Confederate deaths from military causes during the Civil War.[485] A large percentage of the 116,148 registered graves reported by Brevet General M. C. Meigs, the Union Quartermaster General, may represent civilians who suffered and died because of the Union army and deserves future research.[486]

Fascism is a movement of mass psychology that uses lies and propaganda to achieve its goal of expansionism through military domination. The mass psychology of fascism is that persons who believe in it have a character disorder that enables their defective moral and ethical belief system to cease from inhibiting them to commit acts of cruelty and sadism.

Their defective moral and ethical belief system leads them to believe the lies and propaganda of themselves and others. Minor events, real or imagined, are turned into incidents of great magnitude for maximum propaganda effect. If there is no event to capitalize upon, then incidents are intentionally provoked to fulfill a prophecy of aggression by others.

Under fascism, criminal terrorist actions are used by the authorities to impose rigid obedience. Secret arrest and detention, censorship, control of media, invasion of state into church, and the theft of property are

---

[484] *CLNN,* Statutes at Large, 38th Congress, Appendix, page 749.
[485] Wikipedia, "Civil War", accessed 1 January 2007.
[486] *OR,* Series 3, Volume 5, 1900, November 8, 1865, M. C. Meigs to Hon. Edwin M. Stanton, report from page 212 to 249, page 241 accessed 6 December 2006.

their tools of oppression. Their objective is expansionism of a national economic system through the exploitation of labor. The exploitation of labor is achieved by an alliance of fascists and corporate business. The exploitation of labor serves to supply the material needs of the fascist army and corporate state.

To achieve this goal they require military domination. Once they dominate the area under their control their through military domination, fascists turn their expansionist efforts to other geographical areas.

During the American Civil War and after it, certain leaders of the north were infected with the pathological character disorder known as fascism, which is the military dominance of society and expansionism.[487] President Lincoln's power greatly diminished during 1863 and until his assassination in 1865 he acted as a mere figurehead of the government, with Radical Republican military politicians in control of the Union government. When Andrew Johnson became President after the assassination of Lincoln, he took immediate action to inhibit the movement towards fascism by stopping the Union army sales of confiscated property. The United States remained under fascist control until 1876, when Rutherford B. Hayes was elected. His wife, "Lemonade Lucy", put an end to the mischief by prohibiting the consumption of alcohol in the White House. In the words Henry May eloquently said in 1863, "the bright morning star of civil and religious freedom" was beginning to be seen again.[488]

The assassination of Abraham Lincoln elevated him to hagiographic adulation. In Russia, until the disunion of the former Soviet Union, the rigidly enforced hagiography of Vladimir Lenin served to preserve communist power and conceal wrongdoing. In the United States, the hagiography of Abraham Lincoln has served to preserve fascism and conceal the truth about the American Civil War from being known.

---

[487] For an explanation of the concept of fascism as a pathological character disorder, see Wilhelm Reich, *The Mass Psychology of Fascism*.
[488] *CLNN*, Congressional Globe, February 18, 1863, pages 1069 to 1072, accessed 10 December 2006

APPENDIX

CHARTS

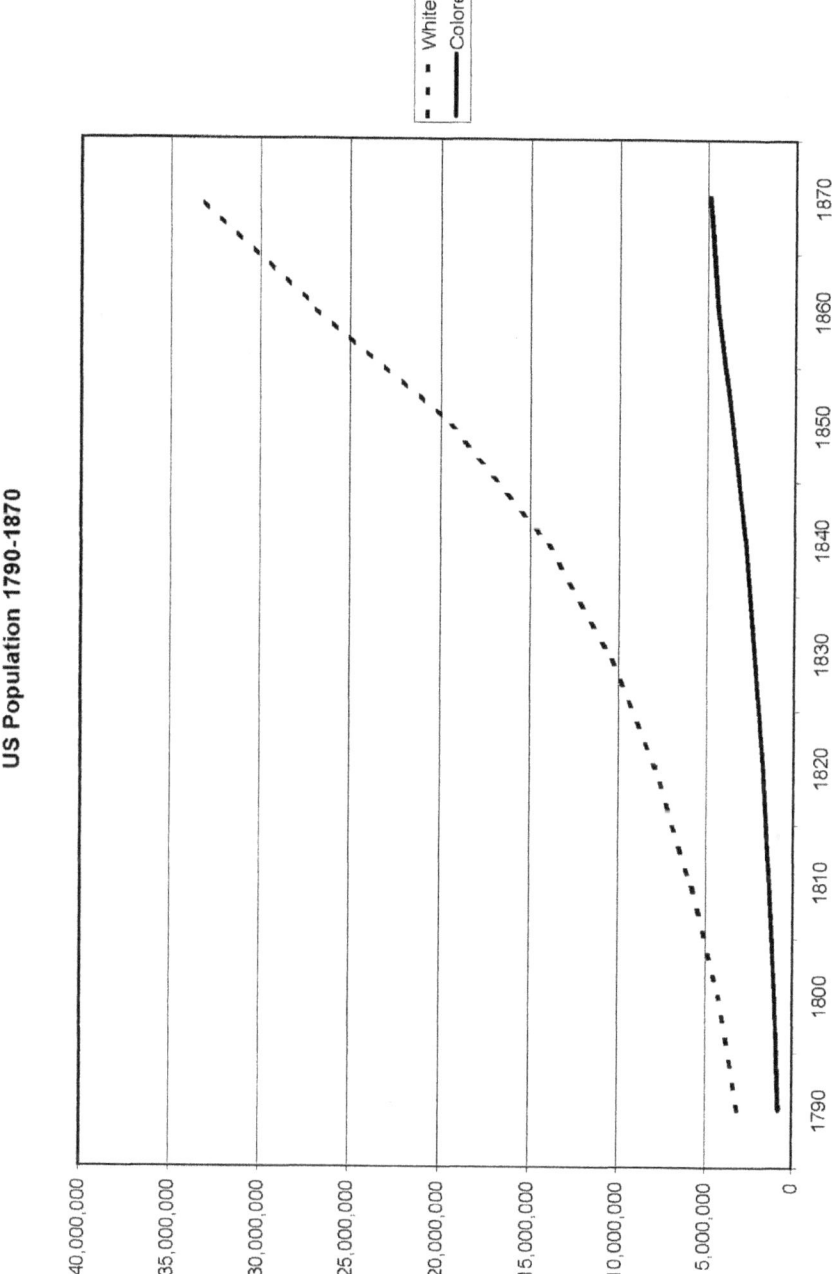

St. Mary's County Freedom and Race 1790-1870

Legend: Aggregate, White, Slave, Free Colored, Total Colored

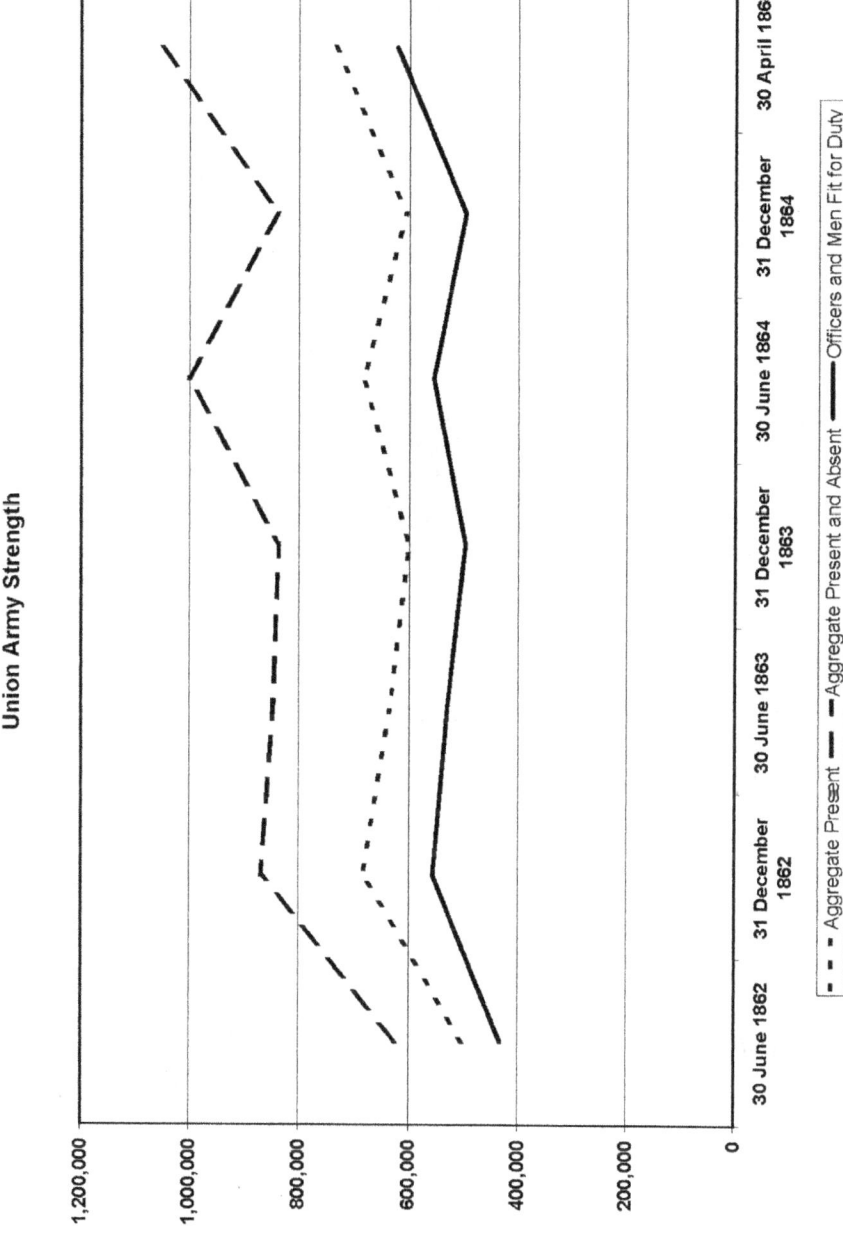

BIBLIOGRAPHY

Please be advised that microfilm copies of the United States Census sometimes have multiple page numbers placed on them. If the reader chooses to search for the Sothoron family they are usually found toward the last pages of the census (on the microfilm reel) in Saint Mary's County, Maryland.

BOOKS

Acts of the Eighty-eighth Legislature of the State of New Jersey, and Twentieth Under the New Constitution, (Newark, New Jersey, printed by R. N. Fuller, Daily Journal Office, 1864).

Acts of the Eighty-fifth Legislature of the State of New Jersey and Seventeenth Under the New Constitution, (Freehold, New Jersey, printed by James S. Yard, 1861).

William Frayne Amann, *Personnel of the Civil War, Vol. I*, (Thomas Yoseloff, Publisher: New York and London, 1961). Library of Congress Catalog Card Number 60-9890.

Anonymous, *Record of the Services of the Seventh Regiment, U.S. Colored Troops, from September 1863 to November 1866 by an Officer of the Regiment* (Providence: E.L. Freeman & Co., Printers to the State, 1878), reprinted in 1971 from a copy in the Fisk University Library Negro Collection, Library of Congress catalog number 79-168518.

Appendix to the Congressional Globe, (Blair and Rives: City of Washington, for the years 1861, 1862 and 1864). Available on microfilm.

John Bakeless, *Spies of the Confederacy*, (J.B. Lippincott Company: Philadelphia and New York, 1970).

Roy P. Basler, editor, *The Collected Works of Abraham Lincoln, Vol. VI, Vol. VII* and *Supplement, 1832-1865* (Rutgers University Press: New Brunswick, New Jersey, 1953, *Supplement*, 1974).

Ira Berlin, editor, Joseph P. Reidy, associate editor, Leslie S. Rowland, associate editor, *Freedom, A Documentary History of Emancipation, 1861-1867, Series II, The Black Military Experience*, (Cambridge University Press: Cambridge, London, New York, New Rochelle, Melbourne and Sidney, 1982).

Biographical Directory of the United States Congress, 1774-1989, (United States Government Printing Office, 1989).

Mark M. Boatner III, *The Civil War Dictionary*, (Vintage Books, A Division of Random House, Inc.: New York, 1991).

Boyd's Washington and Georgetown Directory for various years.

Helen W. Brown, compiler, *Indexes of Church Registers 1686-1885, Volume II, Saint Paul's Parish, Prince George's Parish* (Prince Georges County Historical Society: Maryland, 1979).

Gaius Marcus Brumbaugh, MS., M.D., Litt. D., *Maryland Records, Colonial Revolutionary, County and Church from Original Sources* (Genealogical Publishing Company, Inc.: Baltimore, Maryland, 1975).

Burke's Presidential Families of the United States of America (Second Edition: London, 1981).

Agnes Kane Callum, *Black Marriages of Saint Mary's County, Maryland, 1800-1900* (Mullac Publishers: Baltimore, Maryland, 1991)

John M. Carroll, editor, *Register of Officers of the Confederate States Navy, 1861-1865* (Mattituck, N.Y.: J.M. Carroll and Company, 1983).

Civil War Naval Chronology 1861-1865 (Navy History Division, Navy Department, U.S. Government Printing Office: Washington, 1971).

The Congressional Globe (Blair and Rives: City of Washington, for the years of 1847 and 1848; available on microfilm).

Congressional Record (Government Printing Office: Washington, D.C. for the years of 1874 and 1875; available on microfilm).

Jefferson Davis, *The Rise and Fall of the Confederate Government*, (Thomas Yoseloff: New York and London, 1958)

Frederick H. Dyer, *A Compendium of the War of Rebellion, Vol. III, Regimental Histories*, (Thomas Yoseloff: New York and London, 1959).

James W. Elliot, *Transport to Disaster* (Holt, Rinehart and Winston: New York, 1962).

William J. Evitts, *A Matter of Allegiances, Maryland from 1850 to 1861* (John Hopkins University Press: Baltimore and London, 1974).

Byron Farwell, *Ball's Bluff, A Small Battle and Its Long Shadow* (EPM Publications: 1003 Turkey Run Road, McLean, Virginia 22101, 1990)

H. Chandlee Forman, *Early Manor and Plantation House of Maryland* (Bodine & Associates, Inc.: Baltimore, Maryland, 1982).

Margaret K. Fresco, *Marriages and Deaths, Saint Mary's County, 1634-1900* (Margaret K. Fresco: Ridge,

Maryland 20680, copyright 1982).

Anne S. Frobel, *The Civil War Diary of Anne S. Frobel* (EPM Publications: 1003 Turkey Run Road, McLean, Virginia 22101; 1992)

Joseph T. Glatthaar, *Forged in Battle, The Civil War Alliance of Black Soldiers and White Officers* (The Free Press, a Division of Macmillan, Inc.: New York, 1988).

W.W. Goldsborough, *The Maryland Line in the Confederate Army*, (originally published in 1900, Butternut Press: 12137 Darnestown Road, Gaithersburg, Maryland 20878, 1983).

Mrs. Ulysses S. Grant, *The Personal Memoirs of Julia Dent Grant*, (G.P. Putnam's Sons: New York, 1975).

Regina Combs Hammett, *History of Saint Mary's County, Maryland, 1634-1990*, (Regina Combs Hammett: P.O. Box 393, Ridge, Maryland).

Thomas L. Hollowak, compiler, *Index to Marriages in the (Baltimore) Sun, 1851-1860* (Genealogical Publishing Company, Inc.: Baltimore, Maryland, 1978).

Joan Hume, Editor, *Maryland Index to the Wills of Saint Mary's County, 1662-1960, Somerset County, 1664-1955* (Magna Carta Book Company: Baltimore, Maryland 21215, 1970).

Virgil Carrington Jones, *Grey Ghosts and Rebel Raiders* (EPM Publications, Inc.: 1003 Turkey Run Road, McLean, Virginia 22101; 1956, reprint 1984).

Virgil Carrington Jones, *Ranger Mosby* (EPM Publications, Inc.: 1003 Turkey Run Road, McLean, Virginia 22101; 1944, reprint 1987).

E.B. King with Barbara Long, *The Civil War Day By Day, An Almanac* (Doubleday and Company, Inc.: Garden City, New York, 1971).

Harry C. Knott, *Saint Mary's County Coroners Inquest, 1821-1921* (privately published, Harry C. Knott, 7320 Bond Street, Saint Leonard, Maryland 20685, 1993).

Richard M. Lee, *General Lee's City, An Illustrated Guide to the Historic Sites of Confederate Richmond* (EPM Publications, Inc.: 1003 Turkey Run Road, McLean, Virginia 22101, 1987).

Richard M. Lee, *Lincoln's City, An Illustrated Guide to the Civil War Sites of Washington* (EPM Publications, Inc.: 1003 Turkey Run Road, McLean, Virginia 22101, 1981).

Harold R. Manakee, *Maryland in the Civil War* (Maryland Historical Society: 201 West Monument Street, Baltimore, Maryland, 1961).

Bayly E. Marks and Mark N. Schatz, Editors, *Between North and South: A Maryland Journalist Views the Civil War*, the diary of William W. Glenn (Fairleigh Dickinson University Press: Cranbury, New Jersey, 1976).

Official Records of the Union and Confederate Navies in the War of Rebellion, Series I, Volume 16 and *Volume 17* (published under the direction of the Hon. William H. Moody, Secretary of the Navy, by Mr. Charles W. Stewart, Superintendent Library and Naval War Records, Washington: Government Printing Office, 1903)

Preliminary Report of the Eighth Census, 1860, (Washington: Government Printing Office, 1862).

Edward J. Renehan, Jr., *The Secret Six, The True Tale of the Men Who Conspired with John Brown*, (Crown Publishing, Inc., 1995; University of South Carolina Press, Columbia, South Carolina, 1996).

FitzGerald Ross, *Cities and Camps of the Confederate States* (edited by Richard Barksdale Harwell, University of Illinois Press: Urbana, 1958).

J. Thomas Scharf, A.M., *History of Baltimore City and County* (Philadelphia: Louis H. Everts, 1881; Baltimore: Regional Publishing Company, reprint 1971).

J. Thomas Scharf, *History of Maryland, from the Earliest Period to the Present Day* (Baltimore: published by John B. Piet, 1879).

J. Thomas Scharf, A.M., LL.D., *History of the Confederate States Navy* (New York: Rogers and Sherwood, 1887; Freeport, New York: Books for Libraries Press, reprint 1969).

Stewart Sifakis, *Who Was Who in the Civil War* (Facts On File, Inc.: 460 Park Avenue South, New York, New York, 10016, 1988).

John Y. Simon, Editor, *The Papers of Ulysses S. Grant, Volume 16, 1866* and *Volume 18, October 1, 1867-June 30, 1868* (Southern Illinois University Press: Carbondale and Edwardsville, *Volume 16*, 1988; *Volume 18*, 1991).

Philip Van Doren Stern, *The Man Who Killed Lincoln* (New York: The Literary Guild of America, Inc., 1939).
Southern Historical Society Papers (Richmond, Virginia, published by the Society, 1876-1959).

William A. Tidwell, with James O. Hall and David Winfield Gaddy, *Come Retribution, The Confederate Secret Service and the Assassination of Lincoln* (University Press of Mississippi: Jackson & London, 1988).

William A Tidwell. *April '65, Confederate Covert Action in the American Civil War* (The Kent State University Press, Kent, Ohio London, England, 1995).

Daniel Carroll Toomey, *The Civil War in Maryland* (Toomey Press: Baltimore, Maryland, 1990).

Maxine Turner, *Navy Gray, A Story of the Confederate Navy on the Chattahoochee and Apalachicola Rivers* (The University of Alabama Press: Tuscaloosa and London, 1988).

University of Virginia, *A Catalogue of the Officers and Students of the University of Virginia*, Three catalogues: Second Session, commencing 1 February 1826; Third Session, 1 February to 20 July 1827; Fourth Session, 1827 to 1828 (Charlottesville, Virginia: Chronicle Steam Book Printing House, 1880).

Charles Lewis Wagandt, *The Mighty Revolution: Negro Emancipation in Maryland, 1862-1864* (The Johns Hopkins Press: Baltimore, Maryland, 1964).

John L. Wakelyn, *Biographical Dictionary of the Confederacy* (Greenwood Press: Westport, Connecticut, 1977).

Roberta J. Wearmouth, *Abstracts from the Port Tobacco Times and Charles County Advertiser, Volume Two, 1855-1869* (Heritage Books, Inc.: 1540-E Pointer Ridge Place, Bowie, Maryland 20716, 1991).

Jeffry D. Wert, *Mosby's Rangers* (Simon and Schuster, Inc., 1990).

Charles H. Wesley and Patricia W. Ronfro, *Negro Americans in the Civil War, From Slavery to Citizenship* (Publishers Co., Inc.: New York, Washington and London, 1968).

Who Was Who in America, Historical Volume, 1607-1896 (Chicago, Illinois: A.N. Marquis Company, founded 1897, revised edition, 1967)

ARCHIVAL SOURCES

Maryland State Archives (MSA), Hall of Records:
1. Seventh Census of the United States, 1850. Agricultural Schedules, Saint Mary's County.
2. Seventh Census of the United States, 1850. Mortality Schedules, Saint Mary's County.
3. Eighth Census of the United States, 1860. Agricultural Schedules, Saint Mary's County.
4. Ninth Census of the United States, 1870. Agricultural Schedules, Saint Mary's County.
5. Tenth Census of the United States, 1880. Agricultural Schedules, Saint Mary's County.
6. Saint Mary's County Grand Jury Papers, SM 1602, 1866 November term (MSA: 20,280-11, Location 1/57/7/28).
7. Saint Mary's County Register of Wills, Orphan's Court Proceedings, PHD #1, i, p. 134 (MSA C1667, MSA: 16,516, Location 1/60/14/38).
8. Saint Mary's County Register of Wills, Administration Bonds, JBA #1, p. 187 (MSA C1507, MSA: 40,151-6, Location 1/60/12/33).
9. Saint Mary's County Register of Wills, Guardian Bonds, 1862- 1912, pp. 303-304 (MSA C1604, MSA: 40,155-5, Location 1/60/4/6).
10. Saint Mary's County Register of Wills, Orphan's Court Proceedings, PTB #1, i, pp. 255-258, MSA: 16,517, Location 1/60/14/39).
11. Saint Mary's County Certificates of Freedom 1806-1864, Microfilm CR 47,251.

National Archives and Records Administration (NARA):
1. Civil War Confederate military service record for Webster Sothoron.
2. Civil War Confederate military service record for Marshall Sothoron.
3. Civil War Confederate military service record for S. Webster.
4. Civil War Union military record for Lieutenant Eben White.
5. Civil War Union pension record for Lieutenant Eben White.
6. Claim against the Quartermaster Corp by Colonel John H. Sothoron, 1868, Record Group 92: Records of the Office of the Quartermaster General, Correspondence and other papers relating to claims received pertinent to

rent, forage, fuel and to claims in general, H-4104, 1871-1877, Entry 812, File: box 131, unnumbered package. This package contains the original claim.

7. Claim against the Quartermaster Corp for Colonel John H. Sothoron, 1868, Record Group 92: Records of the Office of the Quartermaster General, Entry 820, File: box 111, package 29. This package contains the thirteen page letter summarizing the claim that was returned to the Quartermaster Corp from the Treasury Department.

8. Sixth Census of the United States, 1840. M704. Saint Mary's County, Maryland (Microfilm 170).

9. Seventh Census of the United States, 1850. M432. Saint Mary's County, Maryland (Microfilm 296).

10. Seventh Census of the United States, 1850. M432. Slave Schedules, Saint Mary's County, Maryland (Microfilm 302).

11. Eighth Census of the United States, 1860. M653. Saint Mary's County, Maryland (Microfilm 479).

12. Eighth Census of the United States, 1860. M653. Slave Schedules, Saint Mary's County, Maryland (Microfilm 485).

13. Ninth Census of the United States, 1870. M593. Saint Mary's County, Maryland (Microfilm 594).

14. Tenth Census of the United States, 1880. T9. Saint Mary's County, Maryland (Microfilm 514 & 515).

15. Eighth Census of the United States, 1860. M653. District of Columbia (Microfilm 56).

16. Military Service Record for John R. Sothoron, Records Group 94, enlistments 1848.

17. Records of the Army Transport Service, ship "Cecil", Records Group 92, Office of the Quartermaster General.

18. War of 1812 military and pension record for Hezekiah Burroughs.

19. Letters Received by the Confederate Adjutant and Inspector General, M474 (Microfilm 49).

20. Unfiled Papers and Slips Belonging in Confederate Compiled Service Records, M347 (Microfilm 73).

21. Confederate Papers Relating to Citizens or Business Firms, M346 (Microfilm 964).

22. Turner-Baker Papers, M797 (Microfilm 126).

23. Congressional Serial Set, Senate Claims Report Number 119 (24th Congress, 1st Session, Volume 280).

24. Congressional Serial Set, Senate Claims Report Number 127 (29th Congress, 2nd Session, Volume 495).

25. Congressional Serial Set, Senate Claims Report Number 57 (30th Congress, 1st Session, Volume 512).

26. House Report 47 (43rd Congress, 2nd Session, Record Group 287).

27. Accompanying Papers File of John H. Sothoron from the 43rd Congress (Record Group 233).

28. H.R. 1975, 16 February 1874 (43rd Congress, 1st Session, Record Group 233).

29. House Executive Document 281, 12 June 1874 (43rd Congress, 1st Session, Record Group 233).

30. Civil War Confederate military service record for J.M. Dent.

31. Civil War Confederate military service record for William W. Goldsborough.

32. Civil War Union military service record for John W. Bantum.

33. Civil War Union military service record for Lewis Ledyard Weld.

34. Civil War Union military service record for William Birney.

35. Civil War Union military service record for Benjamin Black.

Saint Mary's County Historical Society
1. All Faith Parish Register, microfilm.

PERIODICALS AND PAMPHLETS

Chicago Tribune, available on microfilm.
National Intelligencer, microfilm at Alexander Library, Rutgers University, New Brunswick, New Jersey.

The New York Times, microfilm available at public libraries.

Richmond Enquirer, microfilm available at Alexander Library, Rutgers University, New Brunswick, New Jersey.

Saint Mary's County Beacon, microfilm at Saint Mary's County Historical Society, P.O. Box 212, Leonardtown, Maryland 20650. On the same microfilm are issues of the *Gazette* also. The *Gazette* replaced the *Beacon* when the *Beacon* ceased publication because of pressure from the Union authorities during the Civil War.

The Washington Post, microfilm available at Alexander Library, Rutgers University, New Brunswick, New Jersey.

INTERNET SOURCES

A Century of Lawmaking for a New Nation: U.S. Congressional Documents and Debates, 1774-1875 (cited as *CLNN*), at the Library of Congress (Washington, D.C.: American Memory Project, [2000-02]), available on the Internet at
http://memory.loc.gov/ammen/amlaw/lawhome.html

Abraham Lincoln Papers at the Library of Congress (cited as *ALPLC*). Transcribed and Annotated by the Lincoln Studies Center, Knox College. Galesburg, Illinois (cited as *ALSC*), Library of Congress, Manuscript Division (Washington, D.C.: American Memory Project, [2000-02]), available on the Internet at
http://memory.loc.gov/ammem/alhtml/alhome.html

Alumni Records of the Virginia Military Institute, available on the Internet at
http://www.vmi.edu/archives/alumni.html

Annual report of the American Anti-Slavery Society : by the executive committee, for the year ending May 1, 1860., American Anti-Slavery Society., New York, 1861, available on the Internet at the Cornell University Library, Samuel J. May Anti-Slavery Collection (cited as *SJMASC*),
http://dlxs.library.cornell.edu/m/mayantislavery

Anonymous, *The Bastille in America; or, Democratic Absolutism, London, 1861, by an eye-witness*, available on the Internet at the Cornell University Library, Samuel J. May Anti-Slavery Collection (cited as SJMASC),
http://dlxs.library.cornell.edu/m/mayantislavery

Biographical Directory of the United States Congress, 1774-1989, available online as the *Biographical Directory of the United States Congress, 1774 to present*, (cited as *BDUSC*), available on the Internet at
http://bioguide.congress.gov

The Erie Observer, The Pennsylvania State University, Pennsylvania Civil War Newspapers, available on the Internet at http://www.libraries.psu.edu/digital/newspapers/civilwar/

Fort McHenry prisoners, available on the Internet at

http://www.itd.nps.gov/cwss/fortdetail.cfm

The Huntington Globe, The Pennsylvania State University, Pennsylvania Civil War Newspapers, available on the Internet at http://www.libraries.psu.edu/digital/newspapers/civilwar/

Indiana Historical Bureau website, available on the Internet at http://www.statelib.lib.in.us/www/ihb/govportraits/baker.html

National Park Service, Soldiers and Sailors System (cited as *NPSSSS*), *NARA*, Microfilm group number, various rolls, available on the Internet at http://www.itd.nps.gov/cwss/

Official records of the Union and Confederate Navies in the War of the Rebellion., various Series, various Volumes, United States Naval War Records Office, Government Printing Office, 1896 (cited as *ORN*), available on the Internet at http://cdl.library.cornell.edu/moa

Philadelphia Press, The Pennsylvania State University, Pennsylvania Civil War Newspapers, available on the Internet at http://www.libraries.psu.edu/digital/newspapers/civilwar/

Frederick Phisterer, *Statistical Record of the armies of the United States* (New York, Charles Scribner's Sons, 1883), available on the Internet at http://books.google.com/

Donn Piatt, *Memories of the Men Who Saved the Union* (New York and Chicago, Belford, Clarke & Company 1887), available on the Internet at http://books.google.com/

Preliminary Report of the Eighth Census, 1860, United States Bureau of the Census, available on the Internet at http://www.census.gov/prod/www/abs/decennial

United States Census Bureau, Census of Population and Housing, Census of 1870, available on the Internet at http://www.census.gov/prod/www/abs/decennial/index.htm

The War of the Rebellion: a Compilation of the Official Records of the Union and Confederate Armies, United States War Department, United States, Record and Pension Office, United States, War Records Office, *et al.*, Government Printing Office, (cited as *OR*), various Series, various Volumes, various years, at Cornell University Library, Making of America, available on the Internet at http://cdl.library.cornell.edu/moa

The Washington Post, 2006, available by subscription on the Internet at http://pqasb.pqarchiver.com/washingtonpost/search.html

William Whiting, *War Powers Under the Constitution of The United States*, 43rd Edition, (Boston, Lee and Shepard, Publishers; New York, Lee, Shepard and Dillingham, 1871), available on the Internet at http://books.google.com/

Wikipedia, available on the Internet at http://en.wikipedia.org/wiki/Main_Page

Jennings C. Wise, *The Military History of the Virginia military Institute, from 1839 to 1865* (Lynchburg, Virginia, J. P. Bell Company, Ire., 1915), available on the internet at http://books.google.com/

INDEX

A

A Concise System of Instruction Regulations for Militia and Volunteers of the United States, 27
Abercrombie, John Joseph (1798-1877), 69
abolitionism, 33, 61
Accomack, VA, 49
Adams Express Company, 24
Adams, Benjamin, 89
Adela, 84
Adreou, Thomas & Co., Auctioneers, Baltimore, 103
advice and consent, 93
Albert., William Julian (1816-1879), 105
Albion, 1
alias, 21, 22, 82, 83, 109, 115
All Faith Church, 6, 82, 112, 113
All Faith Church Parish Register, 82
Alvey, George, 11
American, 101
amnesty, 63, 73, 92, 103
Amnesty and Reconstruction, Proclamation of, 63, 117
An act for the more easy partition of lands held by co-parceners, joint tenants and tenants in common., 14
An Act to provide for compensating parties whose property may be injured or destroyed in consequence of mobs or riots., 68
Anderson, Virginia, 12
Andrews, George. L., 82
Annapolis, MD, 3, 20, 25
anti-Semitic, 40
Apalachicola River, 84, 129
Appomattox, 53, 80, 82, 90, 113, 116
Army of Northern Virginia, 79, 82, 84, 116
arrest, false, 29, 71, 97, 104
assassination, 19, 51, 55, 70, 80, 90, 91, 95, 97, 118
Atlanta, GA, 85
Auditors Office, 4, 105
Augusta, GA, 85

B

Baker, Conrad (1817-1885), 43, 44
Baker, Lafayette C. (1826-1868), 26, 51, 52, 107
Bantum, John W. (?-1864), 64, 65, 66, 107, 131
Barnes, Thomas alias Jordan, 109
Barney, Joshua (1759-1818), 1
Barns, Charles, 14
Barrack, Henry, 88
barrack, military, 3, 95
Barry, W. F., 69
Bartley & Jenner, 106
Bartley, T.W., 106

Barton, Seth Maxwell (1829-1900), 78
Barton, T. B., 78
Barton, William S., 78
Bastille, 23, 25, 28, 37, 132
Battle of Antietam, 42
Battle of Ball's Bluff, 27
Battle of Bull Run, 23, 85
Battle of Chancellorville, VA, 85
Battle of Fredericksburg, 40
Battle of Gettysburg, 27, 52
Battle of Manassas, 23, 27, 28
Battle of Shiloh, 34
Battle of Spotsylvania, 80
Battle of the Crater, 108
Battle of Winchester, 28, 69
Battle, Second Bull Run, 85
Beacon, 112, 132
Beast Butler, name for Butler, Benjamin Franklin, 20
Becker, Thomas A. (?-1899), 37
Ben Hur A Tale of the Christ, 75
Benedict, MD, 1, 4, 24, 51, 56, 59, 63, 64, 65, 66, 72, 90, 94, 106, 108
Benjamin, Judah Philip (1811-1884), 26
Benjamin, Judah Phillip (1811-1884), 41
Berret (Berrett), James G., 34
Berry, W.W., 98
Bill of Rights, 1
Birney Barracks, Baltimore, MD, 57
Birney, James Gillespie (1792-1857), 42
Birney, William (1819-1907), 42, 43, 46, 47, 48, 49, 52, 53, 54, 55, 57, 60, 62, 63, 66, 67, 68, 70, 72, 95, 105, 106, 107, 108, 116, 117, 131
Black, Benjamin, 64, 65, 131
Blackiston, James T, 97, 104
blackmail, 41, 72, 105
Blakistone, James T., 96
Blatchford, Richard M., 21
Blockade, 24, 31, 87, 115
Bloody Angle, 80
boards, 17, 65, 110
Bond, Hugh Lennox (1828-1893), 46, 47, 49, 59, 107
Boone County, IN, 43
Booth, John Wilkes (1838-1865), 90
Border States, 17, 19, 35, 36, 40, 48, 60, 61, 92, 115, 116
Boston, MA, 21, 45, 74
Boteler, Alexander Robinson (1815-1892), 80
Bowie, Robert, 7
Bradford, Augustus W. (1806-1881), 46, 47, 48, 61, 72
Bragg, Braxton (1817-1876), 79
Bragg, Capitan, 26, 55
bribery, 57, 87, 117
Bridgford, David B., 80
Brown County, IN, 44

Brown, James M., 89, 98, 100, 102, 103
Brown, John (1800-1859), 16, 17, 23, 27, 45, 129
Bryantown, MD, 66
Buchanan administration, 21
Buchanan, Franklin, 80, 81
Buchanan, James (1791-1868), 74
Buckley, F. F., 90
Bucktails, see 13th Pennsylvania Reserves, 28
Bull Run, VA, 23, 25, 85
Bureau for Organizing Colored Troops, 48
Bureau of Freedmen and Government Farms, 102
Bureau of Government Farms, 89
Bureau of Refugees, Freedmen and Abandoned Lands, 93, 94
Burnside, Ambrose Everett (1824-1881), 40
Burroughs Creek, 104
Burroughs, Eliza C., 6
Burroughs, Hanson, 2
Burroughs, Hezekiah, 5, 6, 11, 131
Burroughs, Hezekiah Duncan (1847-1927), 6
Burroughs, John B., 2
Burroughs, Joseph B., 2
Butler, Benjamin Franklin (1818-1893), 5, 20, 21, 25, 45, 63, 67, 68, 74, 87, 88, 89, 115, 116
Butler, Darky, 5
Butler, Peter, 5
Butler, Susanna, 5
Byron, Mr., 89, 90, 127

C

California treasure ships, 21
Calvert, Charles Benedict (1808-1864), 8, 36, 56, 62
Cameron, Fairfax County, VA, 27
Cameron, Simon, (1799-1889), 21, 25
Camillier, Benjamin, 112
Camp Birney, 108
Camp Delaware, OH, 60
Camp Hoffman, see Point Lookout, 102
Camp Howard, Hanover Junction, VA, 79
Camp Maryland, Staunton, VA, 79
Camp Stanton, see Benedict, 51, 63, 64, 66, 67, 72, 94, 106, 108
Canada, 40, 59, 80, 82, 85, 86, 91, 96, 116, 117
Canby, E. R. S. (Canby, Richard Sprigg?), 1808-1895), 81, 82
Caperton, Allen Taylor (1810-1876), 78
Casey, Silas, 25, 28
censorship, 26, 30, 117
censure, 21, 75, 91
Census of 1840, 4
Census of 1850, 7, 10
Census of 1860, 10, 12, 15
Census of 1870, 17, 94, 109, 112, 133
Census of 1880, 110
certificate of freedom, 15, 16
certificates of freedom, 1805 Maryland law, 17, 18
Chancery Court, 3, 106
Chapman, John Lee, 44
Chapman, Richard, 91
Charles County, MD, 3, 4, 5, 11, 16, 25, 90, 91, 97, 130
Charleston, 88
Charlotte Hall Academy, 11, 91, 109
Charlotte Hall School, 3
Charlotte Hall, MD, 3, 11, 28, 53, 78, 91, 94, 109, 112, 113

Charlotte Military Academy, 12, 26
Chase, Salmon Portland (1808-1873), 47
Chattahoochee, C.S.S., 84
Chesapeake Bay, 20, 22, 87, 90
Chicago Tribune, 55, 131
Chiffelle, Th. P., 104
Chiriqui Improvement Company, 35
Circular No. 1, 59
City of Albany, 83
civilian recruiters, 43, 45, 46, 47
Clara (Hutchins), a servant of Colonel Sothoron, 16
class warfare, 49
Cleveland, OH, 11, 44
Cleveland, Stephen Grover (1837-1908), 11
Clipper, 101
coal, 35, 82
coastal islands, 33
Cocoran, John, 7, 8
Coles farm, 88, 95, 101
colonization, 34, 35
colored, 4, 5, 17, 44, 45, 49, 54, 58, 59, 64, 89
Columbus, 84
Columbus, Georgia, 84
Combs, George, 1, 6, 128
Come Retribution, the Confederate Secret Service and the Assassination of Lincoln, 82
Commander in Chief, 21, 37, 70, 72
Committee of Claims, 1, 2, 4, 6, 7
Committee on Military Affairs and the Militia, 58
Committee on War Claims, 105, 107
compensated emancipation, 33, 34, 35, 36, 37, 116
Compton, Barnes (1830-1898), 11, 93
Compton, James, 11
condemnation proceeding, 42, 73, 103
Conditional Unionist, 28, 56, 62, 112
Confederate marines, 88
Confederate Secret Service, 78, 82, 129
Confederate States of America, 17, 19, 26, 83
confidential order, 22, 49
confiscation sales, 95
Congressional Record, 24, 45, 105, 107, 127
Conrad, Thomas Nelson (1841?-1905), 90
conscription act, 37, 38, 41
Constitution, United States, 1, 15, 22, 31, 33, 37, 46, 69, 74, 89, 126, 133
contraband settlements, 87, 88
contrabands, 54, 87, 88, 89, 102, 103, 117
Cooper, Samuel (1798-1876), 26, 27, 78, 84
coparcener, 14
corruption of blood, 74
cotton, 24
Countee, Lieutenant, 63
coup d'état, 21, 25, 32, 58, 68, 115
Court of Claims, 98, 106, 107
Cowden, Robert, 25
Craven, Thomas T., 24
Crawford County, OH, 44
Craycraft, Richard M., 43
Creager, J. P., 46
criminal facilitation, 66
Crisfield, Arthur, 62
Cromwell, Oliver (1599-1658), 67

Cummings, Alexander, 21
Curtis, Alice, 12
Curtis, Ann, 12
Curtis, Elijah, 12
Curtis, H. Z., 40, 41
Curtis, Jim, 12
Curtis, Lloyd Woolley, 112
Curtis, Loney, 12
Curtis, Samuel Ryan (1805-1866), 40
Curtis, Sarah Ann, 12
Custom House, 23

D

Dashiell (or Dashiel), John H., 37
Davis, Jefferson (1808-1889), 7, 27, 31, 37, 77, 78, 80, 127
Davis, R. S., 87, 88
De Long, James, 35
De Russy, Gustavus A. (1818-?), 69
deacon, 6
death squads, 17
decider, 39, 70
Declaration of Independence, 1
Delaware, 6, 14, 33, 34, 42, 44, 47, 59, 60
Delaware, OH, 44
Dements Battery, 84
Democratic National Convention, 25
Demopolis, AL, 81
Dent Memorial Chapel, Charlotte Hall, MD, 112
Dent, J. Marshall, 112, 113
Dent, Julia Boggs (see Grant), 100
Dent, Thomas, 100
Department of Virginia and North Carolina, 67, 88
Department of Washington, 89, 101, 102
Department of Washington, 22nd Army Corps, 102
deportation, 15, 40, 63
depredations, 25, 26, 30, 32, 39, 54, 61, 85, 87, 88, 115, 116
Dictator, *U.S.S.*, 67
Dictator, *U.S.S. r*, 67
District of the Patuxent, 91
Diven, Alexander Samuel (1809-1896), 23
Dix, John Adams (1798-1878), 21, 25, 26, 30, 43, 55
Dotson, John, 106
Douglas, Stephen Arnold (1813-1861), 25
draft, 33, 37, 38, 42, 43, 44, 45, 49, 63, 116
draft riots, New York, 45
Draper, Alonzo G., 87, 88, 89, 102
DuPont, Samuel Frances (Commander) (1803-1865), 21
Durant, Clarke J., 25, 26
Dwight, William, 24

E

Eastern Shore, MD, 47, 49, 59
Eastman, Captain, 87
Ebbit House and Hotel Ebbit, 42, 112
ecology, 99
Edwards, O. W., 80
Egerton, Charles C., 2
Eighteenth Veteran's Reserve Corps, 90
Ely, Alfred (1815-1892), 23, 28
Elzey, Arnold, 79

emancipation, 17, 33, 34, 35, 36, 37, 47, 115, 116
Emancipation Proclamation, 42, 46, 47, 61, 115
escheat, 15
Eufaula, AL, 85
Evarts, William Maxwell (1818-1901), 21
Ex Parte Merryman, 22
Ex post facto, 31
executions, 63, 116
Executive Document Number 281, 107

F

false arrest, 29, 71, 97, 104
Farragut, David Glasgow (Admiral) (1801-1870), 81
fascism, 26, 29, 36, 37, 47, 67, 105, 116, 117, 118
Faulkner, Charles James (1806-1884), 24, 28
Favorite., 88
femme covert, 9, 82, 83, 109, 116
Fickling, Charles H., 112
Fifteenth Ohio Infantry, 44
Fifth Massachusetts Militia, 58
Fifth United States Cavalry, 54, 88
Fifth United States Colored Troops, 60
First Maryland Battery, 84
First Maryland Infantry, 27, 28, 30, 52
First Maryland Regiment, 27
First New York (Lincoln) Cavalry, 28
First Regiment Massachusetts Volunteers, 25
First United States Colored Troops, 42, 45
First United States Colored Volunteers, 45
First Virginia Cavalry, 62
fit for duty, 38, 40, 58
Fladeu, J. A., 102
Floyd acceptances, 21, 74, 115
Floyd, John Buchanan (1806-1863), 21, 74
Floyd, William, 2
Foggy Bottom politicians, 34
Ford, William, 2
forfeiture, 74
Forrest property, 88, 95, 100, 101, 104
Forrest, Joseph, 100, 104
Fort Lafayette, New York harbor, 24, 25, 27, 34, 38
Fort McHenry, Baltimore, MD, 22, 28, 31, 37, 42, 52, 132
Fort Powhatan, 20
Fort Sumter, Charleston, SC, 19, 20, 24
Fortress or Fort Monroe, VA, 25, 42, 45, 48, 55, 60, 63, 78, 88
Forty-third Battalion, Mosby's Rangers, 90
Foster, Charles. W. (1830-?), 42, 43, 47, 49, 55, 59, 60, 74
Fourteenth Pennsylvania Cavalry, 89
Fowler, John, 8
France, 24, 40, 42, 62, 68, 116
Freeman, Fletcher, 44
free-negroism, 16
Fremont, John Charles (1813-1890), 34
French insurgents, 40, 44
French mediation, 40
Fry, James B., 38, 43, 44
Fuller, Charles A., 81, 126
Fullerton, General, 92, 93
Fulton, 23
Fulton County, IN, 43

G

Gardener, Henry, 8
Gardner, John, 7, 8
Gates, E. B., 95
General Order Number 53, 62
General Orders No. 329, 48, 49
General Orders Number 12, 39
General Orders Number 38, 40
Georgia, 88
German recruits, 25
Gettysburg, PA, 27, 45, 52, 62
Gholson, Thomas S. (1809-1868), 78
Gibson Randall Lee (1832-1892), 82
Gift, George W., 84
Gillis, John P. (Commander) (1803-1873), 21
Glenn, William Wilkins, 30, 128
Goldsborough, William W., 27, 30, 52, 80, 81, 107, 113, 128, 131
Goodlow (Goodloe), Daniel R., 34
Goodrich, John, 14
Goodwin, R. D., 39
Gordon, General, 95
Gordon, William F., 62
government farms, 87, 90, 101
Grand Jury of Saint Mary's County, 96
Grant, Julia Boggs (nee Dent) (1826-1902), 100
Grant, Ulysses S. (1822-1885), 40, 80, 93, 94, 100, 108
Gravely tobacco, 87
graves, registered, 89, 117
Great Britain, 1, 11, 41
Great Disposer, 68, 117
Green, John, 44
Green, William, 106, 112
Greenhow, Rose O'Neill (1817-1864), 72
Greenwood, 3, 130
Grinnell, Moses Hicks (1803-1877), 21
Gulf of Mexico, 84

H

habeas corpus, 22, 30, 36, 95
Hackensack, NJ, 27
hagiography, 34, 54, 118
Haiti, 34, 35
Halleck, Henry Wager (1815-1872), 35, 38, 40, 43, 45, 55, 69, 70
Halpine, Charles Graham (Miles O'Reilly) (1829-1868), 28
Hamilton, James A., 47
Harriet De Ford, 90
Harris [or Hanson?], Lewis G., 79
Harris, Benjamin Gwinn (1805-1895), 18, 28, 74, 91, 112
Harrison, Edward, 112
Harrisonburg, VA, 28
Haskell, L. F., 58, 66
Hayden, B. L., 27
Hayden, Lewis, 27
Hayes, Lucy Ware, (1831-1889) see Lemonade Lucy, 118
Hayes, Rutherford Birchard (1822-1893), 51, 118
Hazard, E. W., 62
Hazelton, Gerry Whiting (1829-1920), 107
Henry County, OH, 44
Herbert, John C., 96
Herod, David Edgar (1842-1865), 90, 91, 97

Herring Bay, 90
Hicks, Thomas. H., 20
Higgins, Brigadier General, 81
Higginson, Thomas Wentworth Storrow (1823-1911), 17, 27
Hilligoss, Isaac (?-1863), 43, 45
Hilligoss, James V., 43
Hilligoss, Sylvester, 43
Hinks, Edward W., 87
History of the Confederate States Navy, 83, 84, 129
Hitchcock, E. A., 69
Hodges, Benjamin M., 7
Holcomb, Florence, 62
Hollins, George N., 22
Holmes County, OH, 44
Holt, J., 45, 46, 71, 107, 127
home invasion, 29
homelessness, 72, 75, 93
Hoskins, James W., 11
hostages, 17, 20, 24, 63, 71, 72, 116
house burning, 1, 3, 28, 30, 80, 87, 88, 117
House Resolution 1975, 105, 131
household group, 10
Howard, Oliver Otis (1830-1909), 93, 100
Howard, William, 79
Howe, Dr. Samuel Gridley, 17
Hunter, David (1802-1886), 28, 35
Hunter, Robert T. M., 88
Huntington, Louis, 109
Hutchins, Clara, 16
Hutchins, Ignatius, 15, 16

I

Ile a Vache, Haiti, 35
immigration, 36
impeachment, 100
imposters, 29, 71
impressments, 44, 45
indenturing, 33
Indian Creek, MD, 25
informer, 23, 73
Innis, G. S., 20
Ireland, 7, 8, 41
Ireland, enlistments in, 41
Iuka, MS, 60

J

Jacob Bell, U.S.S., 29
Jenner, L.E., 106
Jews, 40
John Tracy, 64, 66
Johns, J., 29
Johnson, Andrew (1808-1875), 7, 49, 85, 91, 92, 93, 94, 95, 96, 100, 103, 107, 118
Johnson, Bradley Tyler, 27, 28, 78, 79
Johnson, E. V., 52
Johnson, Edward, 23
Johnson, Joseph Eggleston (1807-1891), 113
Johnson, Reverdy (1796-1876), 6, 53, 56, 57, 60, 87
Joint Resolution S. R. 102, 74
Joint Resolution S. R. 103, 29, 71

138

joint tenants, 14, 15
Jones, W. K., 43
jousting tournament, 11
Jowles (or Joles), Henry, 3

K

Kane, Thomas Leiper, 28
kangaroo court, 40, 70
Kansas, 16, 17, 21, 68
Kenrick, Frances Patrick (1797-1863), 37
Kent County, MD, 48
Ketcham, A. P., 93, 94
Key, Henry G. S., 6, 92
King, F. F., 112
King, Horatio (1811-1897), 35
Knox County, OH, 40, 44
Kock, Bernard, 35
Krebs, Captain, 91

L

labor shortage, 36, 115
Lane, G. W., 24
Lane, James Henry (1814-1866), 21, 24
Larner, Noble D., 38
Lawrence, Amos A., 17
Lawrence, William (1819-1899), 106
Leadbetter, Daniel Parkhurst (1797-1870), 44
Leesburg, VA, 38
legislation, An Act for enrolling and calling out the national Forces, and for other Purposes, 37
legislation, An Act for the Release of certain Persons held to Service or Labor in the District of Columbia, 34
legislation, An Act relating to Habeas Corpus and Regulating Judicial Proceedings in Certain Cases, 71
legislation, An Act to confiscate Property used for Insurrectionary Purposes, 22, 23
legislation, An Act to establish a Bureau for the Relief of Freedmen and Refugees, 93
legislation, An act to prevent Correspondence with Rebels, 31
legislation, An Act to suppress Treason and Rebellion, to seize and Confiscate the Property of Rebels, and for other Purposes, 30, 73
legislation, Fugitive Slave Act of 1793, 69
Legislature of Maryland, 3, 22
Lemon, Captain, 63
Lemonade Lucy, see Mrs. Hayes, 118
Lenin, Vladimir, 118
Lewis, J. R. C., 81
Liberia, 34
Lincoln, Abraham (1809-1865), vii, 7, 17, 19, 20, 21, 22, 23, 24, 26, 30, 33, 34, 35, 36, 37, 38, 39, 40, 42, 45, 47, 48, 49, 51, 53, 54, 55, 56, 57, 60, 62, 63, 67, 68, 69, 70, 72, 73, 74, 75, 80, 90, 91, 95, 107, 108, 115, 116, 117, 118, 126, 132
Lincoln, Robert Todd (1843-1926), vii, 54, 67, 116
Lockwood, General, 75
Long Branch, 87, 88
Long, Alexander (1816-1886), 74
Lord of the Manor, 11
Lord Russell, 41
Loudoun County, VA, 43
Lowden (or Louden), Robert, 83

Lower Maryland Vigilance Committee, 27
loyalty oath, 25, 41, 61, 63
lurking, 37
Lyon, Alexander, 2
Lyon, Henry M., 12

M

Maddox, Joseph H., 87
Magruder, John R., 7
Magruder, William, 31
Magruder, William T., 31
Majors, Alexander, 21
malaria, 48
Mallory, Stephen Russell (ca. 1813-1873), 83, 84
Manassas, VA, 23, 27, 28, 30
Mansard roof, 7
Mansfield, Richland County, OH, 44
marines, Confederate, 88
Marston, Gilman (1811-1890), 54, 75
martial law, 30, 34, 95
Martindale, F. G., 28
Martinsburg, WV, 28, 37, 69, 70
Mary Washington, 23
Maryland Flying Artillery, 84
Maryland House of Delegates, 16
Maryland Line, 27, 52, 66, 79, 128
Maryland Senate, 16, 72
Maryland slave owners, delegation of, 53
Mason, James Murray (1798-1871), 41
Massachusetts Militia, 20, 58
material support, 17, 23
May, Henry (1816-1866), 23, 25, 36, 37, 118
Maynadier, John H., 62
McClellan, George Brinton (1826-1885), 38, 39
McConnell, G. E., 29
McDowell, Irvin (1818-1885), 39, 66
McElrath, Captain, 30
Mechanicsville, MD, 90
Mechanicsville, VA, 113
Medford, NJ, 11
mediation, French, 40
Meigs, Montgomery Cunningham (1816-1892), 89, 99, 106, 117
memorial, to Congress to increase the pay of Black soldiers, 108
Memphis, TN, 82
mercenary, 41
Meridian, MI, 81, 82
Merryman, John (1824-1881), 22
Methodist Episcopalian, 37
Middle Department, 48, 51, 52, 53, 55, 67, 75, 116
Midwest, 49
military executions, 55, 63, 83
Miller, H., 80
Millersburg, Holmes County, OH, 44
Milroy, Robert Huston, 69, 70
minister to England, 57
Minor Major, 82
Mitchell, Walter, 97
Mix, John, 54, 87
Mobile, AL, 80, 81, 82
monopoly, 24, 115
Moore, Charles C., 62

morale, 38, 40
Morgan, George D., 21
Morris, W.W., 48
Morrow County, OH, 44
Mosby, John Singleton (1833-1916), 94, 100
Mosby, Mrs., 94
Mosby's Rangers, 43rd Battalion, 90
Mount Vernon, Knox County, OH, 40
Mudd, Cecilia, 11
Mudd, Samuel Alexander (1833-1883), 11, 90, 97
Mulatto, 8, 9, 14
Mule Shoe Salient, 80
Murphy, William, 82
Murray, William H., 27

N

Napoleon, Henry County, OH, 44
Narcissus, 1
National Convention, 25, 62, 107
National Intelligencer, 3, 6, 54, 56, 58, 60, 61, 131
Naudain, Arnold (1790-1872), 2
negro, 5, 56
New England, 11, 17, 35, 67
New England civilization, 35
New England Emigrant Aid Company, 17
New Orleans, LA, 20, 67
Newkirk, Schuylkill Township, PA, 43
Newport, R. M., 98, 99, 103
Newton, MA, 58
Nicholson, Colonel, 63
Nicolay, John, 21, 33, 34, 38, 55
Nineteenth United States Colored Troops, 108
Ninth United States Colored Troops, 108
Norfolk, VA, 42, 43, 45, 49, 55, 95
Norris, Owen, 29
Norris, William, 29, 53
Northampton, VA, 49

O

Old Capitol Prison, 41, 91
Opdyke, George (1805-1880), 21
Order Number 214, 89
Order Number 30, 40
Ould, Robert (1820-1882), 77, 78

P

paralysis, 110
pardon, 73, 80, 92, 103
Parker, Theodore, 17
Parrott, Ed. A., 44
passes, 24
Patuxent River, 1, 22, 25, 28, 29, 41, 51, 53, 54, 60, 65, 88, 89, 90, 95, 98, 102
Pawnee, 22
pay, former slaves, 18
Peace candidate, 25
peace convention, 41, 47
peddlers, 40
Peighton, Mrs. Stark A. W., 45

Peninsula Campaign, 38
performance bail bond, 41
Petersburg Mine Assault, 108
Pettit, Captain, 91
Philadelphia Press, 11, 23, 55, 133
Piatt, Donn C., 19, 36, 37, 45, 49, 51, 53, 54, 55, 59, 69, 70, 116, 133
Pierce & Bacon, Boston, Massachusetts, 21, 74
Pilkinton, Benn, 109
Plains of Plenty, 3
Point Lookout, 54, 65, 68, 73, 87, 88, 90, 91, 101, 102
poker, 55
police, 17, 23, 26, 51, 107
political prisoners, 25, 28, 31, 36, 42, 71, 105
Pony Express, 21
Port Tobacco, Charles County, MD, 11, 91, 97, 130
Porter, David Dixon (Rear Admiral) (1813-1891), 83
posse comitatus, 60
Potomac flotilla, 87, 90
Potomac River, 20, 21, 24, 26, 53, 67, 87, 88, 90
Powell, Lazarus Whitehead (1812-1867), 71
Pratt, Thomas George (1804-1869), 63
preliminary Emancipation Proclamation, 42
Prince Georges County, MD, 3, 6, 7, 11, 108, 127
Princeton College, NJ, 11
Princeton Township, Mercer County, NJ, 11
prisoners of war, 45, 71, 100
privateering, 22, 23
proclamation, 19, 22, 23, 24, 30, 34, 35, 44, 47, 53, 61, 63, 68, 73, 74, 95, 96, 103, 117
Proclamation of Amnesty and Reconstruction, 63, 117
propaganda, 16, 20, 23, 26, 36, 53, 55, 61, 105, 116, 117
property, 22, 23, 30, 73
Prostitutes, 20
Protestant Revolution of 1689, 3
Provisional Army Confederate States, 27, 79, 81
Puritan, 67

Q

Queen of Love and Beauty, 11

R

Raley, James, 28, 29
Randolph, George W. (1818-1867), 78
rape, 39
ratio of whites to colored persons, 17
Read, William, 91
reconstruction, 23, 95
Record of the Services of the Seventh Regiment, U.S. Colored Troops from September, 1863 to November, 1866, 108
recruiters, 45, 46, 47
registered graves, 89, 117
religion, 37, 44
rendition, 69, 103
Report Number 47, 107
Republican National Convention, 107
Resolute, 88
Resurrection Manor, 11
Revolution of 1848, Paris, France, 42, 62, 116
Revolutionary War, 1, 11, 19, 22
Richmond Enquirer, 36, 61, 132

Richmond, Virginia, 20, 23, 24, 26, 27, 29, 30, 31, 36, 38, 40, 41, 51, 52, 53, 58, 59, 61, 63, 66, 77, 78, 79, 80, 82, 83, 84, 86, 104, 116, 128, 129, 132
riot, in Baltimore, 20
riots, New York City, 45
Ritter, Captain, 81
Robertson, Captain, 30
Rogers, Robert Lyon, 106
Ross, FitzGerald, 53, 61, 129
Ruffin, Frank G., 79
Rush County, IN, 43, 45
Russell, Jerome, 16
Russell, Lord, 41
Russell, Majors and Waddell, 21, 74, 115
Russell, William, 21

S

S., Colonel, 22
Sacred Heart Church, 15
safe-keeping, 71, 105
Saint Leonard's Creek, 1
Saint Mary's Female Seminary, 8
Sanborn, Anson L. (?-1863), 17, 24, 27, 45, 47
Sanborn, Franklin, 17, 27, 45
Sanborn, John D., 24, 45
Savannah River, 85
Savannah, GA, 84
Scharf, J. Thomas, 28, 46, 47, 56, 61, 62, 63, 75, 83, 84, 85, 112, 129
Schenck, Robert Cumming (1809-1890), 37, 41, 43, 44, 45, 46, 47, 48, 51, 53, 54, 55, 56, 57, 59, 60, 61, 62, 63, 67, 68, 69, 70, 75, 91, 116
school house, 95
Scott, Robert N., 69, 70
Scott, W. B., 6
Scott, Winfield (1786-1866), 21, 22
Second Battle of Bull Run, 85
Second Maryland Infantry, 27, 52
Second United States Cavalry, 88
Second United States Colored Troops, 42, 63
Secret Line, 29, 53
secret police, 26, 51, 107
Secret Six, 16, 17, 27, 43, 45, 115, 129
sedatives, 92
Seddon, James Alexander (1815-1880), 29, 30, 77, 78, 79
Seddon, John, 29
Senate Bill Number 118, 4
sequestration, 89
serf, 14, 15
servant, 15, 16, 26, 27, 28, 33, 58, 63, 66, 77, 104
Seventh United States Colored Troops, 51, 58, 64, 66, 108
Seward, William Henry (1801-1872), 22, 24, 25, 30
Shenandoah Valley, Virginia, 28
Sherman, William Tecumseh (1820-1891), 60, 85
shotgun, 51, 55, 96
show trial, 40, 66, 70
Signal Corps, 29, 52, 53, 61
Skinner, J. D., 30
slave jails, Baltimore, 46
slaves, household groups, 10
slaves, Mulatto, 8, 9, 14
smallpox, 72

Smith, Garland, 90
Smith, Gerrit (1799-), 17
socialism, 115
Somerset, 84, 128
Somervell, Elizabeth Magruder, 3
Sotheron, John Henry (Sothoron misspelled), 6, 105
Sothoron, Amelia Weems (1851-1941), 12, 109
Sothoron, Catherine (Kate) Lansdale (1862-1895), 71, 112
Sothoron, Eleanor, 8
Sothoron, Elizabeth, 5, 109
Sothoron, Elizabeth A., 3, 5
Sothoron, Elizabeth Magruder (1816-1888), 3, 4, 5, 11, 12, 58, 59, 60, 62, 71, 72, 75, 92, 93, 94, 104, 105, 112, 117
Sothoron, Ellen, H. (Hellen) (1853?-1937?), 12, 109
Sothoron, Fannie Bernard (1850-1929), 7, 12, 109
Sothoron, Forbes, 6, 12
Sothoron, Henry, 1, 3, 11, 112, 115
Sothoron, James Forbes (1784?-1847), 2, 4, 6, 7, 57, 93
Sothoron, James Forbes Jr. (1839-1843), 5, 6
Sothoron, John, 5
Sothoron, John Henry (1807-1893), 1, 3, 4, 5, 6, 7, 8, 9, 10, 11, 12, 14, 15, 16, 18, 26, 27, 30, 31, 51, 52, 53, 54, 56, 57, 58, 59, 61, 62, 63, 64, 66, 68, 72, 73, 77, 78, 79, 80, 84, 86, 89, 90, 91, 92, 94, 95, 96, 97, 98, 99, 100, 101, 103, 104, 105, 106, 107, 108, 109, 110, 111, 112, 113, 115, 116, 117, 130, 131
Sothoron, John Henry Jr. (1856-?), 12, 109, 110
Sothoron, Margaret Holliday (1838?-?), 5, 8, 11
Sothoron, Marshall Lyles (1844-1923), 7, 12, 30, 52, 84, 85, 130
Sothoron, Mary Elizabeth (1836-1924), 5, 7, 12, 96, 109
Sothoron, Rebecca Ann Maria (?-1818?), 1, 3
Sothoron, Rebecca Ann Mariah (1835-?), 5
Sothoron, Robert Bowie (1846-1911), 7, 12, 75, 86, 109, 110
Sothoron, S. Webster (1841-1883), 7, 12, 26, 27, 28, 29, 51, 53, 61, 63, 80, 81, 82, 83, 104, 109, 112, 116, 130
Sothron, (Sothoron misspelled), 26, 107
South, Mosses, 109
Southern Historical Society Papers, 80
Southern Republican Association, 46
Southern, John Henry (Sothoron misspelled), 25, 28, 31, 46, 56, 59, 80, 86, 103, 112, 129
Soviet Union, 118
special license and permission of the President, 24
Special Orders No. 346, 69
Spoons, name for Butler, Benjamin Franklin, 20
St. Mary's, 90
St. Nicholas, 22
Stanton, Edwin McMasters (1814-1869), 37, 38, 41, 42, 44, 46, 47, 48, 49, 51, 53, 56, 59, 60, 62, 63, 64, 66, 67, 68, 71, 72, 75, 89, 91, 94, 95, 98, 99, 100, 106, 108, 116, 117
Stantonism, 91
Star, 88
state prisoners, 71
Staunton, VA, 78, 86
Stearns, George Luther, 17, 43
Stearns, Major, 43
Stephens, John F.(?-1863), 43
Steuart, George Hume (1828-1903), 28
Stone, Charles P., 38
Stone, Frederick (1820-1899), 97
Straughn, L. E., 59
Streeter, William, 83
Stuart, Philip (1760-1830), 2

substitutes, 37
Sullivan County, IN, 43
Sultana, 82, 83
Supreme Court, United States, 21, 22, 40, 41
Sykes, George (1822-1880), 25, 28, 38

T

Taney, Robert Brooke (1877-1864), 22
Taylor, Dick, 91
Taylor, J. H., 102
Taylor, Richard (1826-1879), 81, 82
Tecumseh, 81
tenants, 14, 15, 104
terrorism, 16, 17, 23, 32, 50, 55, 115, 116, 117
Thayer, Eli, 17
The Baltimore Exchange, 30
The Congressional Globe, 6, 127
The Great Emancipator, 34
The Maryland Line in the Confederate Army, 1861-1865, 27, 52, 66
The Mechanic's Bank, Augusta, Georgia:, 85
The New York Times, 18, 34, 36, 46, 47, 54, 55, 56, 57, 58, 61, 63, 68, 69, 100, 132
The Rise and Fall of the Confederate Government, Vol. II, 77
*The War of the Rebellion
    a Compilation of the Official Records of the Union and
        Confederate Armies*, 19, 20, 78, 133
Third Maryland Artillery, 81
Thirteenth Constitutional Amendment, 33
Thirteenth Pennsylvania Reserves, 28
Thirtieth United States Colored Troops, 72, 108
Thirty-second Regiment Virginia Infantry, 91
Thirty-sixth United States Colored Infantry, 87
Thomas, C. W., 99
Thomas, Dr., 63, 104
Thomas, Francis (1799-1876), 46
Thomas, John Lewis Jr. (1835-1893), 97, 98, 100, 106
Thomas, Lorenzo (1804-1875), 18, 60, 100
Thomas, Richard, (alias Zarvona), 22
Timmons, Thomas, 59
tobacco, 2, 7, 11, 15, 18, 24, 59, 64, 87, 94, 95, 98, 102, 103, 105, 106, 111, 112, 117
Tod, David (1805-1868), 44
torpedo, 81, 83, 84
Tory, 19
Tower, C., 43
Townsend, Edward D., 42, 43, 48, 49, 60, 67, 69, 89, 91
Travis, John S., 26
treasure ships, California, 21
Tucker, Joseph W., 82
Turner-Baker Papers of the National Archives, 51, 52, 131
Twenty-first North Carolina Infantry, 80
Twenty-second Army Corps, Department of Washington, 102
Twenty-sixth Michigan Volunteers, 91
Tyler, Dan, 69
Tyler, Erastus Bernard, 48

U

Unconditional Unionist, 72, 98
underwater mines, see torpedo, 88
Union National Convention, 62
Union Party, 56
Unionist, 25, 28, 56, 61, 62, 72, 79, 80, 98, 112
United States Colored Troops, 42, 51, 58, 63, 64, 66, 72, 88, 94, 108
United States Colored Volunteers, 45
University of the City of New York, 46
University of Virginia, 3, 56, 78, 129
usury, 89

V

Vallandigham, Clement Laird (1820-1871), 17, 40
Van Vleet, Jacob R. S., 35
Van Vliet, Stewart, 103, 104
Vanderbilt, 74
Vanderbilt, Cornelius (1794-1877), 74
Veteran Reserve Corps, 101, 102, 103, 104
Vickers, George (1801-1879), 48, 49
Vincent, Thomas M., 64, 66
Vinton, Samuel Finley (1792-1862), 34
Virginia Military Academy, 86, 90

W

Waddell, William B., 21
wage slavery, 18
wages, 4, 11, 18, 34, 57, 60, 68, 85, 89, 93, 102, 103, 104, 105, 108, 111, 112
Wallace, Lew (Lewis) (1827-1905), 75
Wallace, William, 44
Wallis report, 23, 25
Wallis, S. Teackle, 26
War Between the States, 19
war is hell, 61
War of 1812, 4, 5, 6, 7, 22, 57, 93, 115, 131
Waring (Warring), James, 28, 41
weapons of mass destruction, 55
Webster, Edwin Hanson (1829-1893), 72
Webster, William, 10
Wecker, 101
Weld, Lewis Ledyard, 57, 58, 63, 66, 107, 131
Welles, Gideon (1802-1878), 21, 24
Wells, Colonel, 91
Weymouth, H. W., 73
Whig political party, 16, 55, 57
White, Albert Smith (1803-1864), 36
White, Capitan, 63
White, Eben (?-1863), 51, 57, 58, 63, 64, 68, 96, 116, 117, 130
Whitestown, Boone County, IN, 43
Whiting, William (1813-1873), 89, 133
Whittlesey, B., 100, 102
Wiegel, Wm. H., 20
Winchester, VA, 28, 69, 70
Winder Rangers, 27
Winder, John H., 78
witchcraft, 11, 20
wood, 81, 82, 93, 98, 99, 112
Woodburn, Michael, 11
Woodhull, Max, 94
writ of Certiorari, 40

Y

Yankee, 88
Yankee government, 77

ABOUT THE AUTHOR

Stephen D. Calhoun is a graduate of Monmouth College (now University). He contributed research to *April '65, Confederate Covert Action in the American Civil War*, by William A. Tidwell. His political and anti-terrorism commentary have been published in newspapers. He lives in Belmar, New Jersey.